"Full of concrete nitty-gritty wisdom about and for interfaith dialogue. A practical how-to guide for interfaith dialogue—and it surely is the best of its kind—it is also rooted in substantive scholarship and can be employed fruitfully in courses on interreligious dialogue in colleges and seminaries to provide students with a deep introduction to the 'on the ground' practice of interfaith dialogue. Mosques, churches, synagogues, temples, and interfaith groups at every level will find in this book a treasure trove of resources for getting about the work of building community through interfaith living. No religious community that aspires to neighborliness can afford to do without this invaluable resource."

—**John J. Thatamanil, PhD**, assistant professor of theology, Vanderbilt University Divinity School

"Offers us the most helpful tools to initiate, sustain, and promote an 'interactive faith' that does not shy away from intense and intentional involvement in interreligious community-building activity. Brings together the wisdom of so many practitioner-thinkers of interreligious dialogue and offers a real boost to the efforts of all those who are committed to a just and peaceful world. You do not have to be a believer in or a practitioner of interreligious community-building to read this book; you will certainly become one as you finish reading it. If you are already involved in such activities, you will gain a broader vision, a deeper understanding, and a renewed commitment to interactive faith."

—**Rev. Dr. M. Thomas Thangaraj**, D. W. & Ruth Brooks Associate Professor of World Christianity, Candler School of Theology, Emory University

"With great clarity and compelling narrative ... brings into sharp focus the well-intentioned but too often fuzzily-defined world of interfaith activity. Whether you are a pastor preparing your first interfaith service bulletin, a community activist rallying religious leaders to a cause, or a curious but confused private citizen seeking the basics on an increasingly religiously diverse world, this book is the place to begin."

—**Rev. Chloe Breyer**, executive director, The Interfaith Center of New York

"This invaluable resource is sorely needed.... A very thoughtful and useful way to help individuals and communities engage in dialogue and embrace our shared values to help make our world more whole."

—**Rabbi Amy Joy Small**, past president, Reconstructionist Rabbinical Association; rabbi, Congregation Beth Hatikvah, Summit, New Jersey

Other SkyLight Paths Interreligious Resources

How to Be a Perfect Stranger, 4th Ed.:
The Essential Religious Etiquette Handbook
Edited by Stuart M. Matlins and Arthur J. Magida

Spiritual Leaders Who Changed the World:
The Essential Handbook to the Past Century of Religion
Edited by Ira Rifkin and the Editors at SkyLight Paths
Foreword by Dr. Robert Coles

Disaster Spiritual Care:
Practical Clergy Responses to Community, Regional
    and National Tragedy
Edited by Stephen B. Roberts, BCJC, and
    Rev. Willard W. C. Ashley, Sr., DMin, DH

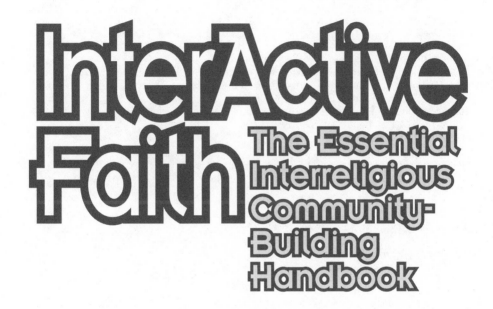

InterActive Faith
The Essential Interreligious Community-Building Handbook

Edited by
Rev. Bud Heckman
with **Rori Picker Neiss**

Foreword by Rev. Dirk Ficca

Walking Together, Finding the Way ®
SKYLIGHT PATHS ®
PUBLISHING
Woodstock, Vermont

InterActive Faith:
The Essential Interreligious Community-Building Handbook

2008 First Printing
© 2008 by Bud Heckman

Grateful acknowledgment is given for permission to use "The Dialogue Decalogue: Ground Rules for Interreligious Dialogue," © *Journal of Ecumenical Studies,* 1983.

Library of Congress Cataloging-in-Publication Data
InterActive faith : the essential interreligious community-building handbook / edited by Bud Heckman with Rori Picker Neiss ; foreword by Dirk Ficca.
p. cm.—(Walking together, finding the way)
Includes bibliographical references (p.   ) and index.
ISBN-13: 978-1-59473-237-9 (hardcover)
ISBN-10: 1-59473-237-X (hardcover)
1.   Religious pluralism—United States. 2.   Religions—Relations. 3.   United States—Religion—1960– I. Heckman, Bud, 1969– II. Neiss, Rori Picker, 1985–
BL2525.I57 2008
201'.50973—dc22
2008017286

10   9   8   7   6   5   4   3   2   1

Manufactured in the United States
❀ Printed on recycled paper

Jacket design: Tim Holtz

SkyLight Paths Publishing is creating a place where people of different spiritual traditions come together for challenge and inspiration, a place where we can help each other understand the mystery that lies at the heart of our existence.

SkyLight Paths sees both believers and seekers as a community that increasingly transcends traditional boundaries of religion and denomination—people wanting to learn from each other, walking together, finding the way.

SkyLight Paths, "Walking Together, Finding the Way," and colophon are trademarks of LongHill Partners, Inc., registered in the U.S. Patent and Trademark Office.

Walking Together, Finding the Way®
Published by SkyLight Paths Publishing
A Division of Longhill Partners, Inc.
Sunset Farm Offices, Route 4, P.O. Box 237
Woodstock, VT 05091
Tel: (802) 457-4000   Fax: (802) 457-4004
www.skylightpaths.com

For our spouses
Laura and Russel
and
for all those who lovingly work for religious cooperation,
deepening their own faith and building bridges in their communities.

Contents

Foreword

There is an underlying sense of urgency to this enlightening yet "practical, hands-on, how-to manual" for the interreligious movement. This is in part because of how the world has changed. Over the past fifty years, the United States has rapidly grown more religiously diverse. This pattern has been mirrored in major metropolitan areas around the world. In the best of times, we might be able to get by without really knowing our new and diverse religious neighbors who espouse different beliefs, engage in unfamiliar practices, and are increasingly from somewhere else in the world. But in a multireligious and post-September 11 world, interreligious dialogue and cooperation are no longer luxuries or options. As Rev. Dr. Francis Tiso says, "There is simply no alternative; we have already seen where the absence of dialogue leads."

Indeed, the consequence of not knowing our neighbors creates a climate of mutual ignorance that can foster misunderstanding and breed mistrust. In the midst of more trying times, this state of affairs can lead to suspicion, tension, conflict, and even violence. As we are all painfully aware, in many places in the world religion is a matter of life and death. We all have a stake and a role to play in determining whether the twenty-first century will be characterized by the now famous Samuel Huntington's catchphrase of a "clash of civilizations" or if we can turn this time of crisis into an opportunity to promote a "dialogue of civilizations."

For that task this handbook is a must. It introduces terms—such as *intrafaith, interfaith, multifaith,* and *multireligious,* or *polyvalence* and *kaleidocultural,* or *religious pluralism* and *civil pluralism*—in clear yet nuanced ways while making direct connections to strategies for advancing better relations between communities. It surveys the field of emerging study on negotiating religious identity in the midst of diversity without ducking the ambiguities involved. It offers a first-class compendium of resources, including brief descriptions of the world's major religious and spiritual traditions, a directory of interreligious organizations and web-based information sites, helpful books to read, and commentary on Leonard Swidler's still helpful "Dialogue Decalogue."

This handbook also offers a multitude of approaches to engage in interreligious dialogue and cooperation—in direct conversation with others, through observance and participation of the practices of others, through the shared process and experience of the arts, in collaborative service and joint action. The steps and strategies for each approach are outlined and explained so that there are no excuses for not trying. There is realism about the goals that may be attainable, and the inevitable pitfalls that may come, so that no one should be surprised when difficulties are encountered or expectations need to be readjusted.

What might be surprising to the uninitiated in interreligious dialogue and cooperation is its power for transformation. This is the heart of editor Bud Heckman's argument and where he has done his best and most inspiring work, collecting stories of individuals, groups, communities, and organizations engaged in this sacred enterprise. What emerges as undeniable is that fostering understanding and trust is something that we can actively work at, and is more often than not within our grasp. Learning how to "agree to disagree" and preventing seemingly irreconcilable differences from escalating into conflict and violence are skills and attitudes that can be cultivated. Discovering about "the other" need not necessarily pose a threat to personal boundaries and ideals, but rather can strengthen one's own convictions and aspirations.

More than anything else, these stories—about the Doorways to Peace program organized in Philadelphia to strengthen social cohesion in local neighborhoods; the interfaith service in support of those suffering from AIDS crafted by the InterFaith Conference of Metropolitan Washington; the issuing of a call for young people to engage in service-learning by the Interfaith Youth Core; engaging in active advocacy for religious freedom by the Interfaith Alliance; and others—are a reason to read this book.

One such story has to do with a group of teenagers—Jewish, Christian, and Muslim—participating in a class to share and write poetry about their visions for the world. One student, Clare, wrote this haiku:

> *Do we always think,*
> *To hold open the world's door*
> *For people unknown?*

A good question with which to start. An equally good aim for which to work. This handbook helps us get there.

Rev. Dirk Ficca
Executive Director
Council for a Parliament
of the World's Religions

Acknowledgments

There are more things in heaven and earth, Horatio,
Than are dreamt of in your philosophy.
—WILLIAM SHAKESPEARE, *HAMLET, ACT I, SCENE V*

InterActive Faith came together as the shared vision of a handful of national leaders and local champions of the interfaith movement in the United States. Our movement, though real and growing, desperately needed a practical, hands-on, how-to manual. We all agreed it should include contributions from some of the very best people in the field and cover a wide range of methodologies.

Rev. Olivia Holmes (Unitarian Universalist Association), Patrick Markey (Focolare Movement), Dr. Tarunjit Singh Butalia (World Sikh Council-America Region), Rev. Dr. Shanta Premawardhana (World Council of Churches), Rev. Dr. Francis Tiso (United States Conference of Catholic Bishops), Rev. Dr. Jay Rock (Presbyterian Church U.S.A.), and Judith Hertz (Union for Reform Judaism) and Martin Hertz (legal counsel) spent hours defining, designing, enabling, and otherwise turning our shared vision into a reality. I thank them for their faithfulness and contributions. As with their other colleagues in the Religions for Peace family, all of them were mentors to me.

Stuart M. Matlins and Arthur J. Magida's pioneering *How to Be a Perfect Stranger: The Essential Religious Etiquette Handbook* (SkyLight Paths), the now classic guide to interfaith etiquette, has been an indispensable resource for all of us in interfaith work. But after that first visit to a Jewish bar mitzvah, Islamic wedding, or Catholic First Communion, what's next? How do we continue to be good neighbors in a religiously pluralistic world? We wanted this book to help its readers take that next critical step, and we felt fortunate when *How to Be a Perfect Stranger*'s publisher, SkyLight Paths, agreed to publish it. A special word of appreciation is due to Stuart M. Matlins, publisher, and Emily Wichland, vice president of Editorial and Production, for leading us gently through new territory.

Speaking for myself, the need for improvement in interreligious relations had been brought into sharp relief when I witnessed firsthand the events of September 11, 2001. My journey into the world of inter-faith work began a few months later when Rev. Dr. Bruce Robbins, at the time the general secretary of the General Commission on Christian Unity and Interreligious Concerns for The United Methodist Church, suggested me for a consulting position at Religions for Peace, arguably the world's largest interfaith organization. Through the generosity of a Rockefeller Foundation grant and with the careful guidance of Dr. Tony Kireopoulos, then executive director of Religions for Peace in the United States, I was given the opportunity to do interfaith work in a variety of communities.

I had learned a great deal about world religions and theology as a student at the University of Chicago's Divinity School and Boston University's Division of Religious and Theological Studies. But Religions for Peace was interfaith boot camp. As local leaders and I focused on issues of special concern to them, I gained new perspectives on religious structures and relations. Plus, I discovered a yearning—in myself and in those good and faithful people whom I encountered—to help people of different faith traditions find their way to live and work together.

A year later, when Dr. Kireopoulos became associate general secretary for International Affairs and Peace at the National Council of Churches, I had the great privilege of becoming executive director of Religions for Peace-USA (RFP-USA). For more than three decades, dozens of senior religious leaders and interreligious affairs officers of American religious communities have been coming together in this organization to work for peace. It was an honor to lead them and learn from them.

Somewhere in between, Lynn Szwaja, then at the Rockefeller Foundation and next at the Henry Luce Foundation, helped give me the freedom to push, test, and learn about enabling religious coopera-tion. Being a program officer in a grant-making foundation is not as easy at it sounds. For her gentle guidance and trust, for her sensitivities to the value of establishing healthful interreligious relations, I am deeply indebted. In fact, during the final stages of work on this book I was leading a national Interfaith Academy for Religious Leaders via the generosity of a Henry Luce Foundation grant.

Here is just a sampling of the issues and people I worked with through the auspices of RFP-USA: Native American language and cultural loss with a consortium of religious and Native groups in Oklahoma City; religious intolerance and public education with Dr. Carl Evans of Partners in Dialogue in Columbia, South Carolina; immigrants and hospitality with Dr. Abraham Peck of Interfaith Maine in a broad community gathering in Lewiston, Maine; workers' rights and living wages with Bruce Jay at the local affiliate of Interfaith Worker Justice in Miami, Florida; the death penalty with Rev. Dr. Clark Lobenstine and the InterFaith Conference of Metropolitan Washington in Washington, D.C.; and interfaith education with Rev. Dr. Vern Barnet of Community Resources Engaging the Spirit in Kansas City. Each community, though often underappreciated and underrecognized for the bridges they build, taught me valuable lessons; all of them are part of the story that led to this book.

I also learned much from colleagues in the National Association of Ecumenical and Interreligious Staff, the North American Interfaith Network, and Hartford Seminary. Josef Walker of Kansas City Harmony jokingly talks about us interfaith workers as "running around with flashlights in the dark." If that is so, then the annual meetings of these organizations were the warm campfires we gathered around together when we had finished running and had begun, instead, to swap notes and ideas.

The leadership of Religions for Peace-USA allowed me to develop the organization to include a broader table of religions, a richer tapestry of resources, and a whole new legion of young people who came to serve as interns and volunteers. Without these interns, this book would have never come into being. I am also grateful for the tireless efforts of my associates—Lori Calmbacher, Kinza Ghaznavi, and Rori Picker Neiss. An Evangelical Christian, a progressive Muslim, and an Orthodox Jew, they represented the diversity that we sought to model. Each excelled in their understanding of the mission and purpose of Religions for Peace. Whenever I become doubtful about the prospects of increasing interreligious understanding, I think of them and their peers and I am renewed with hope. Rori deserves to be singled out. She carried the administrative responsibility of this book during a challenging period of life transitions for the both of us. Without her, I am not certain it would have come together.

These three co-workers were joined over the course of three years by more than four dozen other interns and volunteers who joined me on a hunt for information, methods, and resources. These volunteers gave joy to everyone associated with Religions for Peace. Some of those who need to be especially thanked for their contribution include: Alicia Allison, Erin Anderson, Nadia Bolkin, Katherine Clark, Caitlin Deschenes-Desmond, Maheen Farooqi, Asya Gribov, Anne Hillman, Rabia Ibtasar, Briana Kramer, Erna Leslie, Evelyn Lu, Rubina Madni, Andrew Olsen, Krishan Vijay Patel, Zachary Shaeffer, Stacy Smith, Yuko Shiomi, Joanne Tien, and Kimberly Ann Vassilatos. And a mothering presence to all of us was Dorothy Savage, a trusted friend, colleague, and neighbor. She was interfaith before interfaith was cool.

The high-level diplomacy and unwavering grace with which Very Rev. Leonid Kishkovsky, Rev. Kyoichi Sugino, and Dr. William Vendley carried out the work of Religions for Peace were a constant inspiration to me. They brought me into contact with high echelons of leadership at the United Nations and with religious communities that I probably would not have otherwise had access to. And the erudite Rev. Robert Smylie helped me make sense of it all.

Friendships with colleagues in sister organizations provided me with another avenue of learning. In addition to the contributors to this book, Rev. Paul Chaffee (Interfaith Center at the Presidio), Rev. Dirk Ficca (Council for a Parliament of the World's Religions), Jeffery Huffines (National Spiritual Assembly of the Bahá'í), Sister Joan Kirby (Temple of Understanding), Professor Yehezkel Landau (Hartford Seminary), Rev. Sam Muyskens (Inter-Faith Ministries of Wichita), Rev. Chloe Breyer and Matt Weiner (Interfaith Center of New York), and Monica Willard and Dr. Charles Gibbs (United Religions Initiative) each opened themselves up to me, sharing both their sincerity and camaraderie.

This publication was aided by the insights and feedback of an advisory board of professionals in the field of interfaith relations. Dr. Lucinda Mosher is to be especially thanked for her editing savvy, for example. From Bahá'ís to Zoroastrians, they bring different eyes and voices to our common work for peace.

Members of the advisory board are:

Dr. John Berthrong, Institute for Dialogue Among Religious Traditions, Boston University

Rev. Dr. C. Welton Gaddy, Interfaith Alliance (ex officio)

Homi Gandhi, Zoroastrian Association of Greater New York

Judith Hertz, Commission on Interreligious Affairs, Union for Reform Judaism

Jeffery Huffines, National Spiritual Assembly of the Baha'is of the U.S.

April Kunze, Interfaith Youth Core (ex officio)

Rev. Dr. Clark Lobenstine, InterFaith Conference of Metropolitan Washington (ex officio)

Patrick Markey, Focolare Movement

Dr. Lucinda Mosher, Anglican Communion Network for Inter Faith Concerns

Dr. Paul Numrich, Theological Consortium of Greater Columbus, Ohio

Dr. Eboo Patel, Interfaith Youth Core (ex officio)

Rev. Dr. Shanta Premawardhana, World Council of Churches

Dr. Louay Safi, Leadership Development Center, Islamic Society of North America

Rev. Koichi Saito, Rissho Kosei-kai (Engaged Buddhism Community)

Dr. Tarunjit Singh Butalia, Interfaith Committee, World Sikh Council-America Region

Arunima Sinha, Hindu Community of South Carolina

Abby Stamelman Hocky, Interfaith Center of Greater Philadelphia (ex officio)

Rev. Susan Teegen-Case, Arts & Spirituality Center (ex officio)

Rev. Dr. Francis Tiso, United States Conference of Catholic Bishops (ex officio)

Director-General Yoshimi Umeda, International Shinto Foundation

Arvind Vora, Federation of Jain Associations in North America

Each of these board members was given opportunities to make corrections and comment on the contents of this book, but the ultimate responsibility for any errors, oversights, or other shortcomings rests solely with me as editor. I welcome any feedback that will aid in its improvement. Please visit www.interreligious.org/InterActiveFaith to add your voice.

Finally and most importantly, my beautiful wife Laura has been a loving and faithful companion in our journey together. I love her dearly and see in my children's eyes her zest for life. If my mother, Lena Heckman, enabled me to believe that I could do whatever I set my mind to, I couldn't have accomplished anything without my wife's steadfast patience and encouragement.

BUD HECKMAN

Introduction

Interfaith Dialogue:
What Is It and Why Is It Important?

Some people think that all the equipment you need to discuss religion is a mouth.

—HERMAN WOUK

Coming to Your Backyard

The settings might be different but the underlying issues are the same. In the Deep South, a prominent state school board member refers to Hindus and Buddhists with a derogatory slur while discussing school prayer policy. A small town in Maine at first embraces its Muslim Somalian immigrants, but when they keep coming and coming the mayor says, "No more!" In a city in Kansas, the mayor's prayer breakfast grows to include people of different faiths, but its leaders continue to speak in exclusive and triumphant ways about the supremacy of their own. Outside a gas station in the Southwest, a peace-loving Sikh grandfather is shot to death by a xenophobic bigot. As religious diversity grows, so do interreligious tensions.

Since the 1960s, the United States has been rapidly growing more religiously diverse. No longer relegated to enclaves in major cities on the two coasts, this diversity is finding its way even to small towns in Middle America. Americans are struggling to come to terms with their new neighbors—some, as in the examples above, are implacably hostile. Others want to be better neighbors but aren't sure how they can be. This book is for anyone who is interested in working to foster healthy communities in which positive, forward-looking interreligious cooperation is a key element.

Two young generations (so-called X and Y) of Americans have grown up with religious diversity as a fact of life. But merely living in proximity to people of different faiths does not necessarily equip one to be a good neighbor to them. Faith communities can be insulating enclaves of knowledge and relationships; they often contain a mixture of exclusionary and inclusionary tendencies. Since people fear what they do not know, it is easy for them to cling, consciously or not, to the exclusionary. In other words, if we want to develop deeper and more fruitful relationships with our neighbors, we can't rely on our good intentions. We need to be genuinely motivated and self-aware, and we have to learn specific skills, not all of which are obvious or easy to master.

A Look Inside

This book is divided into three parts. Part I offers guidance on how to achieve interfaith dialogue through different media: spoken dialogue (chapter 1), the arts (chapter 2), and shared "worship" (chapter 3). The contributors to part II focus on putting interfaith into action, either through service (chapter 4) or advocacy (chapter 5). Part III offers a brief overview of major faith traditions, a short guide to some good interfaith organizations and resource centers, and suggestions for further learning.

Each of the chapters is written by the people who I believe are the best in the field. Rev. Dr. Francis Tiso is the staff person responsible for interfaith relations and formal dialogues for the Catholic Church in the United States; few people understand models of formal and informal spoken dialogue as well as he does. Rev. Tiso's appreciation for the integrity and character of institutional relationships stands in contrast to the three women—Abby Stamelman Hocky, Rev. Susan Teegen-Case, and Rabbi Carol Harris-Shapiro—who work together more organically in urban Philadelphia to build interreligious community through use of the arts. In their chapter, you will see how they successfully revel in the "interplay of art, spirituality, and social change."

Rev. Dr. Clark Lobenstine shares some of the best ways he has learned to put an interfaith prayer service together, which is harder to do tastefully than it sounds. The most experienced of our contributors, Rev. Lobenstine has led the InterFaith Conference of Metropolitan

Washington for nearly thirty years, while helping to expand the interfaith movement through the North American Interfaith Network and other organizations. He has thoughtfully mentored dozens of interfaith leaders, including myself.

Dr. Eboo Patel, founder and executive director of the Interfaith Youth Core (IFYC), is one of the interfaith movement's true celebrities. Along with his writing partners April Kunze, vice president of programs for IFYC, and Noah Silverman, one of its most committed field organizers and educators, he lays out the IFYC methodology of helping young people find shared values through engaging in service together.

A prolific author, TV commentator, and newspaper columnist, Rev. Dr. C. Welton Gaddy, head of the Interfaith Alliance and its foundation, also hosts his own radio show on Air America. His chapter focuses on meaningful advocacy work. Many interfaith organizations steer clear of anything political for fear of damaging the fragile relationships between their members. Some engage in what I call "soft advocacy," which is moderate organizing and action (usually educational rather than overt petitioning or lobbying) around broadly accepted issues such as poverty, homelessness, and the environment. As long as it is nonpartisan and broadly interreligious, Rev. Gaddy encourages both this soft advocacy and even what I call "hard advocacy," if warranted. The magic, he finds, is in doing it collectively as religions working together. Altogether, these contributors give you a broad sampling of the types and methodologies of interfaith dialogue.

Did you know that there are board games that teach about other religions? Do you know any nearby interfaith organizations that you might connect to, or if they can provide assistance and models to help you start your own? The resources collected in part III come largely from my own research, as I looked for ways to help myself—and others—do interfaith work.

The interfaith resources section (chapter 6) leads off with short sketches of the world's religious traditions, each reviewed by representatives from or scholars of the traditions. It is meant to give thumbnail sketches of the histories and beliefs of key traditions. While they are no substitute for personal encounter with present-day practitioners, they do offer a very rudimentary map for neophytes exploring their way in uncharted territory.

Those wanting to make their way into even deeper waters, seeking resources and examples to do local interfaith work, will appreciate the list of organizations, websites, and resource centers in the section on interfaith organizations and the web (chapter 7). There are many, many excellent organizations throughout North America and beyond working to promote interfaith understanding. All of them could not be included here. The section concentrates on organizations with: a significant web presence, helpful networks or resources, a noted history in interfaith work, or a broad reach, for example, umbrella or national organizations. Contacting one of these umbrella organizations will likely be your first step in locating local chapters in your area.

The editors and contributors to this book welcome feedback and tips on your favorite resources at: www.interreligious.org/InterActiveFaith. Additional resources and updates will be available on this site. Your contributions may become a part of future editions to this book.

To navigate these resources better, or to nurture your left brain, you may wish to consult appendix A, where there is an analysis of the types of interfaith organizations and activities. To round out this handbook, Rev. Tiso offers two bonuses to his chapter on spoken dialogue. The first, in appendix B, is a contemporary analysis of Leonard Swidler's famous "Dialogue Decalogue." The second, in appendix C, is a detailed model of a formal, structured bilateral (two-way) dialogue.

Getting on the Same Page

So exactly what is interfaith dialogue? On one level it can be as simple as a person of one faith having a conversation with a person of another, a sharing of ideas, values, images, feelings, or beliefs across faith lines. On another level it can be a good deal more complex and nuanced. The terms themselves—both *interfaith* and *dialogue*—can be understood in several ways. As with many things in life, I have learned *not* to expect people to hear them the way that I intend them to be heard, at least at first. In fact, I start my presentations now with short games that help my audiences "discover" and practice the definitions together.

For starters, most people construe the term *interfaith* more broadly and the term *dialogue* more narrowly than a person who already has some experience in the interfaith field. They understand *dialogue* to be whatever comes out of the mouths of "talking heads";

interfaith is broadened to mean anything religious encountering anything differently religious. Professionals tend to broaden *dialogue* so that it encompasses a much wider (and more appealing) range of encounters, and they narrow *interfaith* as a frame for specific types of interreligious engagements. Hopefully, some of this nuancing will be elucidated by the different authors of this book, as they share their own viewpoints about what they consider to be an interfaith dialogue. In the spirit of good dialogue, we don't assume a singular point of view on the issue.

Christians, who still make up more than three-fourths of the U.S. population, are more inclined to talk about "ecumenical" activity or dialogue than members of other groups. The word *ecumenical* comes from the Greek *oikoumene*, which literally means "God's whole created order." This causes some confusion, for though the word's root meaning is broadly inclusive, most people—and that includes those of us in the interfaith movement—construe it in the sense in which it has mostly been used historically, to mean "when Christians talk with other Christians." A little "definition settling" is called for, and this is as good a place as any to make sure that we understand other key terms to mean the same things. In fact, successful dialogue is dependent on it.

Key Terms

- **Dialogue** is when persons of different viewpoints come together and interact. Their "coming together" could be in the form of conversation, sharing a meal, sharing in an experience such as creating art or participating in a religious observance, or some other form of engagement. As you will see more clearly in the models described throughout this book, our image of dialogue is not and should not be limited to "head talk." This is a key point. You'll learn more about the motivations, goals, attitudes, and ground rules for dialogue in the chapters ahead.

- **Ecumenism** is when Christians from different sects or movements within Christianity come together. It is a particularized form of *intra*faith activity.

- **Intrafaith dialogue** is when persons within a tradition come together with other persons of that faith tradition. Christianity has its own term for it—*ecumenical*. Examples of intrafaith would be when Sunni Muslims interact with Shiite Muslims or when so-called "engaged" Buddhists interact with "traditional" Buddhists.

- **Interfaith dialogue** is when persons of different faith traditions or broader religious families interact. This happens by accident all the time, in schools and workplaces, for example, whenever people of different cultures and belief systems share their values and views in everyday interactions. We don't usually think to call such encounters "interfaith dialogues" but that's what they are. School boards and human resource departments are getting wise and learning new ways to address religious diversity issues creatively and purposively.[1]

- **Interreligious dialogue** has a technical meaning within the field of interfaith relations. It doesn't refer to the casual interactions between members of different religious communities, but rather to formal encounters between their representatives. The term implicitly recognizes those leaders' responsibility to represent their respective communities. *Interreligious dialogue* is also used sometimes when the problematic aspects of "interfaith" may be an impediment. Interfaith dialogue is more typically used by the Abrahamic faiths—Judaism, Christianity, and Islam—and it is limited in that Buddhism, Jainism, and Advaita Vedanta (a type of Hinduism) do not refer to themselves as "faiths." Thus, interreligious dialogue can be a worthy term, even when it does not convey either "formal encounters" or "representatives."

- **Multifaith dialogue** may seem like the same thing as *interfaith*, and the terms are sometimes used interchangeably, but within the interfaith movement, *multifaith* has a unique nuance. It is used when people of different faiths come together but without specific articulation or recognition of their individual faiths as an intentionally or conspicuously public part of the effort. In this sense, most enterprises in life where different people come together are by their very nature multifaith.

- **Multireligious dialogue**, likewise, may seem like the same thing as *interreligious*, but, like *multifaith*, it is in fact used to distinguish those occasions when people of different religions come together without special attention to their individual religions, particularly when those involved are leaders or formal representatives of their faith traditions. As an example, there is a multireligious effort underway to try to meet the Millennium Development Goals of the United Nations.

People frequently use some of these terms interchangeably, especially in the popular media but also in the academy. So be conscious of the way you hear and use these words with others. I find that an investment in some simple reflective listening—for example, "What I am hearing you say is …"—usually clears the path to deeper understanding.

A Word about Movements

It is very important to note that the word *interfaith* is sometimes used in a sense that is not yet well known but deeply confusing, if not to say troubling, to many when they do encounter it. Due to cultural shifts in the American landscape, more and more people are developing or claiming more than one religious identity. For example, a person might have grown up with parents of two different faiths (a Jewish father and a Catholic mother) or may have been raised Episcopalian but were introduced to Buddhist practices in college.[2] Scholars sometimes speak of this phenomenon as *double belonging,* but more and more, such individuals refer to themselves as "interfaith." A few seminaries and hundreds of small religious communities resembling the simple house churches of early Christianity have sprung up to respond to the needs and interests of such people in the last few decades. These groups frequently call themselves "interfaith" as well, meaning intraperson, not intracommunity. If you are confused, you are not alone.

As a simple matter of justice, I subscribe to the idea that people should have a right to self-describe. Language is powerful, after all. However, when the choice of words creates a problem for those who have already been using them and in a larger and more popular sense, it engenders confusion and some tension. For a person who strives to bring people of different faiths together, I realize that many good people of faith fear the idea of "interfaith"—even in its intracommunity sense—because they are preconditioned to believe that it will dilute the true sense of their own tradition. It is difficult enough to convince these people that they won't weaken their faith or lose their identity by relating with others of different faiths, even when the boundaries between religions are clearly delineated. It becomes nearly impossible when they encounter people calling themselves "interfaith" who have in fact incorporated more than one tradition into their religious identities. Somehow, we must find another word. I would suggest that *multipath* or *multitraditioned* might cause less confusion than *interfaith*, but whatever new term is eventually selected, it must come from within and be owned by people with multiple religious identities and allegiances before it will catch on.

Another problem that has been of concern to the interfaith movement is its sometimes tense relations with the ecumenical movement. Like the interfaith movement, but a few decades earlier, the ecumenical movement began as a grassroots enterprise. As it grew in strength, it institutionalized and became mainstreamed to the culture. But as mainline Protestant denominations, which were often at the core of ecumenism, began to decline, ecumenical organizations started to suffer as well. Today, ecumenical organizations are consolidating, disappearing, and spending down their endowments. Meanwhile, interfaith organizations are just finding their way into being, trying to develop structures and institutions. The result is that the two movements often find themselves competing for the same resources within local religious communities. Thus, a tension arises between the "E's and the I's."

Unfortunately, the tensions, I think, are rooted in often unspoken arguments about truth claims. They may cloak themselves in political and social organizational issues, but at their root, the disagreements are profoundly theological. Analogies are often drawn using one of two sets of imagery: water (stream, rivers, oceans) or paths (on mountains, connected and/or unconnected). For example, do all rivers flow into the same sea? Are there many paths up one mountain? Are there many paths on many different mountains? Is one path or mountain better or truer than others?

My friend Eboo Patel sidesteps these language hang-ups—of ecumenical vs. interfaith and multipath vs. interfaith—by focusing on religious cooperation as a centering idea. It is a clever approach that appeals even to secular people. It is a technique that skirts theological wranglings to get religious people on a human and sociological plane to work for the common good.

I enjoy trying to explore the answers to these questions, and sometimes I am bold enough to think that I have some of the answers.

At the same time, I have come to learn through many years of theological education that the smartest people I know disagree widely about the answers. Meanwhile the world is really hurting and interreligious strife is rampant. Surely the demand for access to clean water, the effects of poverty and disease, and other serious issues trump these theoretical arguments. Most religious traditions teach their followers to have humility about what they can know and urge them to put the pressing needs of their fellow humans first as the surest way of exercising their true faith.

Why Interfaith Anything?

America is coming to a tipping point, a critical crossroads after which no one will be able to avoid dealing with our growing religious diversity. Using the American Religious Identification Survey, staff at the Ontario Consultants on Religious Tolerance have suggested that, if current trends continue, by as early as the year 2035 the majority of Americans will belong to non-Christian faiths.[3] If you are already interested enough in interfaith work to pick up this guidebook, then you are ahead of the curve. Congratulations!

American educator and author Edith Hamilton once said, "Faith is not belief. Belief is passive. Faith is active." If that is so, and if it is true that no faith stands in isolation, then it stands to reason that interfaith must be interactive. The title of this book came from this stream of thought—that the faith of each person is living in dialogue with that of others. *InterActive Faith* gives people of faith the tools they need to speak across the barrier of their particular class or genus in the human gene pool of faiths; it is a how-to manual for building a respectfully engaged, mutually understanding global community. The only prerequisite is the yearning or will to engage "the other."

How We Got Here

In the grand scheme of things, the interfaith movement in the United States is still in its infancy or, at best, an awkward toddler. While there was the landmark Parliament of the World's Religions in 1893, some early pioneers such as the National Conference of Christians and Jews in 1927, the International Association of Religious Freedom in 1900, and many local interfaith organization that began in the 1960s, there has been an explosion of organizations and activity only since the mid-'90s. We still have much to learn from one another.

If you are anything like me, you are still trying to grow out of the homogeneity and prejudices you learned in your childhood. Abbot Thomas Keating calls this "our tendency to over identification." I grew up in a small town in Ohio. The vast majority of its residents were Protestant Christians and everyone was white. Our idea of "interfaith," if we even knew the term, was that it was a synonym for "ecumenical"—it meant having some sort of engagement with Catholics. No one who was a role model for me ever said that it was important for us to know Catholics or to understand our differences from them. I wish someone had. Simply verbalizing this idea to people whom you influence can make a tremendous difference.

I remember asking a grade school friend if he was a Christian, because I didn't really know what the word meant. Apparently he was as clueless as I was, because he replied, "No, (I am not a Christian.) I am Catholic." And so ended my first exploration into ecumenical understanding. My neighbor David taught me a little more. He was a Catholic and he went to church on Wednesdays and Saturdays. This was clearly mysterious. Everybody in my family's frame of reference went to church at eleven o'clock on Sunday morning. Why would anyone go to church on Wednesdays and Saturdays? They must be up to something! David taught me a little bit about catechism and communion wafers too. Then, when I was in high school, I met a girl at the local mall who lived in the nearby "big city." It wasn't until the end of our fourth date that I realized that this girl whom I was so attracted to was Jewish. Apparently, love is blind. She was so very kind and patient with me, even when I asked her four different times what she was doing for Christmas or what she wanted for Christmas.

These early encounters with people of different faiths, however awkward they might have been, informed my continuing desire to explore interfaith relations. They were my first teachers. People who are from minority faith traditions do not have the luxury of choosing whether or not they should understand and relate to people of other faiths; for them it is a necessity. This is an important point. In contrast, most people who are from a dominant faith tradition—such as Christians in the United States—do not have to understand anything about other faith traditions. For them, it is a privilege of choice, of leisure, of willingness. But as the nineteenth-century philologist F. Max Müller mused, "He who knows one, knows none." That is to say, it is only when we agree to engage the religious other with some depth that we articulate who it is that we are, what it is that we believe. In the process of engagement, we discover not only a richer, deeper, more complex world, but also one in which our own faith is richer, deeper, and more contextualized, and the divine reality is seen in more of its fullness.

Traveling the world, attending many different seminaries, and living in large metropolitan areas, as I came to do, have made me a very different person than I was when I was young. Luckily for me, the graduate program I entered in Boston in 1994 had just been completely retooled to match our changing world so that entering students, who came from many different backgrounds, declared their faith tradition and articulated their theological positions in an interreligious environment. In the first year, we studied together the core texts and motifs of the world's religions.

My family and I have attended a church in New York City whose physical plant houses many things, including a Jewish congregation, a satellite of an Islamic mosque, and half a dozen very diverse congregations of Christians. It's Manhattan—space is tight. The most powerful person in our church is not, as I was taught in seminary, the church secretary, but rather the receptionist/space booker. Living together in such tight quarters on such an around-the-clock schedule has put these traditions into working and loving relationships with each other on a de facto basis, if nothing else.

You will have your own stories of encounter. Sharing them with others and seeking new opportunities is what interfaith work is about.

The Golden Door Opens Wide

One of the seminal documents in the interfaith movement is the *Nostra Aetate* declaration of 1965, which formally changed the stance of the Roman Catholic Church regarding people of other faiths. Its reverberations are still being felt today. But I would argue that another document promulgated that same year has had the most significance for interreligious work in the American context: the Immigration and Nationality Act of 1965. We have only just begun to understand the significance of this piece of legislation, which opened the "golden door" of America to immigrants of all nationalities and faiths. Even with the curtailings and adjustments made in the wake of 9/11, I believe that this act has done more to radically alter the future religious and cultural landscape of America than anything else. It is widely acknowledged that Martin Luther King Jr. was the central figure in eliminating legal racism in the United States. What is less well known is the role he played in creating an interfaith America through his advocacy for this legislation. As time will eventually tell, it may turn out to be his greatest legacy, one yet unrealized or well understood.

A quick review of immigration history is helpful here. When we take into account the religious ways of indigenous or Native peoples and recall that at least 10 percent of the Africans brought into this country as slaves were Muslim and many more were animists (though neither group was permitted to practice its religion openly), we have had religious diversity in America since the first day of colonization.

From 1820 to 1930 the United States received about 60 percent of the world's immigrants, largely from predominately Christian and Jewish Europe. The Chinese Exclusion Act (1882), the Gentlemen's Agreement (1907) with Japan, and more comprehensive quota laws in the Immigration Act of 1924 all codified bias in the form of race and nationality. Even with the elimination of bias on the condition of race with the McCarran-Walter Act of 1952, certain forms of bias were kept intact so that the quota for European immigrants was nearly 150,000 per year as compared to quotas of about 3,000 and 1,400 immigrants per year for Asia and Africa, respectively. And for a long time, those new immigrants had been concentrated in just a few states—New York, New Jersey, California, Illinois, Texas, Arizona, and Massachusetts. Since 1965, however, the growth has been exponential. Now, due to new procedures for immigration and settling refugees occasioned by the Immigration and Nationality Act, they are popping up in other than the typical metropolitan areas. Today substantial immigrant communities can be found in places like Lewiston, Maine; Columbus, Ohio; Kansas City, Kansas; St. Paul, Minnesota; and Spokane, Washington, just to name a few.

The number of practicing muslims has grown significantly as well. Muslim students who came here to study in the 1960s and formed Muslim student associations are now in their fifties and sixties and are leading sophisticated national Muslim organizations. Tens of thousands of American Muslims attend their annual conventions. Similar patterns of institutionalization and growth are visible in Buddhist, Hindu, Jain, Sikh, and other immigrant communities as well.

How is this playing out? Between 1990 and 2001 religious identification surveys and our most recent census-related data show that the number of Americans self-identifying as Christians dropped from 86 percent to 76 percent of the population, even as the overall population grew. While estimates and counts vary widely, there are now as many as 5 million Muslims in the United States. That is more than Episcopalians, Quakers, and Disciples of Christ combined; Islam now may well surpass Judaism as the second largest religious tradition in the United States. Indeed, researchers say that Islam is the fastest-growing religion not just in the United States but in the world. The most recent surveying shows Hinduism may be eclipsing Islam in rate of growth. In any case, more than a sea change is evident. There are now more than a million Hindus, more than 2 million Buddhists, and nearly half a million Sikhs in the United States. Scholars are inventing new terms like *polyvalence* and *kaleidoculture* to keep up with the emerging situation.

Martin Luther King Jr. was masterful because he was able to speak about diversity, harmony, and justice bilingually, in both religious and secular language (though every utterance he made was informed and infused by his religious point of view). To survive and thrive in our changing, increasingly interfaith world, we too must become bilingual and learn to speak from a deeply formed and rich personal faith, but speak in such a way that we can meet and dialogue with others who have journeyed along different paths.

The Generation Gap

My generation and the one after mine, Generation Y or the so-called Millennium Generation, largely take religious diversity as a given, a necessity, or even a preferred option. We are far more likely than our parents to know people of other faith traditions, to engage in and learn about other faith traditions, and, in some cases, to actually pick up the practices of different traditions in an almost eclectic, or even consumerist, fashion.

When I was called to build a program for The United Methodist Church to dispatch young people to different parts of the globe for social justice work, lots of young people sent in flowery letters about their Christian faith along with their applications. When they came to New York for their training, they would share about their faith in more detail and the picture always turned out to be more complicated than their applications had seemed. One would say, for example, "Well, yes, my dad is an Episcopalian priest, and I did grow up in the church, but I have been studying about Buddhism and Buddhist meditation and even done some Hindu yoga." I wound up with lots of "nightstand Buddhists" and other young people whose religious searching had complicated their religious lives.

I think it is absolutely essential that our adult role models articulate and practice a positive and humble posture toward people of other faith traditions, and yet encourage young people to be framed and rooted in a faith tradition. Too many parents of the baby boom generation, dissatisfied with organized religion themselves, have failed to bring up their children in the context of a particular faith tradition.

The glass is either half empty or half full. We are either on the brink of disaster or on the cusp of a great new thing. On the one hand, we have the pluralists. They are represented most preeminently by Diana Eck and the Pluralism Project at Harvard University (which, by the way, offers some of the best resources in the interfaith movement). The pluralists say that endless and increasing diversity is good. It is the American ideal, in fact. They urge us to move beyond mere recognition and explore and enjoy diversity to its depths. On the other hand we have the exclusivists or the "clash of civilizationists," to adapt Diana Eck's famous Harvard colleague Samuel Huntington's catchphrase. Huntington charges that increasing diversity leads inevitably to increasing conflict, socioeconomic unrest, and political instability. He sees civilizations, religions preeminent among them, as the new places of struggle, after the so-called demise of nation-states as mitigating powers.

At Religions for Peace, I learned not to make broad claims about the nature of truth and to resist the temptation to play down the very real religious differences between people of different faith traditions. Interfaith work is at its best when people of faith are in relationship with one another, respecting the integrity of each other's traditions, and addressing together our common challenges as humans.

Lessons from the Field

When I did fieldwork for Religions for Peace in local U.S. communities, most groups that I met with wanted to know how to get "them" to come to "us." In most cases this meant how the "us" of Protestants, Catholics, Unitarians, and Jews, who were already working together in some way, could get the "them" of Orthodox Christians, Muslims, Sikhs, Jains, Hindus, Buddhists, Shinto-followers, and Bahá'ís involved. Many didn't even know where to find "the religious other." New religious communities meet in homes and places they can rent, like schools. Too often they don't have any physical addresses because they are not yet in bricks and mortar. They are not in "the P.O.T."— the plain old telephone book—as Martin Marty, my mentor at the University of Chicago, used to say.

What I learned from my many ventures into American communities is that if you sit in an ethnic restaurant and talk to people and eventually say, "Take me to your leader, please," you will find the diversity that has been under your nose all along. My bet is that Buddhists run that Thai restaurant. A Hindu named Patel owns the local motel. The Greeks at the Greek diner might be Orthodox. If you ask one of these citizens to share with you about his or her faith, you may be surprised where the conversation goes.

I spent a good bit of time with emerging interfaith organizations on the issue of how "we" might make our environments more inviting and hospitable to "them." We had to learn to spend more time just listening, to have meetings that were more focused on building relationships than nailing down agendas, and to allow "our" expectations and standards to be bracketed, de-Westernized even, in the process. We stopped asking the age-old question, "How do we get them to join us?" and learned to ask the real question, which is, "What can *we* do that will meet them where they are and be a benefit to them and (hopefully) to us?"

A major paradigm shift is needed.

Some Practical Ideas

Still trying to figure out exactly where to dip your toe in the interreligious pool? Try some of these practical ideas that I offer to people who are just becoming interested in the interfaith movement. Each one is featured and expanded upon in the pages ahead.[4]

Get Connected

- Attend the North American Interfaith Network's annual meeting.
- Subscribe to interfaith newsletters from Religions for Peace-USA, the Pluralism Project, the Interfaith Center at the Presidio, and the InterFaith Conference of Metropolitan Washington.
- Check out the web resources mentioned in part III of this guidebook.

Open Your Doors

- When I was working in Oklahoma, the Bahá'ís realized that they could help by simply making their community centers available to Native Americans who lacked facilities.
- When a nearby synagogue's roof collapsed, my local United Methodist Church opened its doors to its congregation; more than fifteen years later the church and synagogue are more interconnected than ever.

Learn by Doing

- Service projects are a great vehicle to facilitate interfaith discussion and interaction. Just ask the folks at Habitat for Humanity, Interfaith Youth Core, or your local interfaith council.

Host an Informal Dialogue

- There are so many models to choose from—study circles, living room dialogues, listening circles, and more.

Organize Around an Issue

- Every local community must decide for itself what the issue is, but getting people mobilized and capitalizing on their faith-based motivations for doing good works can be fun and inspiring.

Have a Formal Dialogue

- Host a structured bilateral (two-way) or multilateral (three or more parties) conversation in your community.

Tour Houses of Worship

- Visit each others' houses of worship. The Greater Kansas City Interfaith Council has a clever passport-based program that makes the experience a real adventure.

Share a Meal Together

- Breaking bread together in one another's homes is one of the most memorable of relationship-building experiences. I have developed many lasting relationships at iftars and seders.

Respond to Hate, Violence, and Conflict with a Public Presence

- When the media is covering conflict and controversy, have a visible presence and a positive response. The Qur'an 55 project of the Interfaith Peace Network of Western New York responded to reports about the desecration of the Qur'an with a public press conference at a local bookstore. Religious leaders purchased Qur'ans to show their commitment to interfaith understanding and to the sacred value of religious texts.

Start a Book Group

- Women of Faith groups across the country do this as well as most local interreligious dialogues.

Act It Out

- Consider creating a play from your experiences. *The Children of Abraham Project* in Detroit, *The Hindu and the Cowboy* from the Greater Kansas City Interfaith Council, and the *Same Difference*[5] project in New York each engaged thousands of people in interfaith dialogue in their broader communities by taking a right-brained approach.

Engage Social Justice Causes

- Work on settling refugees, cleaning up the environment, tackling AIDS, or whatever is pressing in your community.

Hold a Festival

- Consider a festival to either welcome a new religious community or celebrate all of them together. An annual community festival with dragon boats in Lowell, Massachusetts, fosters the integration of Southeast Asian Buddhists, particularly Cambodian boat peoples, who settled as refugees in the city.

Celebrate Music and the Arts

- Hold a concert like the one the InterFaith Conference of Metropolitan Washington puts on annually.
- Hold an art contest or community art project like the ones the Arts & Spirituality Center of Philadelphia and the Interfaith Center of Greater Philadelphia do.

Facilitate Reconciliation

- Inter-Faith Ministries of Wichita has a court-recognized mediation and reconciliation program that brings victims and offenders into relationship with one another. It enjoys a very high rate of success, demonstrably reducing its participant offenders' recidivism.
- Religions for Peace-USA's reconciliation program called Return to the Earth brings Native and non-Natives peoples into relationship with one another as they help repatriate the remains of Native Americans that are scattered across the United States.

This profusion of models and options for interfaith engagement hardly scratches the surface of what's possible. You'll encounter a lot more of them in the pages ahead. Don't worry about doing the wrong thing, just dive in. Start small and work your way in. You will make mistakes; everyone does. It's okay, you are human. Seek forgiveness, laugh at yourself, and move on.

Strategies for Creating Interfaith Dialogue

One of the most popular guidelines for interreligious dialogue is Leonard Swidler's "Dialogue Decalogue," which has been reproduced in many forms since it was first published in the *Journal of Ecumenical Studies* in 1983. Father Tiso deals with it in some detail in appendix B of this book. Many other such guidelines have appeared in the intervening decades. In the spirit of Swidler, here are the Ten Commandments that have guided my own interfaith work:

1. *Listen first.* Use the reflective listening techniques developed by relational psychologist Carl Rogers to get the most out of your conversation. Open your body posture, look at your dialogue partner, and seek affirmations that you are hearing correctly what they are sharing. Allow space in the conversation. Don't interrupt.

2. *Speak for yourself and allow others to do the same.* You don't do anyone a favor by trying to speak for them.

3. *Try to see the best in others.* Resist comparing your best self with their worst. In other words, do unto others as you would wish them to do unto you.

4. *Talk about your faith as it is, not as it ideally should be.* Be sober and honest about the worst parts of your tradition. Every tradition has its dark corners. Humility invites deeper understanding.

5. *Know that dialogue is not debate.* There is no contest to prove who is right. Dialogue is about relationships and the process. It is the means, not the end, that matters.

6. *Meet people on terms you can both agree on.* Recognize that your preferred method of dialogue may not be theirs. Dialogue is not all conversation; it can be expressed through service, advocacy, and the arts. It might be framed by song, prayer, meal sharing, or other forms.

7. *Admit what you do not know.* Our religious traditions are large and complex. You can spend a lifetime trying to understand the depth and breadth of a single faith in all its varieties. Admit the limits of your knowledge and leave your assumptions about the religious other at the door.

8. *Accept that you might change somewhat in the process.* In fact, the laws of physics virtually dictate it. Dialogue shapes our understanding of our own self and of the other.

9. *Dialogue is strongest when it is both between (interfaith) and within (intrafaith).* Catholics and Buddhists can learn much from each other, as can Catholics and Protestants. Catholics and Protestants might learn even more if they got together sometimes to talk about Buddhism.

10. *Involve the head, the heart, and the whole body.* The best forms of dialogue move beyond mere "head talk" to heartfelt experience

and vice versa. Participants in interreligious encounters should always seek to see the religious other's viewpoint as completely as possible, to view it from within if possible.

Whatever you do, I encourage you to think about focusing on youth or at least involving youth. There are two trends among Generations X and Y. One trend is toward much greater orthodoxy; another is toward multifaith exploration and experimentation. Both forms have their extremes.

Statistics show that the vast majority of hate crimes are perpetrated by young adults and youth, often on other young adults. From the terrorists who flew planes into the World Trade Center to the vandals who spray-painted swastikas on the local synagogue, too often they are under thirty years of age. This is why Interfaith Youth Core is focused where it is. If we don't help develop positive images of faith development in a religiously pluralistic and, admittedly, sometimes unfair and imbalanced world, then we risk forfeiting our youth into lives of hopelessness and frustration, or even worse, into the hands of people who will channel and feed their disconnect to make human bombs of them.

PART I

Creating Interreligious Community through Dialogue

1

Dialogue through Conversation— Spoken Dialogue

by Rev. Dr. Francis Tiso

In the matter of religion, people eagerly fasten their eyes on the difference between their own creed and yours; whilst the charm of the study is in finding the agreements and identities in all the religions of humanity.

—RALPH WALDO EMERSON

Introduction: What Is Spoken Dialogue?

The topic of spoken dialogue takes us to the heart of the process by which religious people discuss their differences, find common ground, and plan a viable future together. American philosopher Ralph Waldo Emerson, quoted above, lived before the days of ongoing interreligious dialogue; his experience of non-Christian religions came through his readings of translations of classics of Indian religious literature such as the Bhagavad Gita. Emerson wrote of the "charm" of "finding agreements and identities in all the religions of humanity"; today perhaps we are discovering that to ignore our *differences* is not only to risk losing our credibility, but also might even subvert the purposes of interreligious dialogue.

We know from experience that it is possible to find areas in which we agree. We continue to marvel at this. At times it seems as though the highest ideals of all religions converge. On the faces of those who have dedicated a great part of their lives to interreligious dialogue, there is a certain gentleness and patience that comes from having heard "the cries of the world." Yet our experience of dialogue makes us hesitate before Emerson's use of the word "identities." We have learned that something that appears similar across religious lines might have very different meanings for each believer. There could be hidden linguistic and ritual content that we ignore at our peril; the feature might represent an instance of development that only superficially resembles another religion's practice by chance. At best, we might argue for an underlying psychological or biological basis for certain behaviors and beliefs that cross the cultural and doctrinal boundaries of religions. But we are still a long way from achieving a secure theoretical basis for comparative work in religion, and the ongoing debate among scholars of religion on the value of comparison makes the task of dialogue that much more difficult. Spoken dialogue is stronger or weaker than it could be to the extent that its tools—words—are more or less carefully translated and clearly defined. But if words and speech are inherently limited, the key to dialogue is in the hands and hearts of those who are willing to commit themselves to growth in wisdom over decades of effort. Sometimes what we do together matters more than what we say.

In late August of 1219, St. Francis of Assisi, a Roman Catholic friar, left the Crusader encampment at Damietta in the Nile Delta and walked to the Citadel in Cairo, Egypt, to speak to the Sultan al-Malek al-Kamil.[1] The Citadel is a fortress, still standing, that had been built largely by Christian captives of the Muslim rulers of Egypt. Francis could have reasonably expected to be martyred or enslaved. Instead, he and the sultan spoke in peace and respect for one another. To this day, in the treasure room of the Basilica of St. Francis in Assisi, one can see the curved dagger in an ivory scabbard that the sultan gave the saint as a token of friendship and esteem. When I think of all the blood that has been shed across the centuries on both sides of this rare moment of spoken dialogue, I want to cry out for mercy. Had we only continued the conversation without a break from 1219 to 2007, what moral and spiritual progress might we have made together?

Spoken dialogue among persons who adhere to the world's religions is, above all, a means of peacemaking and conflict resolution, precisely because the past weighs so heavily on all of us. Spoken dialogue as it is currently practiced in Europe and North America takes a number of forms, depending on the setting and participants. There are official dialogues, usually annual meetings sponsored by two or more religious organizations, whose primary purpose is to nurture well-informed relationships between and among communities of faith. These official meetings may be local, regional, or national in scope. Participants include official leadership, professional staffs, and prominent members of the scholarly community. Topics can be wide ranging, from high-level theological discussions to the preparation of recommended curricula for religious education programs. Since the participants are often involved in policy making, it is not surprising that social issues and current topics of public concern are also discussed. As my colleague Rev. Peter Cullen, rector of St. Paul's Church in Brooklyn, New York, commented in the "Speaking Across Differences" program of the Dialogue Project, dialogue "involves a disciplined decision to listen to what somebody else has to say. It is a belief that when we hear others speak, we will recognize the fact that we share more in common with the others than we think we do."[2]

The Pontifical Council for Interreligious Dialogue and the Congregation for the Evangelization of Peoples, both of the Roman Catholic Church, issued a document in 1993 entitled "Dialogue and Proclamation" that described the basic meanings that can be attributed to *dialogue*:

> Dialogue can be understood in different ways. Firstly, at the purely human level, it means reciprocal communication, leading to a common goal or, at a deeper level, to interpersonal communion. Secondly, dialogue can be taken as an attitude of respect and friendship, which should permeate all those activities constituting the evangelizing mission of the Church. This can appropriately be called "the spirit of dialogue." Thirdly, in the context of religious plurality, dialogue means "all positive and constructive interreligious relations with individuals and communities of other faiths which are directed at mutual understanding and enrichment," in obedience to truth and respect for freedom. It includes both the witness and exploration of respective religious convictions. It is in this third sense that the present document uses the term "dialogue" for one of the integral elements of the Church's evangelizing mission.

According to the Dialogue and Proclamation, the four forms that dialogue among religions take are:

1. Dialogue of life
2. Dialogue of experience
3. Dialogue of scholarship
4. Dialogue of social service

It should be clear that long-term cooperation among religious people can be built in a trustworthy way only among people who truly know, believe in, and practice their own religion with integrity. Spoken dialogue among activists who wish to engage religious communities in specific social projects is not the same thing as interreligious dialogue, which is really the interpersonal interface between two living communities of faith.

How Is This Dialogue Currently Unfolding?

The experience of recent years suggests that we need to distinguish further among concrete types of working dialogue. For example, we take note of the fact that much local, grassroots dialogue takes place at the inspiration of activists who are not necessarily recognized as official representatives of any religious tradition or institution. People interested in a topic, issue, or activity come together periodically; they are inspired in part by their religious traditions and in part by a sense of social responsibility to address these contemporary issues. In a way, this might be a "dialogue of action," but it is often necessary for these dialogue partners to share ideas and instruct one another in the practices and beliefs of their various religions as well.

Another kind of spoken dialogue can be found in an organization like Religions for Peace. Here, again following the model of a dialogue of action, representatives of religious institutions meet to promote specific activities favorable to world peace and conflict resolution. These representatives are officials of their institutions of origin and have in one way or other the authorization to represent their institutions. They are also usually experts in religious studies, policy making, foreign affairs, conflict resolution, and theology. This kind of dialogue is multilateral—many religious groups are involved.

Another form of spoken dialogue is restricted to a limited number of religious groups. For example, an Abrahamic Roundtable, like that hosted by the Washington National Cathedral, will include representatives and specialists from Judaism, Christianity, and Islam. Often these representatives are selected by the sponsoring agency from a pool of recognized leaders residing in a particular part of the country. It is not uncommon for these trilaterals to include a broad spectrum of schools of thought or denominations from within each of the participating faiths (e.g., Reform, Conservative, Reconstructionist, and Orthodox Judaism; Protestant, Orthodox, and Catholic Christians; Sunni and Shi'a Muslims). Yet another example of spoken dialogue would be the kind of bilateral dialogue that may not occur as often as the others but focuses energy by restricting participation and refining structures that promote good communication, high-level scholarship, and production of publishable results. It is worth noting that aspects of all four forms of dialogue overlap in practice.

On the local level, more frequent dialogue meetings are common. For example, the religious leaders of a particular town or (in the case of a large city) a neighborhood might meet together on a monthly basis for conversation about common problems. Sometimes this is a social event. Such groups, when they involve only Christian participants, may be called ministerial associations. In some areas, however, the membership has been expanded to include rabbis, imams, and Buddhist, Sikh, and Hindu leaders, depending on the ethnic diversity present in the region. These gatherings can become the planning group for an annual interreligious public cultural event designed to nurture mutual respect and cooperation among people of all faiths and of none. Moreover, as trust develops, these groups can volunteer to provide support to local agencies. The interreligious cooperation evidenced during the Virginia Tech massacre in April 2007 is a good example of how previously engaged multireligious chaplains could come together quickly in a crisis to provide vital support. It is easy to imagine that such associations will, from time to time, take up the role of advocacy for human rights and social justice in their communities.

In larger metropolitan areas, efforts to create a more complex version of this kind of association might be patterned on the model established in 1978 in the Washington, D.C., area by the InterFaith Conference of Metropolitan Washington (IFCMW). This gathering has become very highly developed in recent years, in accordance with the exceptional diversity present in the region. It is to be noted, however, that formal spoken dialogue is only one feature of such a large-scale program. Perhaps it would be more accurate to say that in their public events, training programs, social service projects, and in hosting foreign religious dignitaries, everything the IFCMW does is spoken dialogue.

Another model might be called the social approach. Highly effective in neighborhoods, this approach builds on the experience of religious communities in creating a sense of solidarity and belonging. Once a month, certainly not less than two or three times a year, the members of local religious communities plan a shared event around a common meal. Paying attention to each others' dietary requirements reflects the desire of all participants to grow in knowledge and respect for one another's way of life. Sharing a meal allows time for friendships to develop and enhances a sense of common purpose in the neighborhood. A particularly successful example of this kind of dialogue has been going on for many years in Chicago; participants are all women from the local Jewish, Christian, and Muslim communities. The spoken aspect of this kind of dialogue consists of informal conversation and shared prayer. Some social dialogues may invite people from various backgrounds to tell their stories of faith, work experience, immigration, travels, and so forth. From time to time, respected speakers might be invited to offer a keynote reflection to highlight the values that are celebrated in such events. These social dialogues might also be called seasonal dialogues because they require attention to the appropriate time of year. Such events might include a community barbecue event in the summer, a gathering with youth at the start of the school season in the fall, and a winter family event carefully timed not to interfere or compete with religious holidays. In the United States and Canada, Thanksgiving is also a good symbolic moment to link interfaith cooperation to a shared meal that should also include some kind of outreach to the needy. Muslim communities frequently sponsor interfaith iftar dinners, the evening meal at which the Ramadan fast is broken. Inviting members of other religious communities to iftar dinners has become an important form of social outreach for some Muslim communities.

The social approach, in fact, can derive considerable motivation when religious communities cooperate in providing necessities to the needy. In this case, the spoken dialogue will be very practical in nature. It will be about what contribution each of us can make, how we can sustain our cooperation, how we can identify specific needs, and how we can set up appropriate logistics to maintain the program. To be successful, social dialogue requires strong volunteer engagement, with all communities contributing equally. Several religious institutions have also begun to train grassroots leadership (e.g., parish ecumenical representatives) in the practice of interreligious and ecumenical dialogue in order to promote ongoing programs in parishes, mosques, synagogues, and other local institutional settings.

There is also the spiritual dialogue that has typically involved taking a look at religious belief from the point of view of contemplative practice, making possible the creative enterprise of comparative theology exemplified by the work of James Fredericks and Leo Lefebure. The task of this kind of dialogue is to disclose how religious systems with very different historic roots and lines of development can take up perennial human questions. We are often struck by the similarities that emerge in the process of answering those questions, as we are by the ritual forms that acknowledge the human person as a matrix within which answers can be found. For such a dialogue, participants have to be prepared with rare gifts of inner spiritual experience, as well as linguistic and scholarly skills. This dialogue cannot evade the need for theological clarity because such clarity is a sure sign that we take the work of coming to understanding very seriously. At the same time, the manner in which theological clarity is asserted must engage the principles of good dialogue: the respect, the listening, the willingness to seek both commonalities and differences, without negotiating away basic beliefs or making forced attempts to see commonalities by means of theological and linguistic stratagems or relativizing.

Another form of spoken dialogue takes place at national and regional conventions. The Islamic Society of North America, the Islamic Circle of North America, the National Workshop on Christian Unity, the National Catholic Education Association, the National Federation of Priests' Councils, and other associations have all sponsored interreligious panels. Here the approach is to set up a group of expert speakers to present on a topic in interreligious relations. The impact of this form of dialogue on convention participants can be truly electrifying. The participants are often the best informed and most deeply committed members of the association. For this reason, the question-and-answer sessions tend to be very lively and extend beyond the time allotted into spontaneous small group discussions. For many people, the convention setting is the only opportunity they have to be informed on progress in interreligious relations. It is a very important forum for responding to the lingering doubts and questions that, unheard, can lead to conflict in other settings. Sometimes the concreteness and realism of the questions raised can have a salutary effect on the progress of other forms of dialogue.

As spoken dialogue engages a higher level of leadership and increasingly complex issues, the need for professional support becomes increasingly significant. A small, local dialogue can be handled by generous volunteers. Regional and national events require trained logistical staff working closely with experienced professionals in the field of religious studies. One of the great advantages of my position at the Secretariat of Ecumenical and Interreligious Affairs of the U.S. Conference of Catholic Bishops (USCCB) is that I am able to apply the broad background in religious studies that I have acquired over the years to actual dialogue programs that were set up by Dr. John Borelli and others in the previous decades of work in this Secretariat. As a permanent agency of the Catholic Bishops with a full-time staff, the Secretariat is able to provide administrative and logistical support to the leadership of partnering associations that may not be as generously endowed. The Secretariat of Ecumenical and Interreligious Affairs has succeeded in establishing three regional dialogues based on existing local relationships between Catholic and Muslim leaders. These dialogues continue at the present time:

- In the Midwest region, with an ongoing dialogue on values in contemporary U.S. society, including a lively discussion on building interfaith neighborhoods. This dialogue has published the important document *Revelation: Catholic and Muslim Perspectives* (USCCB Publishing).
- In the Mid-Atlantic region, with the drafting of a common study of marriage and the start of a new dialogue on religious education.
- On the West Coast, with an in-depth study of sacred narratives and various modes of their interpretation in the living traditions of Catholicism and Islam.

One of the most important benefits of these dialogue programs is that now at least two hundred Muslim and Catholic leaders know one another well and have a direct and detailed knowledge of how each other's faith communities interpret their own traditions. Should a crisis occur on the local level, a firmly established network of relationships is already in place to provide support and solidarity.

In addition to the programs of dialogue, the USCCB has sponsored three Institutes for Bishops on Islam and Islamo-Christian Relations. Over forty-five bishops have participated in these programs of in-depth study. At a breakfast during their annual plenary meeting in November 2006, nearly seventy-five bishops attended a presentation on the role of interreligious dialogue in the peacemaking process in the Middle East, given by Archbishop Pietro Sambi, the Apostolic Nuncio to the United States and former Nuncio in Jerusalem. A year later, the Archbishop was joined by Dr. Sayyid M. Syeed, Secretary General of the Islamic Society of North America, for a breakfast dialogue before sixty-five bishops. More recently, a panel of twenty Muslim and Catholic scholars led by Angelo Cardinal Scola, the patriarch of Venice, California, and Dr. Musammil Siddiqi of the Islamic Society of Orange County gathered for a theological dialogue on the nature of the human person before God at the Pope John Paul II Cultural Center in Washington, D.C. Nearly two hundred Muslim and Catholic participants were present for the evening presentations of these two distinguished international scholars. It is clearly a time in which the hopes of the late Pope John Paul II and of Pope Benedict XVI are being realized in ever more consistent ways across the spectrum of scholarship and activist commitment.

The impact of this broad dialogue of culture and faith on the peace process needs to increase steadily in the coming years. As Pope John Paul II said at Sarajevo in 1997:

> God is one, and in his justice he asks us to live in conformity with his holy will, to regard ourselves as brothers and sisters of one another, and to commit ourselves to working to insure that peace is safeguarded in human relationships at every level. All human beings are put on earth by God to make a pilgrimage of peace, starting from the situation in which they find themselves and from the cultures in which they live.

The programs of dialogue currently underway are laying the foundations for a wider dialogue of civilizations that will make peace possible through a deeper understanding of what we believe and why we believe. Pope John Paul II reminded Muslim leaders in Nigeria in 1998 that "both Christianity and Islam stress the dignity of every human person as having been created by God for a special purpose. This leads us to uphold the value of human life at all its stages, and to give support to the family as the essential unit of society."

That being said, we may now examine the dynamics of Muslim-Catholic dialogue in the United States in the light of the pastoral concerns of the Church. The Catholic Church's struggle for identity in the great period of immigration continues today, as many Catholics arrive with Vietnamese, Burmese, Filipino, Middle Eastern, and Latino immigrant communities. Our long experience of urban life, ghettoization, institution building, and engagement with political and economic powers is a lesson we are sharing with Muslim immigrants in all three of our regional dialogues and in some local diocesan programs as well. Both sides are aware of the challenges posed by media hostility, political Islamophobia, the war on terrorism, and rapport between Muslims in the United States and Muslims abroad. In our dialogues, we have been able to compare the recent experience of Muslim communities to Catholic experiences of discrimination in the past and present. In view of the widespread and insidious Islamophobia that persists in the mass media at the present time, Catholic–Muslim relations stand as a well-developed bulwark of solidarity, particularly in areas such as moral values and the basic dignity of the human person.

At the same time, we share a great hope that going forward, Muslim teachings about Catholic Christianity will be based upon accurate knowledge of the Catholic faith and that Catholic Christians will reciprocate when they teach about Islam. We are a long way from arriving safely in port, but we have made significant progress. Books by Father Elias Mallon, Professor John Renard, and Professor John Esposito have made a more balanced image of Islam available to Catholic readers. David L. Coppola of Sacred Heart University in Connecticut has edited a substantial volume, *What Do We Want the Other to Teach about Us? Jewish, Christian, and Muslim Dialogues*, that might be helpful to anyone responsible for curriculum development. And for children we now have Sister Donna Jean Kemmetmueller's little jewel, *My Muslim Friend: A Young Catholic Learns about Islam*. Our next round of the Mid-Atlantic Dialogue will explore Muslim efforts in the same direction. We are all aware that curriculum development and the creation of appropriate teaching resources provide a foundation for healthy Muslim–Catholic relations in the future.

In view of the resources that are available through Catholic higher education, our spoken dialogue can begin to evolve a broader notion of the "dialogue of civilizations" that would not only embrace religious, historical, ethical, and political concerns but also take on or sponsor exchanges in the arts, sciences, popular culture, educational institutions, economic development, environmental programs, regional cooperation, and immigration concerns. Many Catholic universities have centers for interreligious dialogue. There is now a great opportunity for these institutions to forge viable links with the dioceses, parishes, mosque communities, and schools, both Catholic and Muslim, so as to make such a broad-based dialogue speak clearly about local social and religious realities. Catholic institutions need to find ways to harmonize their efforts with those of the Holy See, a task that may at times require a recovery of Catholic theological identity as part of the process of making sure that spoken dialogue is truly the interpersonal interface of communities of living faith. Thanks to the challenges of Catholic–Muslim dialogue, Catholics need to be more articulate than ever about salvation, sanctification, the Trinity, the Incarnation, and the nature of revealed scripture.

We need to know what both sides have to offer to each other. We need to discuss honestly what background (including accurate historical information) is required for fruitful dialogue. We need to know about the origins of some of the problematic issues that not only divide us theologically but also continue to sustain misunderstandings on both sides. We need to identify concrete means for bringing about reconciliation and growth in understanding; to identify and pursue possible areas of collaboration in the works of mercy; and to balance a sense of moral solidarity with credible ways to "agree to disagree." Both Muslims and Catholic Christians are aware of the risks of nondialogue. We do not wish to lose this historic opportunity for cooperation.

An Anthropology of Interreligious Relations

When planning, facilitating, and describing these more professional dialogues, there is always the danger that we will drift into abstraction. An exclusive focus on guidelines and advice tends to dematerialize and disembody the dialogue setting, diminishing our appreciation of its value. (For a detailed analysis of one of the seminal works on dialogue please refer to appendix B of this book for my take on Leonard Swidler's "The Dialogue Decalogue.")[3] To do full justice to the concrete, lived experience of a spoken dialogue, a phenomenological approach borrowed from cultural anthropology needs to be employed. Almost as if he or she were entering a village in a remote part of the world, an observer needs to take note not just of what words are spoken, but of everything else that occurs.

Here, for example, is what occurred at our most recent West Coast Dialogue of Catholics and Muslims that convened on May 21–23, 2007, in Rancho Palos Verdes, California, at the Mary and Joseph Retreat Center. (For a more detailed look at this dialogue, please refer to appendix C.)

Twenty-two Muslims and Catholics assembled for a meeting that was designed along the lines of a spiritual retreat, with time set aside for prayer and for attending one another's services. The participants compared narratives from the Qur'an and the Bible, particularly the Joseph/Yusuf stories in the Bible's book of Genesis chapters 37–50 and in the Qur'an's Surah 12. The discussion allowed both sides to clarify their traditional teachings on a number of controversial subjects, such as the infallibility, or more precisely, the impeccability of prophets. The participants agreed that the presentations clarified Muslim and Catholic differences in understanding scriptural narratives about prophets as role models. The conversation about sinlessness led to an examination of the use of the term *infallibility* in Catholic and Muslim theology. In addition, the group explored distinctions between Shi'a and Sunni views of prophets and the infallible imams. Participants also identified common ground in the virtues exemplified in the story of Joseph, such as fidelity, forgiveness, family relationships, integrity, loyalty, perseverance, patience rooted in trust in God, astuteness, compassion, and wisdom.

But it is impossible to do justice to the dialogical interaction, not just in this brief description, but even in the minutes of the conference. Sometimes the best conversations occurred during meals and breaks, or in the hour or two after a meeting adjourned. The role of co-chairs, staff personnel, and moderators as guides to a process is crucial; the more they work as a team, the better the atmosphere and the productivity of the dialogue. It is sometimes necessary to apply pressure to encourage focus and to remind participants of goals and principles. Often the staff person or convener is called upon to act as an orchestral conductor, fine-tuning scheduling, enhancing points of contact, facilitating communication, moving a timetable ahead, noticing the need for a break, supporting a beleaguered moderator, or welcoming a latecomer.

Some Pitfalls

The work of spoken dialogue is never easy. Any number of methodological problems in our spoken dialogue programs can widen existing divisions and open new ones, subverting the whole process. In our early engagement with Buddhism, for example, especially the Buddhism of Western converts, we tended to accede to the critical attitudes of such Buddhists with regard to Western religions and to Christianity in particular. It seemed that the Christian side had little to offer in response without resorting to the then out-of-fashion approach of theological apologetics. The post-Vatican II challenge to be creative and relevant in seeking common ground led at times to a great impoverishment of our own identity, as if the Christian traditions were in such turmoil that they had nothing credible to offer to the modern world except perhaps to mirror its queries and doubts. Frequently, Christians resorted to rereading their own texts in search of Buddhist meanings, despite serious linguistic limitations on both sides. In the decades since we began our engagement, much progress in Buddhist scholarship has been made and, in some cases, that progress has enhanced dialogue, but there is much work yet to be done.[4] We still use excessively imprecise generalizations; we should be more careful to speak of Theravada Buddhists or Sunni Muslims or even traditionalist Roman Catholics.

Another problematic dimension of interreligious dialogue has been at times an undercurrent of polemics. The bad habit of linking Christianity to colonialism, imperialism, dogmatism, and aggressive missionary strategies may have some basis in historical fact, but Christianity has other forms that have not embraced these behaviors and have even successfully opposed them. Unfortunately, most religions have at one time or another succumbed to the temptation to ride on the coattails of political and military movements; we all have good reason for repentance and reform in this area. Even so, dialogue is not advanced by telling any faith community's story in the darkest of terms and with reference only to the basest motives and most eccentric popular beliefs.

The table of spoken dialogue needs to have a strong, self-critical identity as the interpersonal interface of living communities of faith. Spoken dialogue may at times include debate, and certainly needs to address deeply troubling issues, but it is not an exercise in deconstructing the faith of others. Certainly, all participants in spoken dialogue need to know the facts of history, if for no other reason than to be merciful to each other and to be wisely critical of their own positions. It is very important that the difficult topics of history not incline any dialogue partners toward compromises of belief. My students in a course on the theology of interreligious dialogue were quick to point out this tendency in some articles in theological journals. Using dialogue as a crowbar to alter basic Christian beliefs has done a great deal to discredit the whole project of interreligious dialogue.

That said, I am convinced that without difficult conversations, there can be no real learning and listening on either side. To ignore these difficulties is to take no notice of the very real differences that separate both sides, no notice of the historical issues that require a "healing of memories"; thus sanitized, the discourse becomes as bland and featureless as anything that might be heard at a secular ethics think tank. No religious believer should accept the conclusions of a dialogue that brackets truth, that ignores theology, that has no link to authority and tradition, and that does not inquire about soteriology and our "last end."

Hope for the Future

Dialogues that are working seem to include the following elements:

1. They are based on institutions and supported by structures of authority.
2. They are collaborative and project-oriented (e.g., peacemaking, conflict resolution, humanitarian, and pastoral needs).

3. They take advantage of scholarship in support of activism, letting authority structures provide critical oversight to ensure close relationships to real communities of real people.

4. Their goals are related to education and to a broad-based understanding of what each faith is, believes, and does.

5. Their clear identification with communities of faith moderates the Western academic reductionist model of religious studies, and tempers the "religionless" sociological model of human societies entering modernity.

6. They acknowledge social and scientific progress and foster viable cultural exchange as part of the dialogue process.

In the light of these hopeful signs, I would propose a dialogue of civilizations across a wide interface of contacts, including theology, spirituality, and ethics, but also education, scientific exchange, culture, and other institutions. I would borrow from two of my favorite Italian social theorists, Antonio Rosmini and Antonio Gramsci, who might themselves be surprised to find their names in the same sentence: Rosmini for his ideal insight about human motivation—the search for wholeness, fulfillment, dignity, spirituality, and right order in one's personal, social, and professional life; Gramsci for the aspiration for human freedom through informed collective action and for his vision of the worker in all fields as one who learns and who, through learning, becomes a co-protagonist in the creation of a civilization.

I am convinced that a compact faith community, whether territorial or interwoven into the fabric of a neighborhood, aware of its identity and willing to remain faithful to that identity, is the ideal ground within which dialogue can be planted and grow. Such communities constitute viable partners in interreligious dialogue.

We have to recognize the relationship between what we call dialogue today and its roots in history, in the missionary work of the past, in the history of religions as an academic discipline, in past polemics and apologetics, the political aspects that we have inherited (sometimes with a poor memory), and the strong personalities of the recent past who were bridge builders and pioneers. We must also remember that the goal of interreligious dialogue is not to try to create a single world religion. The most obvious purpose of interreligious dialogue would be to diminish that very sectarian impulse through mutual understanding, respect, and cooperation. In particular, religions can work on conflict resolution, humanitarian assistance, education, societal forgiveness processes, and peacemaking. Religions can create the climate within which human cooperation can proceed in a fruitful manner. Religions can also learn from one another. Emperor Ashoka believed as much in the third century BCE, saying in the Twelfth Rock Edict:

> There should be growth in the essentials of all religions ... one should honor other religions because in doing so one's own religion benefits, and so do other religions ... therefore, contact between religions is good; one should listen to and respect the doctrines professed by others ... [the king] desires that all should be well-learned in the good doctrines of other religions.

So what can we learn from one another today? The sociology of religion is rich with examples of the discoveries that the West has made about itself thanks to its encounters with the East. Dietary and hygienic matters, though verified by Western science, in many ways came to us originally from the East. In a similar vein, ecological and medical approaches from the Far East, from traditional Africa and South America, and from South Asia have an increasingly important impact on our ways of acting and thinking.

We have learned a lot about the human body through yoga, both Indian and Daoist. I am convinced that the subtle body (channels or meridians, fluxes of energy, and energy centers: nadis, pranas, and chakras) is a reality that requires further exploration not restricted to the laboratory; it should be explored in retreat centers and seminaries too. It is not only the basis for a mental and physical approach to well-being for the individual; the subtle body and its development also has much to do with our way of interacting with our environment and with other people. It is also a gateway into what Christian tradition has called the "resurrection of the body."

Christian theologians have focused for so long on the resurrection of the flesh that we have neglected the all-important interface between soul and spirit, between soul and embodiment. In preaching and in practice, we have failed to notice that for the "whole person" to resurrect in the kingdom of God, we have to find a way to include the totality of the person, including thoughts, actions, virtues, merits, commitments, and relationships, which have been eclipsed by the historical obsession with the flesh that goes into and comes out of the tomb. As we know today, the "flesh" is a composite of molecules, which are themselves composed of interchangeable atoms, so medieval worries about whether the resurrected flesh was the same as the living flesh were groundless, based on extremely limited scientific knowledge. But things get much more interesting if you have to include in the totality of the person all that a person has been and done; only a contemplative approach will arrive at such a degree of insight, and I think the Chinese, Tibetans, and Indians came to this level of subtle understanding, and perhaps other, nonliterate traditions have as well. Even though I am calling this a "contemplative" discipline, please keep in mind that all that we have said about peacemaking, forgiveness, conflict resolution, health care, humanitarian interventions, education, ecological rescue, and so on requires this kind of sensitivity and cognitive awareness as well; the subtle body is a powerful key, it opens the door of inner development in a way that favors the resolution of all the other challenges that humanity faces. A bleak, cybernetic future awaits us if we do not come to terms with the full splendor of the human person coming to fulfillment (as Rosmini would have put it) in relationship to all other persons and to the creation that is our matrix and whose truths are built into our mind-body complex.

For spoken dialogue to persist within the matrix of the Christian churches, there is a need for a theological basis for dialogue. This cannot be invented anew; it has to arise from foundational Christian convictions about God, creation, humankind, and salvation. The continuing validity of Christianity, and indeed of all the religions that have risen to a glimpse of the universal truth, is precisely in this ability to link thought and inner experience to illuminate the connection between material and immaterial, temporal and eternal. Making that link, religions enable the construction of societies and cultures that enable persons to come to fullness of life. The "love that moves the sun and the other stars," as Dante poetically put it, comes to beat in the human heart and to resound in human thought. The Christian cannot do less than to seek out the Christ who is believed, known, and loved in all religions, all truths, and all phenomena.

Principles of Interaction

The insidious reality of terrorism, political tyranny, and injustice is inescapable. Religious leaders need to seek ways to restore the credibility of our institutions so that we may, together, resume our indispensable role in the work of forgiveness, peacemaking, ethical restraint, and cultural benefit. We must stand collectively for an end to terrorism, oppression, and violence both in the name of religion and against religion. No one should ever advocate violence or coercion for the sake of religion again, nor should any educational institution inculcate attitudes that will bear fruit in dehumanization of any kind. We need to be willing to learn from one another; we need to take the path of forgiveness and humility. This will require an honest look at our respective histories, a renewed effort to find new contexts in which dialogue can take place, and new forms in which healing can be fostered. Let it also be clear that the strands with which peace can be recovered and rewoven can be found in all the great traditions; those strands must be placed in higher relief than other strands in such a way that all believers will recognize themselves in the pathways to peace. The spirit of Assisi (1986) challenges us as religious believers to stand together at this time of great risk. We can no longer pretend that violence is someone else's problem. We can no longer blame secularism or materialism for the misguided conduct of some segments of society. Through interreligious dialogue, and through a wider dialogue among and within civilizations, ethically motivated persons need to find a way to build cooperation through nonoppressive tolerance.

When joining together in dialogue with your neighbors, I ask you to keep the following questions in mind:

- When we have differences of belief or viewpoint, could we not examine those differences more deeply to see if they are matters of substance? Universal questions are often answered in terms that come from particular times and places; when historical and local particularities are taken into account, our answers may have much in common.
- Could we reexamine our grievances about past acts of historical violence with a new willingness to ask forgiveness for our own errors and to forgive those who have harmed us in the past?

- Could we restrain ourselves from polemics, from proselytism, from coercion, from faultfinding when we compare ourselves to others?
- Could we pledge to advise those who come to us seeking to change their inherited religion to search more deeply before undertaking the process of conversion? Could we remember to instruct all converts to love and respect the religion of their birth?
- Could we commit ourselves to teaching our respective traditions in schools and universities with objectivity and fairness? Could professors balance academic freedom with respect for the beliefs and sensitivities of people of faith?
- Could we agree to make positive contributions to world peace through humanitarian interventions for justice so that no one need ever fear loss of property, life, or security because of assertions of power again?
- When it is within our power, could we work to restore property that has been unjustly expropriated and otherwise make restitution for harms done in the past?
- Should we not do penance together in spiritual reparation for the acts of injustice of the past?
- Could we strive to be more humble, more ready to listen than to speak, more eager to learn than to teach, more eager to show respect than to leap into disagreement?
- Could we seek to coordinate what is said in interreligious dialogue with what is said in ecumenical dialogue?
- And finally, can we find it in our hearts to love and respect those of our own faith tradition who do not agree with us, who take the opposite view, who resist change? Peace also starts at home.

Conclusion

It is often said that dialogue is a matter of experts sitting around a table speculating on abstruse topics that do not touch the lives of ordinary people. In actuality, a strong conviction that great ideas do indeed touch the lives of everyone is precisely what keeps leadership returning to the table of dialogue. The joys and hopes, sorrows and triumphs of humanity sit with us as we consider how to apply the principles of belief to the burning questions of our times. We are painfully conscious of the fact that religions have lent their persuasive force to acts of violence down through the centuries. We cherish the memory of the peaceful dialogues of the past, but we are frankly ashamed of the deeds of violence that drowned out reasoned and fraternal dialogue. If it were not for our dialogue today, how could we claim to have a consensus on the conviction that the use of religion to justify violence must be repudiated by all people of faith? If it were not for the just indignation of people of faith, as well as of people of no religious adherence, would we even be talking to one another today? Why has it taken so long for religious leaders to sit down together to work out a way to redress the wrongs of the past and at least come to a basic level of mutual respect and understanding? Because of violence, religion is seen today by many people as a source of societal discord and injustice that must be repudiated or placed under severe state supervision.

Even with scarce resources and, at times, a lack of sympathy in the mass media and even within the faith communities themselves, the dialogue must continue. There is simply no alternative; we have already seen where the absence of dialogue leads. Communities of faith need to revisit their histories and seek reconciliation for the dark sides of their pasts. Spoken dialogue, the interpersonal interface that brings communities of faith together, is the indispensable means to do this.

2

Dialogue through Arts—
"Opening the World's Door"

*by Abby Stamelman Hocky, MSW, Rev. Susan Teegen-Case,
and Rabbi Carol Harris-Shapiro*

> *Religion is the everlasting dialogue between humanity
> and God. Art is its soliloquy.*
>
> —FRANZ WERFEL

Introduction

In these challenging times for intergroup relations, this gathering in an urban church basement is nothing short of extraordinary. This afternoon, teenagers—Jewish, Christian, and Muslim, black and white, male and female, urban and suburban—have gathered for a session of their interfaith service learning group that will draw them into dialogue and reflection through the arts.

The room is filled with the sounds of laughter and lively discussion. A young Muslim with a head covering gestures, smiling, to make her point in a small group composed of other Muslim, Jewish, and Christian teens, all leaning forward, fully engaged. Black and white hands intermingle as participants fill food baskets for homebound seniors. Friendships blossom during the break, as students from very different neighborhoods snack on pizza and fruit and talk about their favorite movies, foods, and sports. Their camaraderie, growing out of mutual learning and community work, belies any separations of religion, race, and class.

In this program, differences are treasured, not feared.

Today, a poetry session allows the participants to express their visions for the world and the future. Dr. Cathleen Cohen, director of We the Poets, a program of the Arts & Spirituality Center that allows children from different cultures and faiths to write and share their poetry, brings copies of inspiring materials: Martin Luther King Jr.'s teachings on love, love poems from thirteenth-century poet Rumi, and rap lyrics from a contemporary artist. When Cathy announces the topic for personal poetic reflection, "Love Your Neighbor," quickly all chatting ceases. As one, the participants look down at the blank pages in front of them and wait for their hands to connect with their thoughts. After only about fifteen minutes, the students have surprised themselves. Each one has created a poem. Cathy invites them to share their poems with one another. Fatima, a ninth-grader at an Islamic high school who had loudly declared, "I don't write poetry" before the session began is the first to share her poem. A Jewish twelfth-grader, Claire, has written eleven haikus, including this one:

> *Do we always think,*
> *To hold open the world's door*
> *For people unknown?*

Dialogue through the arts opens this door, offering a powerful means of personal expression, relationship building, and the seeds of transformation.

Three of us have coauthored this essay, bringing perspectives from diverse experiences and disciplines. The Rev. Susan Teegen-Case, an ordained minister in the United Church of Christ and an artist with a longstanding interest and practice in the interplay of art, spirituality, and social change, is the founder and director of the Arts & Spirituality Center in Philadelphia. Rabbi Carol Harris-Shapiro is lecturer at Temple University, a Reconstructionist rabbi, and a board member of the Interfaith Center of Greater Philadelphia, and has long been involved in interfaith work, both academically and personally. Abby Stamelman Hocky, the executive director of the Interfaith Center, is a community social worker who has worked in the field of interfaith relations for more than two decades. The Arts & Spirituality Center and the Interfaith Center share office space and administrative resources and have collaborated on community projects and organizational development. The stories we relate in this chapter capture the joys and challenges of fostering relationships through the arts, illustrating the many ways that shared creative work can nourish wells of creativity, encourage understanding, and deepen the possibilities of dialogue.

Education reformer John Dewey described how the arts play a critical role in "contributing directly and liberally to an expanding and enriched life." The arts, for Dewey, are about "an experience in which the whole creature is alive."[1] Audre Lorde wrote a powerful essay entitled, "Poetry Is Not a Luxury." It is these notions—extended to all art forms—that guide our work. Art is not a luxury; it is a necessity. Museums and symphony halls are places of respite, spiritual nourishment, and beauty, but the arts are powerful vehicles for social transformation as well. We invite community groups striving to open doors of trust and understanding to use their imaginations and use the arts. Individuals and communities must find ways to express their pain, their hopes, and their dreams before they can effectively join hands to address social problems.

Of course the arts and interfaith dialogue are both dynamic processes with their own integrities. Just as it is wonderful to engage in artistic creativity with no other agenda, dialogue for the sake of dialogue has its own rewards. In our vision of "dialogue through the arts," initiatives offer safe entry points for experiences of mutual enrichment, heightened creativity, enhanced understanding, and strengthened community.

What Do We Mean by "Dialogue"?

At its best, dialogue is a process of honest speaking and honest listening; an exchange that creates trust and understanding. Dialogue is discovering another's story, another's joy, another's pain, and another's hopes. In interfaith work, dialogue means an invitation to a deeper conversation. Social scientist Daniel Yankelovich speaks to the quiet power of dialogue: "By performing the seemingly simple act of responding empathetically to others and in turn being heard by them ... (we fulfill) a profound human yearning."[2]

At its best, genuine dialogue results in people taking their new experiences and perspectives back into their home religious communities where they serve as conscious or even unconscious change agents.

In her book *Encountering Other Faiths*, Maria Hornung writes, "Interreligious dialogue that does not eventuate in action will grow hypocritical and ineffective. Action that does not result in greater understanding and deeper communication will grow sterile and give way to apathy. Neither can survive on its own."[3]

Although dialogue is often seen as a word-bound activity, there is nothing inherent in the dialogue process that limits participants to words alone. There can be honest speaking and deep listening in a nod of the head or touch of the hand, in the shared enjoyment of a meal, or in undertaking a service project at a local food bank together. When a group paints a beautiful design on the wall or brings spiritual voices together in song, these processes respect and transcend differences, unite hearts, and offer powerful environments in which to build trust and understanding. Incorporating artistic modalities allows a group to enter new areas of communication, going beyond words to a different kind of nonverbal fullness.

Dialogue and the Arts: Openings

Why are the arts such a powerful vehicle for interfaith dialogue? They open us to joy and vulnerability. The very act of dialogue is one of risk. Those involved in dialogue share intimate information about themselves, their experiences, and, in interfaith dialogue, their relationships to the Divine: There is always the very real risk of mishearing or being misheard, of opening old wounds or inflicting new ones, of making things worse. Despite this possibility, the arts can also provide an accessible playing field for relationships of difference. By opening us to play, the arts can counteract the typical fear/flight response people usually bring to new and unfamiliar situations. When creating a quilt, singing, drumming, making a collage, or writing poetry, we are engaged in activities that release anxieties and spur our creative minds. As our hands fill with colors, or our hearts pulse in time with the drums, we delight our imaginations beyond our ordinary sensibilities. The process of artmaking opens us to one other.

We Open to Surprise

Sitting before a blank canvas, a painter never knows exactly what will emerge. An interreligous project engaging the arts is also an "opening" experience. Education professionals stress the importance of engaging multiple intelligences that are not always reflected in traditional, verbal forms of dialogue. Spatial intelligence, kinesthetic/physical intelligence, and musical intelligence are only a few that might be drawn upon in an artistic project. Through the arts, participants can bring their whole selves into the dialogue process and "shake them all about!" New realities emerge in the creative processes that surprise us, realities not always accessible using linear, didactic thinking. Our deep knowledge of one another is only improved as we appreciate one other as creative beings, as artists in the fullest sense of the word. Thomas, a resident of New Jerusalem Now, a vibrant grassroots addiction recovery community in North Philadelphia, proclaimed during a mural project, "Wow! I had no idea I was this creative, or that I am living in an entire community of artistic people."

We Open to Trust

Launching into the creative unknown opens potential dialogue partners to trust—in each other and in the process itself. Just as many faith traditions appreciate a sense of mystery, we can bring this sense of humility to our work with people of difference. The Christian scriptures refer to faith as the conviction of things not seen (Hebrews 11:1). As the silent air fills with musical sounds, or the blank canvas takes on light and color, or the page fills with words released from within, we learn to operate in that kind of faith. We touch mystery and begin to trust that a whole new world is emerging. We commit ourselves to the adventure.

We Open to Community

As the Very Rev. James Parks Morton, founder of the Interfaith Center of New York, observed, "The arts are the supreme way of binding people together, of making what is truly important comprehensible—and felt." This shared emotional cohesion is at the heart of building community by incorporating artistic modalities.

Collaborative arts projects have contributed to successful community-building endeavors in such settings as schools, recreation centers, hospitals, and addiction-recovery residential facilities. In each of these unique environments, the constituents step up to be both visionaries and organizers. Individuals with disparate talents and strong opinions learn to work together to transform dreams into reality. Working in the arts fosters thinking outside the box; those involved are given opportunities to generate new ideas and possibilities, discovering pathways that everyone can agree on. Minority religious and ethnic groups, frequently not heard in the dominant culture, find their voices. When people express their experiences through the arts, they can be heard in ways that make defensive walls more porous; they can achieve greater respect and understanding.

We Open to Wonder

As participants and observers pause to reflect on the completed work of art—the musical experience, the quilt, the poetry, or the dramatic presentation—hearts and minds open in new ways, prompting new questions and new lines of inquiry for further dialogue. Hearing someone's struggles, joys, and challenges referenced in their poem or reflected in their collage opens us to empathy, pierces our assumptions, and lodges their story within us. Patterns of colors, shapes, and sounds are emotionally recalled and relived, leading to the spiritual dimensions of wonder, awe, and reverence.

Combining dialogue and the arts allows us to reclaim the power of creative expression. Art has a way of honoring the human spirit and the Spirit that infuses it. It actively furthers the possibility of a world fueled by imagination and vision, rather than hatred or greed.

We Open to Action

As Martin Luther King Jr. said, "The world is in dire need of creative extremists. We live now in extreme times. The question is not whether we will be extremists, but what kind of extremists we will be. Will we be extremists for hate or for love?" Finally, we must say that dialogue through the arts will open us to the creativity that sparks activity, the energy that leads to action.

Opening the World's Doors: Some Stories

These four stories reveal some of the ways that arts endeavors can open doors to strong and meaningful interreligious and intercultural relationships. We invite you to enter these doorways with us, to read the stories, meet the people, feel the ripple effects of work that is rich, evocative, challenging, and enduring.

Walking the Walk: Integrating Experiences through Artistic Reflection in a Youth Service Learning Initiative, Philadelphia

The first youth program begun by the Interfaith Center of Greater Philadelphia was Walking the Walk, the organization's teen interfaith service learning initiative. Launched in the fall of 2005, Walking the Walk brings together Christian, Jewish, and Muslim high school students twice a month throughout the school year to explore the core values of each faith, put these values into action through volunteer service in the community, and reflect upon their experiences through the arts.

The initial Christian, Jewish, and Muslim educator team that helped design the curriculum discovered that dialogue around key religious texts was a way to help youth embrace their own story and core values. Additionally, the texts would help teens gain fluency and comfort in sharing their own language, heritage, rituals, and traditions while learning about those of others. Project director Marjorie Scharf, aware of diverse learning styles and the broad goals of the service learning program, wanted to offer students something besides left-brain language learning.

The Interfaith Center sought the partnership of the Arts & Spirituality Center to help fashion creative forms of reflection that would integrate the new learning, experiences, challenges, and insights of the text dialogue and the community service components. The artistic reflection components included journaling, poetry, photography, collage, music, videography, drumming, drama, and spiritual autobiography. The techniques and art forms practiced in these sessions will hopefully encourage youth to extend their use into others parts of their lives.

A primary goal of Walking the Walk is to give young people the opportunity to gain multicultural and multifaith skills to become leaders in an increasingly diverse global society. Reflection techniques help students articulate their values, grow in their own faith-based identities, integrate lessons learned into their daily lives, and build relationships with peers, parents, clergy/spiritual mentors, and teachers. Reflection allows participants to create new stories about themselves and others, stories that make the new values they learn become a real part of their own life journeys. Such reflection should itself become a lifelong skill that students can take with them in responding to personal and social issues. Dr. Norman J. Cohen writes in *Moses and the Journey to Leadership: Timeless Lessons of Effective Management from the Bible and Today's Leaders* (Jewish Lights) that "leadership involves truly 'seeing'—the ability to perceive the importance of what one experiences, to understand it, and then to internalize it."[4]

The Walking the Walk group gathers at a synagogue for its third session on a Sunday afternoon. The group of Christian, Jewish, and Muslim teens from three congregations is first led on a tour by the rabbi, who clearly enjoys engaging with these curious students, readily answering their flow of eager, intelligent questions. Participants then enter a second-floor classroom for the learning session, where they break up into small same-faith clusters to study short texts from the Torah, New Testament, and Qur'an on the theme of hospitality. To encourage active reading and richer discussion of these ancient texts, students are given colored highlighters and told to mark those words and passages that are distinct to a given faith and those that are universal. A Jewish boy blurts out a new insight: "I honestly never thought of hospitality as a Jewish value!"

It is not until they reassemble in mixed groups that the new ideas and stories come alive. "I have heard about Jesus and the loaves and fish but never knew the whole story," said a Muslim girl, referencing the selected New Testament text, Luke 9:11–17. A Jewish girl says, "This Muslim text reminds me of the story in the Torah of Abraham welcoming the three men at his tent" in Genesis 18. She points to the sheet before her on Islamic teachings and texts on hospitality, citing Qur'an 59:9: "Then He (the Prophet) led the visiting man to his house and said to his wife, 'Treat generously the guest of the Messenger of God.'" Here, a simple visual cue—using colored highlighters—helped to accomplish key aims of Walking the Walk: to highlight the value being taught to ground the value in core narratives and texts of each traditions, to illuminate (literally) similarities and differences among the three religions concerning this value, and to spark curiosity and deeper exploration of those similarities and differences. However, the artistic component of the day goes well beyond using colored highlighters. After the text study segment, the session moves to a multifaceted reflection using collage, journaling, photography, and videography. When told of the upcoming task, both the students and their adult mentors are curious and somewhat skeptical. How will this work?

Their concerns quickly turn to excitement as Susan Teegen-Case and Pam Hooks, artistic leader of the Arts & Spirituality Center, introduce the plan. Centering on the theme of hospitality, they explain, teens will create collages for the covers of their Walking the Walk loose-leaf journals, write in their journals, and take cameras and explore the premises to capture any images that convey the value of hospitality. If they choose, students will be interviewed by Pam on video about what hospitality means to each of them.

This reflection technique goes far beyond arts and crafts, as Susan, an artist herself, shows some examples of her own collage work and describes the intention and processes that underlie this seemingly simple art form. Collage is a nonthreatening art form, accessible to participants with varying levels of comfort with and attraction to creating visual art. This medium is often enjoyed by participants with a wide range of learning preferences and with varying commitments or comfort with the group. Susan encourages participants to consider a question they want to focus on in their collage, and then flip though magazines and collect those images that capture their attention and say yes to their question. The idea is to do this without analyzing, but simply responding to the intuition of the moment.

Susan hands out a list of questions to prompt the students' reflections and broaden their thinking about the theme of hospitality. She suggests, "Choose two questions that you like the most, and one that you don't." The questions include: "Do I welcome all parts of myself?" "Is there a stranger in me?" "What does he/she look/feel like?" "Who welcomes me?" "What images do we think of when we think of hospitality (e.g., open/closed doors, hands)?" "Is hospitality always welcome?" "Is it always safe to be open and hospitable?" "How do we know?" These questions stimulate the teens to reflect on the values in the texts they studied earlier that afternoon and integrate them with their own thoughts and experiences.

Both students and adults now sit around tables strewn with magazines brought from home, their pages filled with colors and images that evoke their diverse cultural heritages and popular interests. These publications jostle for space with scissors, felt pens, colored paper, glue sticks, and photocopies of the translated hospitality texts that had been part of their earlier dialogue. Those seated are initially quiet and thoughtful, but gradually the noise level rises. Sounds of rustling through magazines are intermingled with chatter and laughter.

Throughout the collage sessions students also become photojournalists, taking pictures that reflect answers to the questions posed by the artists: "What gestures or visual cues promote hospitality?" "What do my gestures and other nonverbal expressions say to others?" "Do I invite people in?" "Do others perceive me as hospitable?" "In what ways am I expressing hospitality in the way I act, dress, greet friends, strangers, use body language, share my belongings, invite people to my home, school, and congregation?" They are excited to be videotaped by Pam, who interviews them individually about their experiences of hospitality. The students note the discoveries of the day, as they share their collages and insights. The group also celebrates the beauty that has happened in just an hour, as they view the photographic collage that Pam has assembled from their photos. Later in the year, they will also see and hear themselves on the DVD that Pam created from their video interviews.

The artistic medium allows students to develop their individual visions of the theme and explore them in depth. It also adds creative energy, excitement, and feelings of camaraderie. Just as the collage exercise enabled students to turn fragmented pieces of text and image into a coherent whole, reflection allows them to take fragmented pieces of their experiences and make them whole.

Learning doesn't stop at the doorway to the outside world. Marjorie, the project director, devises a way for students to share their creativity throughout all the sessions by stringing a clothesline on which they hang the poems, collages, and other art they create in their reflections. Students start to bring new work that they create between sessions and report that they are finding new ways to create in their free time.

The students' work is taken to a new level, as they rise to the opportunity to share their poetry and creative work at a large Interfaith Center event with keynote speaker Dr. Eboo Patel, director of Interfaith Youth Core, an organization that inspired the Walking the Walk model. Several students also join with Marjorie and Susan in leading a workshop on Reflection through the Arts at the National Conference on Service-Learning. They beam with pride as they share their poems and collages, offer their insights on how this work has deepened their understanding of their own faith and others and opened doors to new friendships across religions and cultures.

Alternative Spring Break Program: Integrating Interfaith Service Learning Immersion Experiences through Poetry, Philadelphia

In the fall of 2005, North Carolina State University approached the Interfaith Center of Greater Philadelphia with the idea of developing an interfaith service-learning program as one of their Alternative Spring Break options. Consistent with the mission of the agency and eager to experiment with an immersion model, the Interfaith Center staff joined hands with student and faculty leadership at North Carolina State to co-create this annual program.

In March 2007, a group of eight college students spent an intensive week of community service, cooking meals and sleeping overnight in a Philadelphia church housing families in transition through the Northwest Philadelphia Interfaith Hospitality Network. Additionally, they volunteered at Grace Café, housed in an urban church and sponsored by Project H.O.M.E., a respite site for the homeless community. In addition to their service-learning endeavor, North Carolina State students explored the rich religious diversity of the Philadelphia region, celebrating the Jewish holiday of Purim at a synagogue, worshiping at a multiracial Catholic church on a Sunday morning, and sharing Friday prayers at a masjid (mosque). They had opportunities to dialogue with socially conscious clergy from various faith communities and to spend an afternoon with members of a local Bahá'í community.

At the end of the week, it was time to reflect on the different religions encountered, on the service projects that had immersed them in issues of housing, hunger, and homelessness, and on the people they met in life situations and faith communities quite different from theirs. We chose a poetry workshop as a way for them to begin to integrate their learning.

The students and group leaders gather in the comfortable living room of the youth hostel where they have been staying. It is the last day of their spring break week in Philadelphia. Just six days earlier they sat in this same room, eagerly awaiting an orientation to the interfaith and community experiences they would have in the ensuing days. Today they are a changed group, bonded by their time serving soup and coffee to homeless men and women, and the nights they shared with homeless families. As the students now begin to think about the eight-hour drive back to campus and their reunions with their roommates and friends, how can they put into words the new and challenging experiences they had? Even with daily reflection time as a group, so much had been packed into this immersion week, waiting to be integrated.

On this sunny Friday, the Interfaith Center invited Dr. Cathleen Cohen, director of We the Poets, to lead a concluding reflection session. She sits on the couch as the students and leaders gather around, seated on comfortable chairs and the carpeted floor. Cathy introduces the workshop, "Today we are going to focus on 'deep listening.' You have spent a week listening to people with painful life stories, quite different than yours, listening to people from religious communities you may never have met before. And I suspect you have listened with more than your ears—you have taken in these experiences with your full selves, with open hearts and open minds."

After Cathy shares a poem about listening, she invites the students to dive in and take just ten to fifteen minutes to write their own poems. She asks, "Have any of you written poetry before?" Only one young man, Daniel, raises his hand. The leader passes around some pens and lined paper. Cathy gently adds, "Let's sit quietly for a few minutes, and then just write—don't worry about punctuation, don't worry about rhyming. If I have one suggestion, it will be to go back after you have written and figure out your line breaks."

Abby, one of the leaders, wonders what the students are thinking. Do their contemplative expressions mask awkwardness, skepticism, or resistance to this exercise? How can people be stretched to write poetry when they have never done this before? She glances around the quiet room, appreciating each student she has come to know by name. Her thoughts are brought back to moments in a Quaker-Jewish dialogue when she was stretched to understand the experience of silent worship, and the practice of speaking only when "divinely inspired." The concept was so foreign to her, but she momentarily feels as if she is experiencing it.

After ten minutes Cathy asks if anyone needs a few more minutes; some nod, others don't even look up from their writing. One sullen-looking student says to Cathy, "I don't know if I'm doing this right."

She gently walks over to him and says, "It's your poem. It's for you." He shies away from her offer to look at his work; she quietly returns to the couch and he resumes writing.

Then Cathy invites people to pair up and share, if they like, the poem they have written. She reminds everyone that this is just a draft; no one needs to feel that the work is in its final form. Cathy instructs all of the participants to listen carefully as each person reads aloud in order to pay attention to any words or images that jump out at them and share them with the poet before taking their own turn reading.

A civil engineering student, the same young man who didn't know "if this is right," is the first to share in his small group. His poem opens, "As I look at religion I see love; the one thing they all share ..." Tears well up in his eyes as his poem opens a deep place in his personal struggles. Members of his small group silently respect his disclosure, then remember to name the words that strike them. He nods in appreciation.

Next, Cathy asks the group if anyone has a poem he or she wants to share aloud with everyone. Liz, a bio-engineering student, reads first, then Brian. The setting of both of their poems is the street café they had worked in two nights before. Liz has written:

> *We had no interaction other than sharing half-*
> *smiles*
> *As the couple passed by*
> *My smile, a mix of concern and surprise*
> *Her smile, a story of a hard day, a hard tomor-*
> *row to come*
> *They carefully rolled out their worn blanket*
> *upon the hard floor*
> *Placed another upon it*
> *And sandwiched themselves between the pair*
> *The couple, a decade older than me*
> *Kissed each other goodnight*
> *And lovingly rolled away from each other*
> *The woman fell asleep while*
> *The man laid reading,*
> *His sock-covered feet sticking out from the end*
> *of the covers*
> *The scene seems so delicately familiar*

Cathy asks Liz if she wants to say anything about her poem. Liz shares that this couple and this very ordinary scene of retiring to bed reminded her of her parents. Yet this couple's bedtime setting was a cold floor in the middle of a church hall, with seventy strangers around.

Brian, a chemistry student, writes:

> *We talked a while about Chemistry*
> *Myself and this man at Grace Cafe*
> *'Though to all else in the vicinity*
> *It seemed so dull, seemed so passé*
> *But he remembered molecules*
> *As well as some students at my school*
> *Don't get me wrong*
> *His memory wasn't fully clear*
> *It had been so long*
> *But I still had to hear*
> *About aldehydes, ketones and hexane*
> *Our conversation must have seemed inane*
> *He needed this*
> *He needed to know*
> *Another chemist*
> *For his knowledge to show*
> *I listened and wondered about the man I did meet*
> *Where did he err to end up on the street*
> *His interest in science*
> *Showed he wasn't so dumb*
> *From where came his reliance*
> *On us? He's no bum.*
> *Did he get addicted to drugs, booze or wine?*
> *Did fighting in Vietnam impair his mind?*
> *He'd be a chemist if things broke a different way*
> *But instead he's here in a soup kitchen today.*

Geneva then offers her poem called "Brotherly Love?":

> *Beautiful on the outside is the city of Brotherly*
> *   Love, Delicious food to feast upon. Malls and*
> *   shopping centers to shop till you drop.*
> *Ugly on the inside is the city of Brotherly Love.*
> *   Filled with pain grief, tears hurt souls, and lost*

minds. Yet lined with faith and spirituality
that makes living possible each day.
A man said to me "Brotherly love, there is
none."

Cathy closes the workshop, expressing gratitude to each of the poets and pointing out something special and powerful in each. She invites the students to keep writing. There are many nods and smiles and thanks expressed to Cathy for giving the students the opportunity to exercise a new part of themselves. The day ends and the students pack up to go to their van, taking their insights with them to be discussed anew in North Carolina with fellow students, teachers, friends, and family.

The day needed little more than paper, pens, and most importantly, its simple, elegant design. Cathy started off with the theme of deep listening and gave the group a simple listening exercise—to repeat back some of the words of the poems read aloud first in small groups. The simple, accessible instructions, conveyed with ease, created a comfortable space. She invited some silence, and out of the silence of a mere fifteen minutes emerged deeply rich poetry. Reminiscent of Michelangelo's reference to his own work as "releasing the sculpture from the stone," opening space for students to reflect in this way lifted words from deep within them that would otherwise not have been shaped into poems. The artistic process of reflection through poetry proved a powerful means of finding coherence in a very intense immersion week of community service and interfaith relations.

Doorways to Peace: Building Intercultural and Interreligious Bridges through a Community Mural Project, Philadelphia

Doorways to Peace is one of the first projects stemming from the city-wide Arts & Spirituality Center program, MasterPeace, launched on September 11, 2003. MasterPeace brings schools, congregations, and communities together to identify a peace or justice issue that is significant for their community. The issue is then explored in a six- to twelve-month process of art making, interwoven with dialogue, spiritual expression, community organizing, empowerment, training, and advocacy.

First steps. Less than a week after the start of MasterPeace a meeting was arranged between the Arts & Spirituality Center and Al-Aqsa Islamic Society. Al-Aqsa is the largest Arab American masjid (mosque) in Philadelphia. It has a K–12 Islamic day school comprised of fourteen ethnic/cultural groups. Both Abby Stamelman Hocky and Cathleen Cohen had strong and positive interpersonal connections with leaders of Al-Aqsa, which was an important factor in successfully convening the first meeting.

The meeting was attended by teachers at Al-Aqsa Academy, Abdur Rahman Crumpton, the principal of the school, Susan Teegen-Case, Abby and Cathleen. Adab Ibrahim, a parent and art teacher at Al-Aqsa, was there as well as Ahlam Yasin, an AmeriCorps volunteer at the school. The participants took a tour of the school and the men's and women's worship spaces. A few remained to meet around a lunch table, in a room lined with empty cubbies, a familiar school setting.

Susan recalls this first gathering as a meeting of hearts and vision. We learned that the membership of Al-Aqsa felt hungry to be welcomed and known in the immediate neighborhood and in the region. They appreciated the invitation by the Arts & Spirituality Center to embark on the first MasterPeace initiative, which offered their community the opportunity to shine in new and needed ways, to create a good impression for itself among its non-Muslim neighbors. This was especially true given the heightened tensions since 9/11. The idea of creating a mural to beautify the outside of the masjid was proposed and enthusiastically endorsed. With this new vision, the plan moved forward.

The vision swiftly turned into a reality when Joe Brenman joined the planning team as the Arts & Spirituality Center artist in residence. Joe, an accomplished sculptor and muralist, is an active synagogue member. Joe brings his own religious values and perspectives to his art and has a great sensitivity to interfaith work. While many of his drawings and sculptures are inspired by themes in the Hebrew scriptures, Joe has also created sculptural Stations of the Cross. Interestingly, Joe lived right in the Al-Aqsa neighborhood for years, but had no idea that the boxy, former warehouse was a masjid. Clearly, there was work to be done for Al-Aqsa to achieve recognition in the neighborhood, and Joe was delighted to do it. Members of Al-Aqsa met with Joe (including both Abdur Rahman and the lay head of the school, Chukri Khorchid), reviewed his portfolio, and welcomed him to *Doorways to Peace*.

Joe Brenman, Al-Aqsa, and the Arts & Spirituality Center invited the partnership of the Mural Arts Program (MAP), the renowned organization responsible for creating over 2,700 murals in the city of Philadelphia since the mid-1980s. MAP provided significant help as well as another lead artist, Cathleen Hughes, a Catholic resident of the same neighborhood. MAP put this project on the front burner, rather than tabling it for future consideration, because it furthered their goal of peacemaking and their interest in engaging the Arab American community. Expanding the artist cadre to include a lead Muslim presence, the Arts & Spirituality Center invited Fadwa Kashkash to join the nascent effort. Fadwa is an artist from Kuwait and Jordan who immigrated to the United States as an adult. Having lead artists from three Abrahamic faith traditions was a powerful collaborative dimension of the mural project. It was also an important factor in making this mural both authentically Islamic and positively received by the surrounding community.

Early successes, early challenges. During the fall of 2003 and winter of 2004, the lead partners undertook three significant efforts that enabled the project to continue: securing needed funding, engaging the community, and designing the mural.

As the lead partner, the Arts & Spirituality Center ascertained that $50,000 in new funding would be needed to complete this ambitious project. While MAP provided significant resources, the Arts & Spirituality Center and Al-Aqsa were hard at work identifying and soliciting funding from foundations and other constituencies. Second, and equally important, was creating neighborhood solidarity for the mural. Adab served tirelessly as a volunteer community organizer, mobilizing support for the project. She arranged a meeting with key community stakeholders: the Kensington South Neighborhood Association, the Community Development Corporation (CDC), La Salle Academy, St. Michael's Catholic Church, and Hancock-St. John's United Methodist Church and their afterschool program.

Susan remembers the meeting at the CDC building, a renovated factory space that now serves as a communal gathering place.

I saw European Americans, Latinos, African Americans, Arab Americans, all bringing a wonderful spirit and openness to the possibility of neighborhood unity and transformation. Ann, a lawyer who volunteers for the CDC, spoke about the arson against Irish immigrants and their churches that happened in this same neighborhood 150 years ago. It felt right to come full circle and be in solidarity with Arab American neighbors and other Muslim groups who were experiencing alienation today. Rev. Delois Johnson, pastor of Hancock-St. John's United Methodist Church, brought her passion for making the neighborhood vital and safe, and she expressed a commitment to draw neighbors closer together to reduce the potential for crime and gun violence. Her support for the mural project invigorated the rest of the attendees. By the end of the meeting it was clear that the *Doorways to Peace* project would also be the doorway to a strengthened neighborhood.

The design for the mural was among the first issues addressed at this meeting. Muslims prohibit depictions of humans and animals in artwork connected to sacred spaces. Susan explains, "We discussed the importance of creating only abstract images because the mural will be on the side of a masjid. We used this as an opening to explore diverse beliefs about art in our traditions and cultures, explaining the premise for this in Islam, which is that God is the premier artist and no human is capable of creating life forms like God." Given that premise, community members suggested ways that community life could be incorporated in the mural. It was decided that the project would encompass two murals in one: a community mural on one side of the building that would contain individually designed tiles by the neighborhood, and a traditional Islamic design for the front of the masjid. Several ideas were suggested for the theme and/or name of the mural at the community meeting and in conversations with each of the community partners. The name *Doorways to Peace* emerged naturally, as the Arts & Spirituality Center felt it captured the common hopes, dreams, and possibilities that were voiced during the early months of planning.

Later in the planning process, the lead artists gathered with leaders of Al-Aqsa to capture their ideas for the design, soon to become the first installation of Islamic public art in Philadelphia. Joe, the Jewish muralist, enrolled in a class in Islamic art at the University of Pennsylvania and elicited the guidance of a doctoral candidate with this expertise. Adab, along with Chukri Khorchid, the head of the school and a respected leader of his community, guided the process. Syrian by birth, Chukri beamed with pride each time he described what he imagined the building would look like with the traditional colors and designs that would authentically reflect the beauty of their culture and community. There was excitement as the idea surfaced to incorporate Islam's ninety-nine names of God into the design. By using Arabic and English calligraphy on tiles that would begin in the front and wrap around the sides, words naming God's attributes would help to synthesize the design and its meaning. Fadwa Kashkash, the Muslim artist, would oversee and hand paint this part of the project, as well as the special calligraphy of the new large sign for Al-Aqsa.

It is said that the further the progress, the more challenges incurred; the project *Doorways to Peace* was no exception. Like most nonprofit organizations, the Al-Aqsa board moved slowly and cautiously in its approval of each stage of the mural construction and related expenditures. The board, not surprisingly, took some time to warm up to the idea of a joint community mural decorating an exterior wall of their spiritual and ethnic "home." They asked to review the tiles made by children and community members to ensure that the content was fitting for their building. This led to a slowing of the project timetable and changes in the design to meet the new deadlines.

It is important to note that caution and mistrust were not a monopoly of the Al-Aqsa board. Questions surfaced from a small segment of the Jewish community outside of the neighborhood, particularly, "Why would we partner with an organization called Al-Aqsa?" For those Jews, Al-Aqsa signified the controversy around the Temple Mount in Jerusalem, and connoted support for the Palestinian intifadas. They were not completely reassured by the fact that these Philadelphian Muslims chose this name for their masjid long before the recent intifada. Some Christians and some secular community members voiced more general suspicions, questioning, "Why would anyone want to work with Muslims?"

Patience, relationship building, and the passage of time helped to alleviate the tensions and were critical to successfully overcoming these hurdles. The Arts & Spirituality Center invested needed time in lengthy discussion with key community members and worked with liaisons who moved back and forth between constituencies to assuage fears. Community partners and individuals began to be more willing, step by step, to take the risk of trust.

The mural is made. In the spring, summer, and fall of 2004, most of the plans made during the last six months finally came to fruition. Ann wrote an article for the local paper describing *Doorways to Peace*. Abby, Susan, and Joe, with help from Adab, put together a tile-making project that brought together fourth- and fifth-grade students from three schools: a public elementary school, a Catholic school, and a Muslim day school. Students were selected for a series of workshops to engage in dialogue, explore the theme of *Doorways to Peace*, and create tiles to be incorporated into the final mural.

These workshops were rich and emotional. Students poured their creativity and dreams into the tiles, sharing stories of their schools, families, and interests, and dialoguing with one another about their values and cultures. The adults present at the workshops were deeply moved. A teenage volunteer's father, helping out, spoke quietly about his own lack of faith and how projects like this made him think that hope might be possible. A volunteer offered to take photographs of the workshops, and wept with joy at the end of every session. As a culmination of the eight sessions, students invited parents and significant friends and relatives to a celebratory breakfast, where they each received a certificate for their involvement in the project and displayed their newly fired, beautiful tiles.

Both the tile-making project and the mural painting were opened to the community at large over the summer months. Logistical difficulties lessened participation, as it was difficult to plan around times of prayer and religious observance in the Muslim community and it was also not easy to convince adults to come out in the evenings after work. Still, significant numbers of community members came out to make their own tiles and begin painting the mural on parachute cloth that would later be attached to the building's walls.

Joe, the artist who always wore a Jewish star, became a beloved figure to the Al-Aqsa community. Joe also became a personal ambassador of the project to the outside community. Susan tells the story:

One morning, Joe arrives at Al-Aqsa shortly after dawn to begin installation in the cool hours of the day, as the heat of the summer has become oppressive and he wants to get an early start. At this hour, the street is mostly deserted, but one young man walks up and initiates conversation. He has just returned from Iraq where he was fighting in the U.S. Army, and he asks Joe what he is doing. Joe tells him about the mural project, and that it is in collaboration with the mosque. The young man becomes highly agitated. "You need to get out of here! You can't trust these people, they are crazy!" Joe attempts to calm the young man down. "No, you don't need to worry. These are really beautiful, loving people who work for peace and long for it like all of us." At this point in the conversation, Adab walks up, in her head covering, and greets Joe with a wide smile. As the two engage in warm conversation, the young man begins to calm down, as he witnesses a radically different kind of interaction than he was expecting: a Jew and a Muslim in partnership and friendship.

The mural installation continued, and in November plans were made for the dedication. However, here, too, a story shows that despite all of the good will and creative energy that had been dedicated to the mural project, misunderstandings can still arise. Again, Susan recalls, with a chuckle, just how astonishing and ill-timed this particular issue was:

> The Mural Arts Program agreed to provide all of the equipment and set-up needs for the dedication day, including the sound equipment. I am waiting and getting a bit nervous whether everything will show, when a taxi pulls up. The Mural Arts staff person steps out of the cab. There is a huge podium sticking out of the back, and as folks gather to help pull it out, everyone sees that it has a huge cross on it! Some of the Muslim women waiting outside surround me with looks of dismay and even anger; women who had not been volunteers in the project. I imagine that this is the moment of proselytizing they expected all along. My heart sinks to my feet. I am a Christian minister, painfully aware of how my tradition has oppressed other faiths throughout the ages, and how that violates the heart of my faith—to be welcoming to all and to extend hospitality to those whom the dominant culture rejects. At

the critical moment, Amy, of the Mural Arts staff, pulls out a fine gold and turquoise cloth which she attaches to the podium to hide the cross. The women were slightly mollified, but back away, still looking uncomfortable. I could not have imagined the miracle that happened months later. These same women devoted hours participating in another MasterPeace quilt-making project, celebrating the diversity in unity that is Islam, while forging surprising friendships with the Quaker and Jewish artists leading the project.

Despite the podium misstep, the dedication on November 14, 2004, was a beautiful celebration. Al-Aqsa decided to throw a party for the neighborhood, with all kinds of balloons, play equipment for the children, and halal/kosher hot dogs and other refreshments for the guests. About four hundred people attended the dedication, and a total of eight hundred people came by during the day.

The future. Since its completion, the mural project opened several "doorways to peace" between Al-Aqsa and its surrounding community. Some of these doorways include:

- The youth who participated in tile making and their teachers want to continue these relationships, so an interfaith poetry club is formed.
- A Jewish board member of the Arts & Spirituality Center goes into a sandwich shop to order lunch, when one of the traditionally dressed Muslim women behind the counter says, "You were at the dedication!" This leads to a moment of connection and human contact that would not have otherwise taken place.
- A disaffected student at the public elementary school finds the tile making so inspiring that she brings her grades back up and rediscovers her love of learning.
- Adab emerges from this process as a skilled community organizer and an active member of the Arts & Spirituality Center Board. After the mural project is completed, she is inspired to return to school and develop her creative and leadership gifts in a new way.
- Principal Abdur Rahman Crumpton effuses that the student body has a whole new morale and spirit. A place that used to "look like a dump" is now a place of exquisite beauty.

- Al-Aqsa and *Doorways to Peace* is now on Philadelphia's mural tour, serving as a positive representation of the Arab and Muslim populations in the city.
- Pastor Johnson, quietly envious of the mural on the masjid, is approached two years later by the Interfaith Center of greater Philadelphia with an opportunity to create a mural at her church as part of a college service-learning project. Joe Brenman returns to work on this, creating two tile mosaics, "Growing Peace and Justice," in partnership with North Carolina State University Alternative Spring Break students and Hancock-St. John's youth.

The building still serves as a source of pride for the Arab and Muslim communities in Philadelphia. The mural is a lovely addition to the neighborhood and a beacon of hope for interfaith relations.

Annual InterFaith Concert: Lifting Spirits and Creating Bonds through Music, Washington, D.C.

A very different model of dialogue and the arts is provided by the very successful annual InterFaith Concert in Washington, D.C., organized by the InterFaith Conference of Metropolitan Washington. The public performance structure of the InterFaith Concert offers different opportunities and challenges than the more ongoing participatory models described previously, but can serve as an equally desirable method for realizing interfaith dialogue through music and dance. Held on the third Thursday in November, the InterFaith Concert has become an eagerly awaited event. The concert brings together performers from ten faith traditions: Bahá'í, Hindu, Islamic, Jain, Jewish, Latter-day Saints, Protestant, Roman Catholic, Sikh, and Zoroastrian. Of course, even within these divisions, multiplicity is represented. For example, one Protestant choir was composed of Adventists, Baptists, Congregationalists, Episcopalians, Evangelicals, Lutherans, and Methodists.

Rabbi Eugene Lipman, a founding member of the InterFaith Conference and its fourth president, suggested the idea of the concert to Rev. Clark Lobenstine, executive director. As a chaplain during World War II, he helped organize an interreligious concert in Texas that was innovative, popular, and even broke the segregation barriers so entrenched in the South at that time. The InterFaith Conference became excited by the potential of such a transformative event, and since 1979 has seen it grow as both an avenue for dialogue and an important fundraiser. The event regularly brings out more than one thousand Washington, D.C., area residents to experience an evening of interfaith expression.

Beginning six to eight months in advance, a central Concert Planning Committee manages the details of such a large and complex event. But the faith communities themselves choose the performers. Smaller communities often send the same group year after year while larger communities share the wealth by asking different groups to perform in consecutive years. Each group's mandate is to share something meaningful and profound about its religious traditions (in five to six minutes!). The variety is dazzling.

Some groups chant from their religious texts or perform compositions a cappella, others use instrumental music, and a few communities might include sacred dance. Just the willingness of the various faith communities to honor through their performances Lord Shiva, Allah, and Jesus on one stage during one evening is a manifest display of religious cooperation, understanding, and trust. The concert also includes combined choirs, which frequently both open and close the concert.

Rehearsals in the performance venue begin a month before the concert and a dress rehearsal is held two days before the event. On the day itself, dinner is provided for participants, and the InterFaith Conference hosts a reception after the concert at which traditional foods from the member faith groups are provided.

Fundraising is woven into the concert in a number of different ways. A respected leader in the community is recognized every year; money is raised by offering a donor reception with special seating to honor this individual. Well-known media figures, such as Ted Koppel, narrate the evening's events, providing an even greater draw.

Each year the InterFaith Conference attempts to introduce a new, innovative element. The event might host a large-scale choral group, followed by liturgical dance, a handbell choir, and then folk musicians. In 1987 the InterFaith Conference sponsored a Thanksgiving Hymn Competition to create new hymns suitable for interfaith services; the three winners were performed at the 1987, 1988, and 1989 concerts. In 1990 dancers used the banners and symbols of the InterFaith

Conference to call forth each choir and depict its mission statement. The opening of several concerts featured a circular call to prayer from the conch, tabla, shofar, and gong. The 2001 concert opened with "Taps," in honor of those lost on September 11, played by a member of the U.S. Navy. One year the whole concert was dedicated to a specific theme. Titled "Let There Be Peace on Earth," the participating faith communities each performed a piece centered on the idea of peace for all people and for the environment. The impact of one of these concerts was described by a Catholic brother who is a board member of the InterFaith Conference:

> From personal experience I consider the InterFaith Concert a unique, prayerful experience of joy and awareness of unity with people of many faiths expressing glory and praise to our Maker who loves us into life. In personal prayer, focus is on God alone. In this interfaith prayer, there is an accompanying ecstatic feeling that God delights in his people shared in an inclusive way with so many. Usually I think of putting prayer into my life. This experience put my life into prayer and was a true taste of heaven, mindful of the celebrations depicted in [the book of] Revelation.

Creative Planning: Step by Step

What steps should be taken in conceiving and planning an interfaith arts project or event? The guiding principle of successful planning is to approach the project in a spirit of inquiry and discovery. Projects should emerge organically from the constituencies engaged.

The following guidelines should be viewed as a series of loose suggestions rather than a prescription; they are meant to be implemented in a nonlinear, dynamic, and interactive fashion.

1. Bring constituencies together. Step one is to identify the constituencies involved and discern the most effective ways for their community representatives to come to the table. Identify, reach out, and assure the commitment of all community partners. Different partners will inevitably have diverse goals and expectations; it is helpful to acknowledge this at the beginning and throughout the project so this can be a part of the richness of the process versus a stumbling block.

Sometimes there is a single group interested in an arts endeavor. Interfaith and intercultural issues can still be explored in such contexts. We have found richness in bringing together groups within a single school setting or from multiple schools. At later phases of the project they can share their work with their peers in a larger venue or with an adult/community audience, for example via a poetry reading or a theatrical or musical performance.

2. Ask open-ended questions to ascertain needs and goals. The process should be dynamic in order to elicit reciprocal energy and exploration. The following are examples of some guiding questions to begin the conversation:

- Are there different factions or groups that need bridging?
- Are there tensions/problems to be addressed?
- What relationships exist already?
- What are the wounds?
- What have been the obstacles?
- What strategies have worked?
- What are the hopes?
- What are new possibilities for celebration and sharing joy and beauty?
- What methodologies need change?

3. Brainstorm various creative processes/art forms and select facilitating artists. Sometimes the art form is chosen by the community partners or collaborator and naturally emerges along with the initial dream of the project, such as the dream of a mural on the exterior of a building. Sometimes the project begins with the specific desire for a particular art form, such as a poetry workshop. Other times, we begin with the community context and imagine the range of possibilities of art forms that will best match the energy, hopes, and needs of that community or constituency.

We celebrate the versatility of art and encourage creative exploration of art forms such as poetry, collage, journaling, drumming, singing, spoken word, quilting, photography, drama, dance, mosaic, painting, instrumental or vocal performance, theater, or film, embracing whatever means spark the imagination.

In selecting the art form(s), think about budgetary needs, time constraints, and the ages of the constituencies. Consider bringing an artist to the table, along with the related constituency representatives, to be part of the brainstorming. The larger the multidisciplinary planning team, the more likely it is that the complexity of the issues will emerge and imaginative responses will be generated.

In selecting the artist, review the variety of gifts that artists can bring to the table or palette. Some of the following questions might help in discerning which artist(s) seems to be the best match for the project:

- Can the artist invite people into the creative process and make it accessible for a wide range of participants, especially those who may be resistant or frightened?
- Can he or she help people overcome inner barriers to creativity?
- Does the artist exude a connection to the mystery and joy of the creative process, which can then be translated to others?
- Does the artist demonstrate compassion and is he or she aware of the sensitivities that need addressing?
- Is the artist sensitive to the ways that wounds can be inflicted?
- Is the artist able to be patient when dealing with a wounded community?
- What is the artist's skill level in the particular art form? In teaching art and leading a communal process? In working with diversity?
- Will he or she be a strong team player, open to others' ideas and open to collaboration?
- Is he or she respectful of the intrinsic creativity of each participant? As the African proverb says, "If you can walk, you can dance; if you can talk, you can sing."

Are there artists from within the community that can be lifted up and engaged, either as the leaders themselves or as collaborators with a lead artist? Would it be best to choose a dialogue facilitator to carry out reflection processes and work in conjunction with the artist who will focus on artistic design and teaching?

It is a treat to give communities the opportunity to work with professional artists who offer a breadth and depth of exceptional skill. Consider the goals of the end product and the process. Sometimes the end product is insignificant, and sometimes an awe-inspiring creation is the desired result. Have fun, be creative, and take time to create a process that is as inclusive—and as accessible—as possible.

4. Estimate the budget, identify funding possibilities, and choose the lead community partners. As in all successful community organizing efforts, constructive planning will include an agreed-upon timeline, clear scope of the project, budget, staffing, fundraising plan, identification of community partners, artist(s), decision-making process, and communications plan involving all parties.

Who is the lead agency and lead staff person(s)? Are the responsibilities of each party in writing? Who is responsible for raising the money, hiring artists, supervising the project, and monitoring the budget?

Issues of inclusion and participation are always central to any dialogue through the arts. Who is at the table? Are all involved religious groups adequately represented? Are their voices equally valued? Are there ample time and resources to allow a collaborative process to take place? Working with groups with different cultures, expectations, and outlooks can be exciting and invigorating, but surprises, obstacles, and frustrations are often part of the process.

5. Clarify the desired outcomes. How will this dialogue through the arts endeavor improve, enhance, or deepen interfaith and community relations? By the end of the project, what do you want its participants to know, value, question, or challenge? Are there concrete results that the group is seeking—for example, new relationships that bridge neighborhood groups or faith communities, calling attention to the issue of youth violence, or creating a safer neighborhood? Is there a desired art form that can be created through this project, such as a mural, quilt, concert, documentary, photography exhibit, or theatrical performance?

How much should the project be tied into social change? At one end of the spectrum, the desired result is that individuals' encounters with the arts will bring about personal transformation. At the other end of the spectrum, what may be desired is moving devastated communities toward healing and reconciliation, or beginning a new kind of political activism. Again, the goals considered in steps 2 and 5 should guide this decision.

How much is the project one of reflection? An art form can be experienced without it being specifically integrated into a group's dialogue activities; an artistic moment can be designed to promote private contemplation rather than public discussion. On the other hand, individual art projects can be used as springboards for personal reflection and sharing as personal artistic expressions are discussed in a dialogue context. Neither alternative is wrong—it depends on the needs and desires of the dialogue group.

6. Choose your project(s). How participatory should the project be? The dialogue group can view meaningful art, listen to music performances, or walk through a garden. Or the group can create visual art, perform its own music, or design and plant its own garden. The planning team responsible (which could be the entire group, depending on its size) must chart a course.

How structured should the project be? Again, there are myriad possibilities. At one end, the project can have minimal structure and guidelines, allowing participants to design the experience as well as the result. At the other, a firm structure (think of dance choreography or strict rhyme schemes in some forms of poetry) might be valued as a framework within which to access creativity.

7. Design the flow of the process and also let the process emerge. No matter how much a group plans, there will always be contingencies—events, circumstances, and outcomes that are surprising and sometimes wonderful! Be open to discovery; expect the unexpected. There will be unanticipated issues among constituencies. Learn to respect the needs of diverse constituencies and to be flexible. Remember that the grain of sand, which in the moment of irritation feels unbearable, can turn into a pearl over time.

Although goodwill and a vision for success are indispensable for any interfaith dialogue project, sound community planning and non-profit management skills are equally critical to move any project forward. It is extremely helpful to have one or more trained facilitators, either volunteers or paid staff, who are able to structure meetings and discussions to lead to productive and satisfying results. Educators, social workers, community organizers, psychologists, and clergy are among the professionals that have some background in successful group facilitation. We often pair artists of different disciplines—such as a poet and musician or musician and painter—to contribute to spirit and community building as well.

On the practical level, different choices for the arts component of any dialogue require a certain investment in time, energy, and finances. Is the group able to initiate and sustain the chosen project? Are there ample funds and/or fundraising potential to truly bring this project to completion? Are there fruitful collaborations with other organizations that can provide complementary strengths and benefits? (For example, the Interfaith Center of Greater Philadelphia and the Arts & Spirituality Center share talents, resources, and staff to be able to extend the programming of both organizations.) Is the planning adequate to prepare for potential obstacles? Is the burden of time and finances appropriately distributed among the participating communities? Are there creative fundraising activities that can build community, spirit, and financial resources simultaneously? Again, it is very helpful to have individuals on your planning team who are attentive to budget and design implications to keep the project focused and on track.

8. Reflect upon and evaluate your results. Evaluation has become a watchword in the nonprofit community to make organizations accountable for meeting their goals. Although you may not be required to provide funders or boards with a formal evaluation, the group should take the opportunity to reflect upon and, if possible, quantify results from the project. Were the goals met? Outcomes achieved? How do you know? What means of measurement were built into your process? What can you learn from this project to improve future art/dialogue endeavors? Gathering for the purpose of evaluation and reflection can also offer important community building, engagement, and closure opportunities for community partners and participants.

Reflecting on Opportunities and Challenges

There is no cookbook for art/dialogue programming. The varied projects, experiences, and stories offered here demonstrate that positive outcomes can be achieved through a wide range of structure and participation, and whether or not the project has the specific purpose of reflection or social change. These stories help us to see, however, that many dialogue-through-the-arts programs face a number of common challenges. They also share a number of elements that lead to their success.

One of the critical underpinnings of successful interfaith endeavors is building relationships of trust. Project leaders have to create conditions for trust, be patient and persistent for trust, and serve as midwives of trust. Challenges arise when lack of trust gets in the way of meaningful interactions. The stories we have told illustrate key contexts where trust was lacking, and the relationships and processes that helped to build foundations of trust.

From Fatima, the ninth-grader who "didn't write poetry," to the sullen college student who was afraid that he wasn't writing his poem about his spring break experience correctly, there is something about the arts that causes fear and impedes confidence for some. Most of us have gone through an education system that gives us grades that define our worth. Early on, we learn that we are either good at certain things or not. A little boy might be told by his preschool teacher that his art efforts were just "scribble scrabble!" It is difficult for some participants to let go of such early conditioning and rediscover the joy of uninhibited creativity. Much reassurance, coaxing, and empathy may be necessary with diverse groups to encourage them to try new modalities of expression.

"Who Is This Artist and What Does He or She Know about My Community?"

Why this artist? Who is this artist, anyway? Why is this person telling me to do things that are uncomfortable? How can I trust this person who is from a different ethnicity/culture/religion than me? Thought must be given in any participatory project to introducing the artist(s) and establishing a minimum level of trust. Artists themselves, ideally, have experience not only in their medium but also in teaching and group facilitation. Consistency in artists can help build group cohesion in a long-term project, although it is also good to expose people to a variety of art forms. In a more audience-focused project, careful framing—such as the narration at the InterFaith Concert in Washington, D.C.—can allow viewers and listeners to understand and appreciate what they experience. What is initially strange needs to become familiar, and that includes the artist(s) and his or her art form(s).

"Do I Trust the Process? Do I Trust Those in Charge?"

In a long-term project, how much collaboration can and does take place is very important for getting buy-in from communities and individuals. It is also important for all developments to be shared in as open a manner as possible. Open communication, direct community involvement, and working with trusted partners are essential. Mistrust is not quickly surmounted, as the podium story and the community reactions to the mosque mural in *Doorways to Peace* amply demonstrate. Reversal is always possible, but it can only happen over time.

"Who Are These People in the Room with Me?"

Just as in spoken dialogue sessions, participants in artistic projects will encounter those who look, sound, and dress differently. Each may have little knowledge of the other; the potential for misunderstanding abounds. The Army veteran is an excellent example of someone encountering the surface of an art project centering on a mosque. His first reaction was the sense of danger; thus he urgently advised the Jewish artist to "get out." It was not until he saw that Joe's Star of David and Adab's hijab did not foreclose a close friendship that he was given a vision of a new kind of relationship. Unless fear of the unfamiliar is addressed as part of the event/project from the beginning, the arts/dialogue program may not bear its full fruit.

Opening Hearts and Minds: Common Elements of Success

There are common elements in all of these projects that helped people surmount the resistances and challenges implicit in community work, especially work that values the full engagement of diverse constituencies and interests. Building relationships of trust and understanding are both the means to and the results of a successful project.

All of the projects were clear in their purpose, vision, and goals, and aligned the scope of the project to meet those goals. The InterFaith Concert brings D.C. area residents together for a remarkable evening of interfaith celebration and fundraising, while the intimate poetry workshop at the end of the Alternative Spring Break allowed students to process their feelings about their week together. The students would have been ill-served by an interfaith concert, and the InterFaith Concert by a thousand-person poetry workshop. All of these projects benefited because leaders and organizers fit means to ends. They understood what they wanted to accomplish, how to organize their projects for the best results, and how to gather the appropriate resources to make their projects possible.

All of the projects used artists who had the sensitivity and people skills to actualize the plans. One of the most important resources available to dialogue through the arts is the artists themselves. An artist working in an interfaith environment, faced with a high level of diversity, needs to have exceptional listening skills, artistic flexibility, and inclusiveness, as well as an ability to nurture the creative sparks and to lift out the artist within everyone. Having artists of that caliber involved in any art/dialogue endeavor is indispensable.

The projects' organizers brought them to fruition through persistence and a spirit of possibility. It is natural to become discouraged with slow progress and unexpected obstacles. Each of the projects encountered some difficulties, either in the project itself or the support work behind the scenes. Project leaders who follow through, who find ways to meet immediate and long-term needs, who respect and seek to understand the barriers and challenges of all constituencies, will be those who most readily build trust. In these kinds of endeavors, organizers must keep a focus on the big vision and remember that people generally want to overcome challenges, see success, and be called upon to do their best.

"Bridge" persons are especially critical. Adab and Joe in *Doorways to Peace* are examples of bridge persons. They are individuals who serve as liaisons between different constituencies, iron out difficulties, communicate between parties, and bring communities together. Sometimes a volunteer or participant will serve this function, while other times designated leaders are the appropriate individuals for this role. It is inevitable, however, that one or two people will bear the labor-intensive investment in conversing, scheduling, calling, meeting, and handholding. The faith communities in interfaith endeavors cannot stay in their silos; as they reach out and take risks to promote dialogue, they need individuals whom they can trust to further the process.

All of these projects actually furthered interfaith dialogue. It is always possible that an interfaith concert can be viewed by its attendees as entertainment alone, or that a planned reflection through the arts can devolve into a mere arts and crafts project. There is real evidence, however, that all four of these interfaith ventures moved and even transformed their participants, leading to greater interfaith understanding.

Conclusion

Interfaith dialogue through the arts is itself an art form, subject to all the vagaries of the artistic process; creative bursts, creative blocks, careful design, and wild spontaneity are all to be expected. It is an art form much needed in the modern world, beset by social problems, fragility, and mistrust, and that so often seems to be on the brink of destruction. In *Free Play: Improvisation in Life and Art,* Steven Nachmanovitch writes that:

> The only capacity our species has that is powerful enough to pull us out of this predicament is our self-realizing imagination. The only antidote to destruction is creation ... Precisely because the standing of posterity is so tenuous, art is more relevant now than it has ever been ... not just art but artfulness: playfulness, seriousness, connectedness, structure, wholeness, and heart.

It is difficult work, but it is essential and deeply fulfilling. And when it works, it infuses new breath, fresh winds, and vital energy into places that are desperately in need of hope and joy.

3

Dialogue through Observation and Participation—Interfaith Prayer Service

by Rev. Dr. Clark Lobenstine

The problem to be faced is: how to combine loyalty to one's own tradition with reverence for different traditions.

—ABRAHAM JOSHUA HESCHEL

America is one of the most religious nations in the world. It is also one of the most religiously diverse. The opportunities to visit a Christian or Jewish congregation during a formal worship service or a Buddhist Sangha during a meditation session are myriad. Yet it is usually only when we are asked by a family member or a friend that we go to a place of worship or meditation that is not our own, assuming we have one. Often that happens in the context of a life-cycle event, such as a naming ceremony for a baby, a confirmation service, a wedding, or a funeral. Such visits provide rich opportunities to learn about other religious traditions; they are important ways of dialoguing through observing and sometimes participating. I believe firmly that a deepened understanding of what profoundly motivates other people is an essential prerequisite to developing the respect and trust necessary for being good neighbors, colleagues, or fellow students—not to mention citizens in a democracy.

It has been my joy to observe the worship services of many traditions throughout my life. And during my nearly thirty years as the executive director of the InterFaith Conference of Metropolitan Washington, it has been my privilege to create, co-create, and participate in dozens of interfaith prayer services. The title of this chapter,

"Dialogue through Observation and Participation," is very important because it expresses the substantive difference between being an observer in the worship service of another tradition and being a participant in an interfaith prayer service. In doing either, we are challenged to deal with the problem articulated by Rabbi Abraham Joshua Heschel, one of twentieth-century Judaism's greatest leaders: "how to combine loyalty to one's own tradition with reverence for different traditions."

Some Important Definitions

To me, the terms *worship service* and *interfaith prayer service* are distinct. A worship service takes place within a particular tradition and includes certain elements that reflect its key beliefs, whether or not they are shared by any other faith. A person of a different faith may participate in one or a few parts of a traditional worship service. For example, a Jew might read a passage from the Hebrew Bible or Old Testament during a Christian worship service. But in other parts of the service, those that have to do with explicitly Christian beliefs or practices, she or he will be an observer.

An interfaith prayer service, on the other hand, includes participants and elements from two or more religious traditions. Representatives from these traditions are equals during its planning. The service does not include elements from one tradition that people of another religion might find offensive. Also, such a service would not include elements from one tradition in which those from other traditions could not participate, such as communion for Christians.

A further distinction is important in interfaith prayer services: we can either come together to pray, or we can come to pray together. Do you hear the difference? When we come together to pray, we each pray in our own tradition; we do not unite in joint prayers. That is one way of dealing with Rabbi Heschel's question. It was the model that Pope John Paul II and his staff used when they hosted the top leaders of many religions in Assisi in 1986 and The Return to Assisi in 2002. The representatives of each participating religion first prayed by themselves, using the many different chapels in Assisi. Later, all the traditions came together to pray in one place. Participants from each religion offered a brief prayer from their own tradition. No unified prayers were said by all.[1]

Dialogue through Observation

Frequently, it is the distinctiveness of a tradition's worship service that makes the deepest impression on a person of another faith. For example, a Bahá'í shared this memory:

> My most moving memory of such a service took place when I attended a Quaker boarding school, where we had a silent meeting every Wednesday afternoon in our dormitory and a schoolwide meeting every Sunday morning. Having been raised a Bahá'í, I had only a superficial knowledge of the Quaker faith, but my parents assured me that I would enjoy a Quaker environment, and they were right. The small Wednesday meetings were relaxed but often more profound than I had expected. The silence itself was a novelty for me (silences being rare in Bahá'í services), and I came to enjoy both the silences and the occasional inspirations shared by my schoolmates.
>
> The Sunday meetings were more formal, with elders facing us from the stage, and few students ventured to break that weighty silence. But there came a Sunday that led many of us to speak, perhaps not entirely from divine inspiration. A kind and much-admired senior student had suddenly been expelled, just weeks before her graduation. The nature of her misdeed was never revealed but few students could believe that she deserved to forfeit her graduation. So the students spoke that Sunday and the elders listened and the meeting lasted an extra half hour. I was left with a lifelong appreciation of Quaker inspiration and dialogue in good times and not so good.

When I attend a worship service in a tradition other than my own, I want to learn about that faith through observing what is and is not done, said, or sung. If there is a worship book I do my best to follow along, perhaps with the help of someone sitting nearby. I may find that there are parts of the service that I can comfortably join in with the members. Yet I encourage you not to feel any need to do so.

The Importance of Showing Respect

When you attend a worship service or another religious event in a tradition other than your own, it is very important to show respect for the practices of the congregation or group. Simply knowing some of the basic terminology can be an important sign of respect. When I used the word *Sangha* (the community of teacher and students) in speaking with a Buddhist teacher, she told me, "Just using that name, which means so much to me, is a sign of respect. I feel seen. I feel honored."

If you attend a service with a member of a tradition unfamiliar to you, it's helpful to ask basic questions in advance about how to dress and what to expect during the service. Refer to *How to Be a Perfect Stranger: The Essential Religious Etiquette Handbook* (SkyLight Paths), or search the web.

Modest dress is always appropriate, although exactly what this means will vary from religion to religion. Covering one's head and/or removing one's shoes are practices a variety of religious traditions observe during worship. Wearing shorts, a tank top, or very tight-fitting clothes, for example, would be inappropriate almost anywhere. Appropriate clothing for a woman visiting a mosque would include a dress or a blouse with at least short sleeves. In some mosques, the sleeves should come well below the elbows. Dresses or skirts should come to at least the knee. Most mosques require women to cover their hair. Pieces of cloth to do so are almost always available at the entrance. Women typically sit separately from men.

Similarly, when entering a synagogue, it is often required for a man, but not a woman, to cover his head by wearing a yarmulke or *kippah*, a small, thin cap on the top of his head. When I go to the Sikh *gurdwara* (place of worship), everyone takes off their shoes. Men and women will either be wearing turbans or will use a piece of cloth that has been provided to cover the head. Again, you can count on cloths being available when you arrive to do this. Men and women also sit separately.

Yet even something as simple as wearing a yarmulke can have complications, as a rabbi friend discovered. He had invited a Palestinian scholar to address his congregation during a service. When the scholar learned that he would be required to wear a *kippah* in the sanctuary, he balked. This very simple head covering had such negative associations with Orthodox Jews in Israel that he could not wear one. After a long discussion, he compromised by putting on a baseball cap!

By observing carefully, you can notice and follow what others are doing. Some practices, like the ones discussed, present no problems for most people, but there may be others that you are not comfortable with. The first time I entered a gurdwara, for example, I noticed that people were going to the front and prostrating themselves in front of the Guru Granth Sahib (the Sikh scripture) and donating money. To be respectful, I joined the line. When I came to the front, I stood respectfully before the scripture for a moment before finding a place on the men's side of the floor. I chose not to prostrate myself because it was not my scripture. Such conflicts are present even within the Christian Church. For example, Catholic Church teaching makes it clear that, as a non-Catholic, I am not to partake in the communion in their services and that Catholics are not to share in the communion in worship services in other Christian traditions.

It is also very helpful to find someone with whom you can sit. They can help you follow the service and perhaps answer your occasional, whispered questions. Usually, you will go as an invited guest of a member of the congregation. If you are among many guests and cannot sit with your host, such as at a bar or bat mitzvah (the coming-of-age ceremony for a boy or girl in the Jewish faith), it can be helpful to ask an usher if there is someone familiar with the service with whom you might sit.

If you are interested in attending a religious service by yourself, I recommend that you call the congregation in advance to find out if they welcome visitors. You can also ask if they have any special considerations for visitors, such as having someone to welcome you or even a member to sit with you. Visiting the congregation's website, if it has one, or doing some appropriate reading can be especially useful in such a situation.

Dialogue through Participation

This section will focus on occasions when people come to pray together. Note that I use the words *interfaith*, *interreligious*, and *multireligious* interchangeably in describing such prayer services. Some use *interfaith* to refer only to services or events involving Jews and Christians, or perhaps Jews, Christians, and Muslims, that is to say, persons of the monotheistic, Abrahamic-rooted faiths. They want to reserve the terms *interreligious* and *multireligious* for events or services involving other faith traditions. Neither approach is right or wrong, just different.

Established relations of trust among religious leaders and/or congregations of diverse faiths make an enormous difference when planning any interfaith prayer service. For example, communities across this nation and around the world struggled to find appropriate ways to pray and reflect together in the aftermath of the terrorist attacks of September 11, 2001. However, many people who wanted to pray with Muslims did not actually know any Muslims in their community. Muslims had a similar dilemma. They wanted to reach out to their neighbors and clarify that those who flew the planes into the World Trade Center and the Pentagon did so in opposition to Islamic teachings, no matter what they might have claimed. Yet many Muslims had done so little outreach before the crisis that they had no relationships to draw upon afterward.

One good thing that emerged from that horrendous destruction of life and property was a marked increase in interfaith awareness and relationship building. For the week or two after 9/11, the Qur'an was the most purchased book on Amazon.com. Numerous mosques held open houses for the first time ever in the months after 9/11. They invited their neighbors to visit to see for themselves what was taking place in these centers of prayer, to learn more about this religion that about one-fifth of the world follows.

The crisis challenged the complacency of many other religious leaders and congregations around the world, making clear how important it is to build respectful relationships of mutual trust and understanding, especially with Muslim neighbors and mosques. A great many congregations called us for a Muslim speaker in the fall of 2001. I coordinated these requests during the first half of 2002, providing 107 speakers to three dozen congregations, schools, and community groups.

Guidelines for Interfaith Prayer Services

The model for interfaith prayer services that the InterFaith Conference has used since its founding in 1978 is that we come to pray together. Our "Guidelines for Interfaith Prayer Services" was prepared in our very early years; parts of it are reprinted below.[2] The guidelines define an interfaith prayer service as liturgy that includes clergy and/or laity from different faiths *as full and equal participants*. A denominational service to which clergy or members of other faiths are simply invited does not qualify.

The goal of these guidelines is to assist those planning interfaith prayer services to do so in ways that will enable all those present to feel included and to participate wholeheartedly—to promote the highest level of inspiration, without any compromises of conscience. A concern for inclusive language will serve the planners well. It is important to draw on the universal and unifying aspects of our various traditions and to use prayers, readings, litanies, hymns, and other elements of a service that lift up the commitment to peace and justice in the world and to any event or person who may be commemorated in the service.

Scripture and Prayer

Readings from the sacred scriptures of each tradition involved in the service is most appropriate. As with hymns and every other part of the service, they should be selected with their inclusive nature in mind.

Prayer is most helpful when all feel included and can say "Amen." Some appropriate ways of addressing God are: "Creator," "Source of All Life," "Our God and Sustainer," "Eternal Creator," and "Source of Our Being." Some appropriate closing addresses include: "In Thy name we pray," "In the Name of God," or simply, "Amen."*

The Setting

Interfaith events set in a church, synagogue, mosque, or other sanctuary acknowledge the physical integrity of the house of worship. Consideration should be given to the temporary removal of symbols or objects that might cause others distress and that can be easily removed. Similarly, the addition of banners, symbols, or expressions of welcome that may make guests feel more at home should be explored.

Some Guidance on Choosing Prayers, Scripture, and Music

We have consistently included readings of diverse faiths in our interreligious prayer services. For many attending, it will be the first time to experience such texts. For others, it will be a time of renewed acquaintance, perhaps even with a scripture reading from their own tradition. We stress the importance of avoiding passages in many

---

*Please note that the language suggestions of these guidelines were adopted at least twenty-five years before the Washington Area Buddhist Network became a member of the InterFaith Conference.

sacred writings whose exclusivity would likely offend members of other traditions.

I do not mean this restriction to exclude passages that name a person holy in that tradition, such as Abraham, Moses, Jesus, or Muhammad, or a reference to God when nontheistic traditions such as the Buddhists are part of the service. Instead, you should avoid, for example, passages that emphasize that one must follow a certain path to be saved or that condemn people of another tradition.

There is frequently a concern about using Jesus's name. Years ago, a Jewish neighbor and leader in her faith community was talking with me about the InterFaith Conference's work. Wondering how a Presbyterian minister could provide executive leadership for it, she said at one point, "You must not pray in Jesus's name." That was the only way a Christian's leadership in interfaith work made sense to her. To the contrary, Jesus is essential both to my faith and to why I can be the executive director of the InterFaith Conference. I am blessed to have a deep sense of partnership with Jesus. I am not shy about saying that I have the privilege of knowing God's love through Jesus, whom I experience as God's Son.[3]

At the same time, how I express my faith with others is crucial. When offering a prayer in a group that includes people of faiths other than Christianity, I gladly follow our "Guidelines for Interfaith Prayer Services" so that all may be able to say "Amen." As a part of the largest faith community in America, I make a point of first inquiring about others' experience of the holy one or of sacred truth and share my own experience afterward, especially if asked to do so. When I share that I have the privilege of knowing God's love through Jesus, I make clear that each of us have our glimpses of God, our experiences of the divine or of sacred truth, whom none of us can know fully. I emphasize that as we share our glimpses of God, we each come to know a bit more fully the source of our life. I am convinced that God's love is so much wider and deeper than I can grasp. I know in my heart that God is so appreciative of each person's path of worship and right living.

Sometimes the Greatest Impact Comes without Words

An Episcopal layman active on our board and at Washington National Cathedral was present for the national interfaith service held a few days after 9/11 at the request of President George W. Bush. What really struck him that morning was something very simple and yet very eloquent:

> As profound an interfaith experience as I ever witnessed was a small but, in my eyes, enlightening part of the September 14, 2001, Remembrance Service at the Washington National Cathedral. The service was a virtual who's who of national political and religious leaders, with words from the president and Rev. Billy Graham. Yet the key message of that day, for me, came from two small, elderly men who spoke not a word. One was a rabbi and the other an imam. As senior leaders of their respective faiths, they processed in together—side by side—in a long line of faith leaders. They were critically positioned in the middle of the procession and the spacing between those whom they followed and those who followed them accentuated the meaning of their walking together. Leaders of other faiths seemed larger in status and circumstance. These two men were both short and elderly with graying beards, dressed in simple business suits and distinguished as religious only by shawls and headdress. Even the vestments of their respective faiths were virtually identical in color and modesty. They could have easily been twin brothers. I thought to myself that they must realize that their common links were not just to Abraham in the past but what they each probably wanted for their respective grandchildren and generations to come. I felt hope at that moment.

The Difference Made by a Simple Change of Words

I had the privilege of performing the wedding of Melody Fox and Umar Ahmed, the son of American University Islamic scholar Dr. Akbar Ahmed. We worked together on ideas for what would make this marriage ceremony between a Muslim man and a Christian woman both appropriate and special. The challenge was to find a way to show reverence for both faith traditions.

The simplest thing I did turned out to be the most important. Each time I used the word God, I also said Allah. I explained at the beginning of the service that Allah was the Arabic word for God and that Arabic-speaking Christians as well as Muslims used it. Afterward, there was deep appreciation expressed for the wedding ceremony by the couple, their families, and friends. Often, people mentioned my use of both names for the Creator.

Selecting Appropriate Hymns

In planning interfaith services in which songs are sung either by the congregation or by a choir, it is important that the texts be carefully reviewed. For example, in an interreligious service, Christian hymns that praise Jesus are not appropriate. However, just scanning the texts for the word Jesus or Christ is not enough. Other references, such as "the risen one," "the Resurrection," or "he died on the cross," are all clearly references to Jesus Christ. The lack of his name does not make them acceptable in this context. Sometimes it is appropriate and easy to substitute words such as "God" for Christ, or "Holy One" for Jesus Christ, without doing violence to the basic message of the text.

Hymn tunes that are familiar to more than one tradition are also helpful. For example, the musical text for "The God of Abraham Praise," known to many Christians, is a slight revision of the "Yigdal" tune, known to many Jews. Since its words are appropriate for an interfaith service, we have used it frequently. Many older hymns are in the public domain and permission to use them is not required. However, it is important to respect copyright restrictions and seek permission to reprint a copyrighted song in a program you are preparing for a service or other event. If, however, the song is included in a hymnal that is made available to the participants, it can be sung from that hymnal, since permission has already been obtained by the publisher.

It may be helpful to know some of the hymns that we have used in our interfaith services and annual interfaith concerts as a guide for developing your own interfaith prayer service. Here is a partial list:

"We Gather Together to Ask the Lord's Blessing"
"Father of All" (Charles Callahan)
"Jesu, Joy of Man's Desiring" (J. S. Bach)
"Praise to the Lord, the Almighty" (Lobe Den Herren)
"Shout for Joy!" (A. Peloquin)
"Precious Lord, Take My Hand"
"This is the Day" (Dmytro Bortniansky)
"Come You Thankful People Come" (G. J. Elvey)

"Holy God We Praise Thy Name" (Ignaz Franc)

"Great Is Thy Faithfulness" (William M. Runyan and Thomas O. Chisholm)

"All Creatures of our God and King" (R. Vaughn Williams)

"The God of Abraham Praise" (Daniel ben Judah Dayyan)

"From All That Dwell Below the Skies"

"God of Creation"

"For the Beauty of the Earth" (Conrad Kocher and Folliott S. Pierpoint)

"Joyful, Joyful, We Adore Thee" (Henry Van Dyke and Ludwig Van Beethoven)

"Now Thank We All Our God" (Martin Rinkart)

"Amazing Grace"

"We Shall Overcome"

"Lift Ev'ry Voice and Sing" (James W. Johnson and J. R. Johnson)

"O God of Every Nation" (William W. Reid Jr.)

"America the Beautiful"

"This Little Light of Mine"

"O Freedom" (Hall Johnson)

"Great Is Thy Faithfulness"

Different Styles of Prayer in Different Traditions

In some faith communities, spontaneous prayer is natural and expected. In others, such as Episcopal, Islamic, and Jewish traditions, standard prayers from a prayer book or scripture are the norm. When a Muslim is called on to give a prayer, it is very often the Fatiha, the first chapter of the Qur'an, which is recited in each of the five daily prayers. In the Bahá'í faith tradition, prayers recited in public always were written by the founder or the founder's son. A rabbi explained the challenges that often face him when he participates in an interfaith service:

> Jewish prayer in general, although not exclusively, is part of a daily series of services in the morning, day and night in which fixed prayers form a very ordered way of worship. There is room for only some freeform addition. Within that fixed form, the importance of prayer comes out of the intention and feeling that one is able to put into those fixed prayers. For Jews, the method of spontaneous interaction with God and community comes through

study. One rabbi stated it this way: "When I pray, I speak to God; when I study, God speaks to me." As a result, interfaith prayer services often give us some unusual challenges. Rabbis may choose to reinterpret prayers from parts of our services. We may write a prayer that takes some of the form of the less used, more informal style of prayer. We may do readings from a psalm or other canonical text, or we may do a short text study. I have noticed over the years that rabbis often end up just a little out of step with the other clergy for this reason.

Thus, in asking persons to offer prayers in a service, it is wise to consult with them in advance, if they are not part of the planning committee, to be sure that they are comfortable offering the kind of prayer you are expecting of them or to decide whether an alternative is better.

A Responsive Reading for Many Occasions

Written for the service for the first anniversary of the InterFaith Conference, our "To Our Common Cause" responsive reading has been used in many multireligious gatherings. I have often ended presentations about our work by asking those gathered to read it out loud with me. It lifts up many of the highest common denominators we share as people of diverse faiths. You may find it helpful to use as well, adapted for your situation and community. (Endnote 4 for this chapter explains the use of the asterisk and theistic language).

TO OUR COMMON CAUSE
A Responsive Reading of the InterFaith
Conference of Metropolitan Washington

In an era when the forces of division and decay abound, we as religious communities in the metropolitan Washington area have dared to come together.

We come together because our love for God or our particular experience of sacred truth* inspires it; our commitment to humanity insists upon it; our concern for justice, freedom, and peace demands it; and what we can learn from each other requires it.

Bahá'í, Buddhist, Hindu, Islamic, Jain, Jewish, Latter-day Saints, Protestant, Roman Catholic, Sikh, and Zoroastrian, we have begun to listen together to the spirit within our varied and venerable traditions.

In spite of our differences, we share many principles which spring forth from the teachings of each of our faith traditions.

A conviction of the fundamental unity of the human family under God* and the equality and dignity of all human beings.

A sense of the sacredness of the individual person and each one's conscience.

A sense of the value of human community.

A realization that might is not right; that human power is not self-sufficient or absolute, and that in God is our trust.*

A belief that love, compassion, selflessness, and the force of inner truthfulness and the spirit have ultimately greater power than hate, enmity, and inordinate self-interest.

A sense of obligation to stand on the side of the poor, the hungry, and the oppressed, and to serve the cause of justice.

A profound hope that good finally will prevail.

Because we affirm these convictions held in common, we also affirm one another in our different religious and cultural expressions. Because we affirm our differences, we also affirm the validity of the diverse efforts and gifts which we each shall bring to the common cause of improving our metropolitan community. Because we affirm our metropolitan community, we also affirm our commitment to stand together as a unified force for its social and moral benefit, and to be a symbol of the living together in diversity which the Creator intends for all creation.*[4]

Services for Different Purposes

Interfaith prayer services are developed to meet many needs. I will discuss examples of services in a variety of situations, especially ones that the InterFaith Conference has prepared or cosponsored. They include:

- Immediate response to an event or crisis
- A service as part of a larger event or program
- Annual services that celebrate a particular occasion
- Anniversary services
- Services designed to not only pray for a situation but increase awareness of it as well

It is my hope that by discussing the different elements in these services and sharing brief reflections by people of several faiths, those using this book will be better able to develop their own interfaith prayer services.

Immediate Response to an Event or Crisis: A Service After 9/11

After 9/11 the InterFaith Conference used its well-established relationships to quickly develop a moving, multireligious service on the morning of September 13 in Georgetown University's Gaston Hall. The service engaged leaders and other people from our member faith communities at the time—Bahá'í Faith, Hindu, Islamic, Jain, Jewish, Latter-day Saints, Protestant, Roman Catholic, and Sikh Faith. Even though Cardinal Theodore McCarrick was a relatively new leader of the Roman Catholic Archdiocese of Washington and had not yet been formally involved in the work of the InterFaith Conference (IFC), the commitment of his predecessors as well as the nature of this crisis made him a ready participant.

Major planning was needed to design the service, choose appropriate hymns, and prepare the eight-page program for printing in just one day. The service had four sections, each with a spoken prayer, a scripture reading, a three-minute reflection, and time for silent prayer. The themes of the four sections were:

- Those who died and their loved ones
- Those who were injured and all those in need of comfort
- Justice, reconciliation, and unity
- Thanksgiving for God's sustaining power as we move through this crisis

Members of the New Hastinapura Hindu Temple chanted, then people from the Bahá'í Faith chorale sang as nearly seven hundred people gathered from around the community and across many lines of faith, race, and nationality. The procession of speaking participants was accompanied by the IFC's banners of diverse faith symbols, which were placed behind the podium on the stage to visually transform the secular auditorium into a more prayerful space. The IFC's responsive reading "To Our Common Cause" was jointly led by a longtime member of our board of directors and the President of the Georgetown University Student Association. The mayor of the District of Columbia was asked to share a few words, a closing hymn was sung, and a shofar was sounded for healing. Our service that day ended by encouraging everyone to greet their neighbors with a word or sign of peace. The program included guidance that could be easily adapted for other interfaith services:

> Please be aware that, for religious reasons, some people do not wish to be touched by those of the opposite sex. A word of greeting is always appropriate. You may also offer your hand and simply withdraw it if the person you are greeting does not offer you his or her hand.

A Service as Part of a Larger Program: The Million Mom March

We were asked to create an interfaith prayer service to begin the Million Mom March on the National Mall in Washington, D.C., on Mother's Day, May 14, 2000. You may remember that the major focus of this march and of the organization's continuing work is the adoption of sensible gun laws.

This was the largest service we had ever conducted. Even though we printed 3,000 copies of the program, we quickly ran out. We received many requests from musicians and other performers from around the country who wanted to participate—too many to include them all. We decided to have an hourlong musical program from 9 a.m. to 10 a.m., and then the interreligious service from 10 a.m. to 11 a.m. While the last group in the musical program was still singing, participants in the interfaith prayer service began to process through the audience to the stage, led by three jubilation streamers and the banners of eleven faith communities. The banners were then put in stanchions at the back of the stage, helping to transform it into a prayerful space.

Given the nature of this huge event, we were careful to include children, youth, and people who had been directly impacted by gun violence, as well as members of diverse faiths. For example, the Islamic call to prayer was given by a fifth-grader from the Clara Muhammad School in Washington, D.C. One of the reflections was given by the leader of MOMS (Mothers on the Move Spiritually), begun by a Catholic church as a support group for mothers who had lost a child to gun violence. During a period of silence in the prayer of remembrance led by a youth minister from Bronx, New York, the congregation was invited to say the names of loved ones and friends who had been killed by guns. During the prayer for courage and thanksgiving, those present were invited to speak the names of elected officials for whom they wanted to pray for courage on this issue or for whom they wanted to give thanks. At the conclusion of the service, an African drumming group from Richmond, Virginia, led mothers and other marchers toward the main stage ten blocks away.

Annual Conference of the National Alliance of the Mentally Ill (NAMI)

This annual conference brings together people who live with mental illness and their families. It combines elements of education, mutual support, and advocacy. One year we were asked to prepare an interfaith service for the end of the conference. The group was meeting in a hotel in downtown Washington, D.C., and a room had been reserved for our use. As with some of the services already described, one of the challenges was creating a space that was fitting for such a service. In this case, we used holy books of several traditions along with candles on a table at the front of the room.

A second challenge was finding people of diverse faiths who would be sensitive to the needs of those attending. Through our collaboration with the Clinical Pastoral Education (Chaplaincy) Department at Washington Hospital Center, I was able to engage three graduate student chaplains to do this. Their five- to seven-minute reflections as a Jew, a Christian, and a Muslim were deeply appreciated.

This was also a setting, it turned out, where flexibility was critical. Toward the end of the service I received a written note that a young man at the conference who was mentally ill had wandered off from the hotel. No one knew where he was. I invited the prayers of everyone present for this man. This impromptu lifting up of prayers was experienced as another highlight of the service.

Annual Services That Celebrate a Particular Occasion

Let me share two examples of annual interfaith services. One is the observance of Yom HaShoah, or Holocaust Commemoration, jointly planned by the Silver Spring Presbyterian Church and Tikvat Israel Synagogue, a conservative Jewish congregation. The second is the Washington region's only multireligious service for Dr. Martin Luther King Jr.'s birthday.

An Interreligious Commemoration of the Holocaust

As a parish associate or volunteer assistant to the minister of Silver Spring Presbyterian Church, my primary responsibility has been to work with our church on interreligious matters. This has focused primarily on our relationship with Temple Israel, five blocks away. Once again, the value of well-established relationships of trust cannot be overestimated. These are nourished by at least fairly consistent contact and the willingness to move deeper in the relationship over the years. Without a doubt, the commemorations of the Holocaust that began in 1984 have been the most consistent and deeply moving ways of connecting with each other. A planning committee of clergy and laity from both congregations meets two or more times each year to plan it. We choose a theme and define how we will develop it through the speaker, music, designation of an offering,[5] or in other ways. We alternate hosting the service in our respective sanctuaries.

In the annual services, we light not only the traditional six candles in memory of the 6 million Jews who were killed in the Holocaust but also a seventh candle to remember the other victims—the mentally ill and physically disabled, gays and lesbians, Christians who hid Jews or in other ways sought to rescue Jews from the death camps, and others who were deemed inferior to Hitler's vision of an Aryan race. In 2007 an eighth candle was lit for the hundreds of thousands of people killed in the genocide in Darfur.

Our theme in 2007 was "No More Bystanders: The Holocaust and Darfur." A volunteer at the U.S. Holocaust Museum who is a member of congregation in Tikvat Israel Rockville spoke for ten minutes about why so many people remained indifferent during the Holocaust. A college student active in STAND, the intercollege campaign against the genocide in Darfur, also spoke for ten minutes to help us better understand what was going on in that tormented region of Africa and what could be done about it. A sixth-grader from congregation Tikvat Israel was introduced because she had started her own protest, making origami cups and getting others to join her. Each cup represents one of the six thousand people who die in Darfur each month. Many of us learned how to fold the little squares of paper to make a cup during the reception after the service in the church's fellowship hall.

Also during the reception, people watched pictures from the Holocaust and Darfur projected on a wall and picked up flyers encouraging them to call the White House. The flyer included a phone number to use and a suggested paragraph to read, urging the president to act promptly to stop this genocide. The printed programs given to everyone as they entered included an insert on the rally at Lafayette Square, across from the White House, to be held on the following Sunday afternoon. The two congregations were planning to hold a collaborative vigil outside the Sudanese Embassy.

Music is always an important part of the service. The cantor sings the Kaddish, the traditional Jewish prayer for the dead that praises God. Choirs from both congregations also participate. Recently, they have formed a single, conjoined choir. Both congregations love the fuller sound of the bigger group and appreciate the symbolism of their singing together. A member of the church wrote a hymn for everyone to sing for this service and we often include it. The Silver Spring Handbell Choir is a perennial favorite when the service is held in the church.

Observing Dr. Martin Luther King Jr.'s Birthday

For more than twenty years, the InterFaith Conference, working closely with the Dr. Martin Luther King Jr. DC Support Group, has coordinated the national capital area's only multireligious service for King's birthday.[6] For several years before 1983, the DC Support Group held its own service. This group advocated for a federal holiday before it became law, and continues to work today to lift awareness of King's accomplishments and support the King Center in Atlanta.

Our services have almost always been held on the Sunday afternoon before the federal holiday, but occasionally it has been a week earlier. While they have usually been held in African American churches, we have also held them in a synagogue several times, the Washington National Cathedral, the Basilica of the National Shrine of the Immaculate Conception, or another Catholic church. The themes often reflected those chosen by the King Center, especially in the 1980s and 1990s. They have included:

- The Challenges of the 1980s: Jobs, Peace, Freedom
- Focus on World Hunger
- Living the Dream: Let Freedom Ring
- Remember! Celebrate! Act!
- A Day On, Not a Day Off!

- Races Faithfully Working Together for Justice
- Repentance and Reconciliation: A Non-Violent Struggle
- Building the Beloved Community by Building Homes and Drug-Free Neighborhoods

The services have consistently included scripture readings from diverse faiths by members of those traditions. As noted earlier, this is often the first time many of the worshipers will have heard a portion of a sacred writing from one or more of the participating faiths. But it also can have a significant impact on the readers themselves. A Buddhist on our board wrote after one of the services:

> Each time I am part of an interfaith prayer service, such as when eleven faiths come together under the umbrella of the IFC to honor King's legacy, it is an opportunity for me, as a Buddhist practitioner, not only to renew my commitment to my own faith and to share the Dharma with the community at large, but also to practice my belief that each faith has values that I honor too.
>
> This practice is in line with the spiritual message of Thich Nhat Hanh, my teacher who, through Engaged Buddhism, encourages everyone to find common ground at the level of spiritual awareness to solve the ethical and social problems the world is facing. For example, at this year's memorial service, which was addressing violence in the community, I read the Fifth Mindfulness Training about mindful consumption: "Aware of the suffering caused by unmindful consumption, I am committed to cultivating good health, both physical and mental, for myself, my family, and my society, by practicing mindful eating, drinking, and consuming."
>
> Being part of an interfaith service or dialogue nourishes me in the spiritual reality of the common ground between faiths, and encourages me to be involved in this reality even more.

An interfaith children's choir has attracted elementary-age participants from many religions, helping to pass on King's dream to the next generation. Participating congregations and schools are given music to practice in advance. Their one combined choir rehearsal is an hour before the service. For years we have also had a separate children's educational program during the majority of the service that usually lasts about ninety minutes. The children return to the sanctuary before the end of the service, stand across the front, and lead us in singing

"We Shall Overcome" as we cross arms and join hands. For many of us, it brings back memories of our experiences in the civil rights movement. Several years ago we encouraged children to create a poster about King in advance and then process in with it ahead of the speaking participants at the beginning of the service.

There has always been an adult choir in these services as well. Usually it is a choir from the host church or an interdenominational church choir, but sometimes it is interreligous. While the music usually follows the "Guidelines for our Interfaith Prayer Services," sometimes it's overtly Christian. As a service for King that usually takes place in an African American church, there seems to be a greater acceptance of such anthems by people of diverse faiths than there would be in other interreligious services. As one host pastor said, "They expect that. They want that."

High school students of diverse faiths lead the congregation in a responsive reading about King's leadership of the civil rights struggle. For the last three years we have briefly highlighted the work of community groups that are helping to make King's dream a reality. Each group's representative reads a two-sentence statement about his or her group after the congregation's response. The statements are printed in the program along with the text of the responsive reading. Some further information about each of the groups is in the back of the program, and groups are encouraged to bring information and handouts for display tables in the reception hall afterward.

One of the most moving moments in these services came in 2006 when the opening prayer was given by a Sikh girl in high school. She read something that her Indian father had written and she was moved to tears because of how much King meant to her. Even though we have had people from many faiths participating in the services, especially in scripture readings, that prayer and her tears helped all of those present really understand the global impact that King had and still has.

The sermons have been delivered by a wide variety of people, almost all of them clergy or people functioning in that role from the Islamic, Jewish, Protestant, and Roman Catholic faiths. Several have been bishops. A particularly striking service was the year Imam W. Deen Muhammad, the leader of the largest group of African American Muslims in America, spoke at Washington Hebrew Congregation, the area's oldest and largest synagogue.

The reception afterward is a very important time to continue the fellowship that has been experienced in the service. For years, the planning committee and InterFaith Conference staff coordinated the collection of food donations. Several years ago, when a lack of donations required a last-minute run to the grocery store, the planning committee agreed to ask the host church to provide the reception.

Funds received from the offering at the service, advertisements in the program, and endorsing congregations and organizations (with gifts of $25 to $200) and cosponsoring ones (with gifts of $300 or more) are used to pay for the mailing to about one thousand congregations in November or December, promoting the service and soliciting participation; for the printing of the program; for honorariums, if any, for the speaker and choir directors; and to make a donation to the host church to defray the costs of the reception. The planning committee always designates two or three recipients of the bulk of the funds. One year, for example, DC Habitat for Humanity received $3,300, while $1,100 was sent to the organization that is building a memorial to King on the National Mall in Washington, D.C.

The Children's Defense Fund's Annual Children's Sabbath Service

The Children's Defense Fund (CDF) has very effectively encouraged congregations, ecumenical and interfaith organizations, and others to lift up the great needs of children in its Children's Sabbath Service each October. For years, the organization has provided the most extensive printed resources that I am aware of for any such occasion.

For example, one year the CDF published 8½- by 11-inch, 105-page paperback books for use by African American churches, Catholic parishes, Jewish congregations, and Protestant churches. They also issued a volume of multiethnic, multifaith resources. Each book shared the same introductory section but the later chapters were customized for particular audiences. These chapters included bulletin inserts and worship suggestions, sermon ideas, prayers and other resources, and a shared discussion of the theme for the year: "A Moral Witness for Children: Still There Is a Vision." The books also provided lesson plans and activities for different age groups. They all concluded with follow-up suggestions, resources, and a form to complete and return with comments. The multiethnic, multifaith resources book included an interfaith service in Spanish and in English that could be copied and used as well as a bilingual discussion of the theme.

Later, the CDF provided a two-hundred-page book of worship, educational, community outreach, and advocacy resources for Protestant, Catholic, Jewish, and other faith traditions. Other books include *Wonderfully Made: Preparing Children to Learn and Succeed* and *Providing What God Requires and Children Need: Justice, Kindness, and Faith*. The opening chapters provided background on the Children's Defense Fund, materials for "Planning and Promoting Your Children's Sabbath," and separate sections on resources for Christian, Jewish, and interfaith worship and education. They included sample homilies or sermons for use in Catholic, Jewish, and Protestant traditions, and a sample sermon for children. The "Interfaith Worship Resources" chapter added resources related to children from the Bahá'í Faith, Buddhist, Hindu, Islamic, Native American, Sikh Faith, and Unitarian Universalist traditions. The Children's Defense Fund also makes these resources available online.[7]

Anniversary Services

You may well have occasion to participate in or help plan an interreligious service commemorating a significant year in the life of an organization, a community, or an event. The InterFaith Conference has held such programs on its first anniversary and every five years thereafter. One of the most interesting of our many multireligious services was held on the first and tenth anniversaries of the Chernobyl disaster in the Ukraine.

Anniversary Services for the Chernobyl Disaster

Shortly before the first anniversary of the world's worst nuclear disaster, the IFC received a call from a leader of a Ukrainian American organization asking if we would prepare an interfaith service for it. Its members were painfully aware that the devastation caused by this accident affected people not only in the town of Chernobyl but also throughout the world and that its repercussions would be felt for generations. The service was held on April 27, 1987, in the sanctuary of the Ukrainian Catholic National Shrine of the Holy Family. Another anniversary was well noted in the service, as 1988 marked the millennium of Christianity in the Ukraine.

This service was unique in our several decades of work because it took place in a Ukrainian Catholic church and engaged a number of Eastern Orthodox priests. We have had Orthodox choirs in our InterFaith Concert on a couple of occasions, and Orthodox priests and bishops were present as observers during the formation of the InterFaith Conference, but since the Orthodox Christian Clergy Council was divided on whether or not to join, they never did. The Eastern Orthodox community, with its many churches separated primarily by nationality (e.g., Russian, Greek, Serbian, Ukrainian), has rarely been involved in interfaith work in the metropolitan region. I can still remember the looks of surprise and discomfort on the faces of several of the Orthodox priests and bishops when they realized they were going to be participating in a service led not only by other male Christians but also by a woman Presbyterian minister, an imam, a Jewish lay leader, and a member of the Latter-day Saints!

The service included music from the church's choir, which sang a modified version of the Great Prayer (Divine Liturgy) of the Eastern Churches written by St. John Chrysostom in the fourth century, a prayer that has been used in Ukrainian and other Orthodox churches for a millennium. The modifications made it appropriate for this inter-religious service and included a reference to all those who had died or were suffering because of the Chernobyl disaster. While the priests leading the Great Prayer from the Ukrainian Catholic and Ukrainian Orthodox churches spoke in English, the response (*Hospodi Pomiluy*, "Lord Have Mercy") was led by the choir in Russian and joined by the congregation in Russian or English. The prayer of remembrance for the victims of Chernobyl was led in turn by a clergy or layperson from a Latvian Lutheran church, an Estonian Evangelical Lutheran church, and the Lithuanian Catholic Mission.

The service opened and closed with hymns. The second hymn also included specific references to the victims of Chernobyl and was first sung in Ukrainian by the host church's choir and then by everyone in English.

Another service was held on the tenth anniversary of the disaster, this time at St. John's Episcopal Church, Lafayette Square, in Washington, D.C. Much of the text from the first service was used again and several additional Ukrainian Catholic and Ukrainian Orthodox priests participated, including one from Baltimore, Maryland. The service again included readings or other leadership from a variety of traditions, including Hindu, Islamic, Jewish, Latter-day Saints, Protestant, Roman Catholic, and Sikh.

This service also had the support and presence of leaders from seventeen embassies from Eastern and Western Europe. The Ukrainian ambassador was the only secular representative to speak during the service, sharing why we gathered that day. But after the benediction, there were remarks from a Chernobyl survivor, two members of Congress, a representative of First Lady Hillary Clinton, a special advisor to the president, and the director of the Ukrainian National Information Service in Washington, D.C. Then an eleven-year-old survivor lit a candle and led a candlelight procession to the Chernobyl Tree in Lafayette Square, where there was a moment of silence and a Ukrainian prayer (*Bozhe Velykyi,* "O Thou Great God") was said.

IFC's 25th Anniversary Service: The Use of Silence and Symbols

Of the many anniversary services the InterFaith Conference has held to commemorate its development, the most moving was also the shortest. For our twenty-fifth anniversary we planned a half-hour service just before the Third Snowdon Lecture by James Wolfensohn, who was then the president of the World Bank. The service was designed as a time of recommitment and included several founders of the organization and most of its current leadership. In planning it, we followed a Quaker leader's suggestion that we use silence.

The founders charged their successors and the leaders of the faith communities that had joined the InterFaith Conference to carry on its pioneering mission. In silence, the current leaders signed a document of recommitment and then went to the central table to light a candle representing their religious community. Once these ten candles were lit, the leaders jointly lit a center candle representing the InterFaith Conference.* The congregation then read out loud and was asked to sign their own declaration of commitment, an insert in their program.

---

*When including a shared candle-lighting element in an interfaith service, it is wise to consult with Jain participants about their perceptions and expectations. Full participation in advance planning helps avoid problems with these particularities of tradition.

In another period of silence, the diverse faith community leaders lined up in front of the congregation. One by one, they stepped forward for about fifteen seconds, holding or doing something central to their tradition, and then returning to their place. The printed program enabled everyone to understand what was being done and why. For example, our Bahá'í vice president stepped forward holding a vase of beautiful flowers because beauty is a sign of the Creator. The Zoroastrian priest stepped forward and lit a sandalwood fire in an open urn because fire represents the purity of God. A Protestant leader took three steps toward the audience holding a bowl of water and a towel, a symbol of servant leadership because Jesus washed his disciples' feet during his last supper with them. A Hindu priest blew a conch shell because that is done on all auspicious occasions. Several other faith leaders did something special from their tradition. It was a powerful and creative service and had the extra blessing of giving our distinguished speaker a unique way to learn something important about us.

Not Just Prayer, but Awareness as Well

I want to share two examples of prayer services intended to raise awareness as well. The first was our interfaith prayer service on AIDS. The second was an interreligious service at Washington National Cathedral for the Alexandria Declaration for peace in the Middle East.

Cry Pain, Cry Hope

The InterFaith Conference's Task Force on AIDS pioneered interreligious work on this issue in the mid-1980s, when hardly any faith communities were confronting this devastating disease. In fact, when we began this task force, the Episcopal Caring Response to AIDS was the only AIDS organization that had been created by one of our member faiths. There was one other religious organization, established by a Roman Catholic, but it was not recognized at the time by the archdiocese.

In part because of our efforts, many of our member groups began to consider how they could educate their communities to overcome fear and become welcoming those with HIV or AIDS. They also learned about the special dimensions of pastoral care for people with AIDS and they engaged in advocacy to change governmental policy. Therefore, our multireligious service, "Cry Pain, Cry Hope," was much more than an opportunity for interfaith prayer in response to the crisis of AIDS. It was a pace-setting model that was shared throughout the country. The program even included a note inviting others to use and/or reproduce the words in the service.

The service was divided into three parts: Lamentation, Remembrance of God's Solidarity with the Suffering, and Celebration of God's Mercy and Love. Periods of silence and times of reflection both in music and with words were integral to the service. Readings from our diverse faith communities, responsive readings or prayers, and hymns sung by everyone present were also important. A shofar was sounded to begin the third section, the Celebration of God's Mercy and Love. The program included an explanation of what the shofar was and when it was used. It read in part:

> The sounds of the shofar, like the sounds of a trumpet, call us to action. Often times a shofar was sounded to call for people to change their ways. We hear the shofar to revive our faith in Almighty God who will bring the final victory of life and freedom over death and despair. May the sounds of the shofar we hear tonight bring us renewed hope and consolation to continue our battle in confronting AIDS.

In the service for the Alexandria Declaration described below, another insight was given about the sounding of the shofar:

> The shofar, or ram's horn, is an ancient instrument often mentioned in the Bible. Its sound is a call to gather and a sound of warning and liberation. This call serves to inspire a renewal of hope in a messianic age when all humankind will be as one.

An Interfaith Service for the Alexandria Declaration

The Alexandria Declaration was an amazing step toward peace in the Middle East. It was signed by key Jewish, Islamic, and Christian leaders in the Middle East on January 21, 2002, in the city of Alexandria, Egypt.[8] It recognized the sanctity of the Holy Land for all three faiths while calling for an end to the violence and bloodshed that denies the right to life and dignity. These religious leaders of the Holy Land were convened by Dr. George Carey, the archbishop of Canterbury.

Yet this signature process of dialogue and the declaration that resulted were hardly known in this country. Therefore, in March 2002, leaders of Washington National Cathedral convened people to plan a service of prayers for the Alexandria Declaration and its implementation that would be held on May 5 of that year. Sixteen people from the faith communities who signed the declaration were participants, along with Jewish and Muslim choirs and a Cathedral organist.

After the Adhan, or Islamic call to prayer, and a welcome by the dean of the Cathedral, the hymn "God of Our Fathers" was sung—its lyrics changed to "God of Creation" to avoid sexist language. That was followed by readings from the Hebrew Bible, the New Testament, and the Qur'an, along with brief reflections on them.

Everyone present then read in unison the Alexandria Declaration, followed by a time of silent reflection. Six leaders from the Abrahamic traditions took turns in leading the congregation in a responsive reading on peace. During the offering, which raised funds to support interfaith Middle East peace work, offertory anthems were sung by the Clara Muhammad School Children's Choir and by two Jewish choirs. Sharing the Peace—the priestly blessing in the Hebrew Bible (Numbers 6:24–26)—and the sounding of the shofar ended the service.

A Jewish lay leader whom I asked to help lead the responsive reading in the service told me that while she had agreed to do so, she remained quite skeptical. She had a son serving in the Israeli military and took very seriously the need both for peace and for appropriate safeguards for the security of Israel. However, afterward she shared how deeply moved she was by the service. She spoke for all of us.

Pilgrimage: A Dialogue by Observing and Participating

The InterFaith Conference has organized a number of pilgrimages, or Time for Faith Sharing programs (what we initially called them). The first few took a busload or two of people to visit sanctuaries of different faiths in Washington, D.C., Montgomery County, or Northern Virginia. The most ambitious of these, The Landmark Tour of Significant Montgomery County Religious Sites, was a daylong program that visited five congregations—Jewish, Buddhist, Latter-day Saints, Islamic, and Ukrainian Orthodox. Other pilgrimages that we organized included opportunities to experience some aspect of each congregation's worship. This enhanced the visits and encouraged some people to return and experience more fully a service in that tradition.

The value of these journeys was brought home by a colleague who lived two blocks from a synagogue for more than twenty years and yet had never visited it. She worked regularly with Jews on legislation on Capitol Hill as part of her professional work with a Christian advocacy office. She told me how excited she was to be part of this program because she had never known if the synagogue would welcome her.

The fullest experience of visiting congregational worship services of different faiths was a yearlong program developed in collaboration with the Washington National Cathedral's Spiritual Perspectives Committee. One congregation of a different faith was visited during a time of worship each month for a year. During these visits, we made sure that someone greeted and oriented those new to the service, sat with them, and discussed it afterward. These steps proved to be very beneficial and made the worship site more welcoming to such visitors. Each quarter began with a speaker who gave an overview of and orientation to the three faiths to be visited next.

In the late 1990s my wife, Rev. Carole Crumley, and I led three pilgrimages. Inspired by her leadership of pilgrimages in other countries and elsewhere in the United States, we agreed it was high time that we did this in Washington, D.C.! She described pilgrimage in this way for the participants in our first one, to Three Sacred Gardens, in 1998:

> One of the elements common in our religious traditions is the sacred journey, the pilgrimage. There are many destinations, but a shared journey; many paths, but a common way.
>
> The destination has been marked as a sacred place, a place where God's presence has been particularly experienced. Others have gone before. The pilgrim usually travels in the company of other pilgrims, although she may not know them. Yet they have a similar intent—to seek the holy, to be in the presence of God, to deepen their spiritual life, to touch back into the vision glimpsed there before, perhaps to lift up a special intention, whether for healing or forgiveness or peace.
>
> It is usually an outward journey, frequently to a far destination. For example, Jews especially go to Jerusalem, Muslims to

Mecca, Sikhs to Amritsar, Hindus to the Ganges, Mormons to Salt Lake City, Bahá'ís to Haifa, Christians to Jerusalem or Rome. Yet the pilgrimage is always also an inward journey. It is the inward journey which differentiates pilgrimage from travel. Thus, you can go on a pilgrimage and never leave home.

I have described pilgrimage in this section as a way of understanding dialogue both through observation and participation. For example, in visiting the gardens at the Franciscan Monastery, the Washington Hebrew Congregation, and the Kahlil Gibran Park, there were distinctive elements from different faith traditions. Yet people could participate in a meaningful way in these visits because they each remind us that every place is holy ground, that the entire universe is sacred, that our intentions really do matter, that our actions really do make a difference.

Two years later, we invited people to share in a pilgrimage called Praying by Hand: The Devotional Use of Beads in Four Faith Traditions. In this program, we stayed in one place but were encouraged to experience by observation and/or participation the ways in which beads are a compact, powerful tool for personal spirituality. As our brochure said: "With only a set of beads, you can transform time spent waiting, traveling, or sitting into a potent devotional space."

An opening plenary session gave our presenters and workshop leaders from the Buddhist, Hindu, Muslim, and Roman Catholic faith communities the opportunity to explain the use of prayer beads in their traditions. Then, after a light supper that provided opportunities for lots of conversation among the participants, everyone chose to attend a forty-five-minute workshop in two of the four traditions. During these workshops, in which leaders demonstrated how the beads were used in devotions, those attending were asked if they wanted to hold and/or use a set of prayer beads from that tradition. During the closing ceremony, in an outdoor garden of the cloistered convent and school where we gathered, people shared brief yet moving reflections of thanksgiving as we stood in a circle of prayer.

The 9/11 Unity Walk

The annual Unity Walk on the Sunday closest to September 11 is the largest pilgrimage in the metropolitan Washington area of which I am aware. The InterFaith Conference was a cosponsor for its first two years and began coordinating it in 2007.

The Unity Walk is an expression of the commitment to peace by people of very diverse faiths and no particular affiliation. It is a dramatic way of reclaiming this day of great tragedy that transformed America and the wider world. The 1,000 to 1,500 participants each year gather at Washington Hebrew Congregation, the region's oldest synagogue. After a welcome and orientation, the walkers begin the pilgrimage to the Islamic Center, the area's first mosque, and then to the Gandhi Memorial. During this mile-long walk, they are greeted by members of nearly a dozen different congregations along Massachusetts Avenue (this section is also called Embassy Row), each sharing bottled water or a song or chant or some other way of supporting these pilgrims. On the front steps of the Islamic Center there is another program with a few speakers and a song by the two cantors from the synagogue. The Muslim community generously provides sweets and other food as well as more water. Many participants stay after the program for the opportunity to see the mosque itself.

The walkers are encouraged to continue to the Gandhi Memorial at Dupont Circle, a journey of over a mile. Perhaps a third to half of the pilgrims keep going. The Indian community, especially the Hindu, Jain, and Sikh Faith traditions, naturally plays a lead role in providing hospitality in the program there. In 2006 the walk to the Gandhi statue had particular significance because it was on September 11, 1906, that Gandhi first announced the Satyagraha or truth-force/non-violence campaign in South Africa—an idea that was recommended to him by a Muslim. One of Mahatma Gandhi's grandsons joined us at the statue to speak about his grandfather.

As the InterFaith Conference coordinates each Unity Walk, we continue to find ways to increase interfaith dialogue in planning meetings by starting each one with a half hour in small groups focused on a specific question. This emphasis will continue on the walk itself, when each person is given a couple of questions to discuss quietly as he or she makes the pilgrimage, hopefully with someone that he or she does not already know. We will encourage these pilgrims to sign up to be participants in an ongoing neighborhood interfaith dialogue in the following months. We are also working to engage more deeply the cosponsoring congregations that greet us. Finally, we will identify justice themes that need to be more clearly highlighted in the walk without detracting from its primary emphasis on our unity.

Conclusion

Increasingly we have opportunities for dialogue through observation and/or participation, occasions when we can learn about another tradition by being observers at its worship services or by coming together for an interfaith prayer service or another kind of multireligious celebration. These remind us of how much binds us together even as we grow in our appreciation of how different we are. In diversity is the unity that can change the world. How can you help create that transformational unity?

PART II

Living Interreligious Dialogue through Service and Advocacy

4

Action through Service— From Shared Values to Common Action

by Dr. Eboo Patel, April Kunze, and Noah Silverman

Never doubt that a small group of thoughtful citizens can change the world. Indeed, it is the only thing that ever has.

—MARGARET MEAD

Introduction: The Interfaith Youth Core Approach to Interfaith Youth Work

On an ordinary spring afternoon in 2005, two groups of young people got together for a party. They ate pizza, played games, and read books out loud. Around the room young children sat on older children's laps while the older children struggled to hold the book in that elusive position—the trademark of grammar school librarians—that enables everyone to see the pictures at once. Some of the younger children, just learning to read, scrunched their faces as they strained to sound out the words for themselves. Parents looked on with pride and sounds of laughter, giggling, and the scraping noise of turning pages filled the room. In many ways, it was an ordinary party for ordinary people in the ordinary city of Chicago.

There was something quite unusual, however, about this particular party. First, the two groups seemed out of place. The children of the younger group, ages three to twelve years old, were refugees—Somali Bantus who had fled their homes and communities thousands of miles away to escape persecution. With their families, they had traveled by foot, train, boat, and plane to reach Chicago, searching for a place where they would not be hated simply for who they are. The second group was equally remarkable in its composition. It consisted of high school and college students from around the city who were choosing to spend this afternoon—and countless other afternoons before—serving at a refugee resettlement agency rather than studying, hanging out with their friends, or enjoying the inspiring beauty of the Chicago lakefront on a warm day. Perhaps not surprisingly, each of the members of this latter group possessed a deep faith and commitment to their religious community and the values it called them to live out in the world. Rather uncommonly, however, they belonged to not one, but three different religious traditions and several more congregations across the city.

The main activity of the day—reading children's books—was also noteworthy, for they were all reading the same book and it was no ordinary book. It had just been published and its authors were the very same people who now sat around reading it to each other, a dozen teens of different faiths and a dozen Bantu refugee children. The book was about them. It told their respective and collective stories of belonging and not belonging, of home and of loss, of service and of fulfillment, of making great journeys over land and of making great journeys of the heart. The book was entitled *Why Are You Here?* and the answer, contained in beautifully illustrated pages that the Bantu children had drawn themselves, was plain. Despite the seeming contradictions and their apparent out-of-placeness, they were there because it was precisely where they belonged. It was a space where all of them could be fully who they were without fear or reservation, where they could come for inspirational relationships, and where they could work collectively to create more such spaces in the world.

The members of the older group were participants in the Chicago Youth Council (CYC), an annual intensive interfaith leadership program run by the Interfaith Youth Core. The nine-month program pairs religiously diverse college and high school students for weekly meetings, alternating between facilitated interfaith dialogue and service-learning volunteering. The theme for this year of the CYC was "Welcoming the Stranger," an exploration of the value of hospitality as found in the three Abrahamic faiths, a theme that intentionally corresponded with the year's service-learning project: working with the group of Somali Bantu refugee children who had been recently resettled in Chicago. The refugee agency already had an afterschool program for the refugee kids in place; the CYC's involvement was intended to take as much burden as possible off the agency's overworked staff. On a biweekly basis, the CYC participants designed games, led arts and crafts projects, and tutored and helped the kids with their homework. On the alternate weeks, the CYC members gathered for interfaith storytelling, utilizing the service-learning methodology of the Interfaith Youth Core. The culmination of the project, described above, originated in the CYC members' desire truly to live out their theme by composing a children's book for the Bantu children.

This chapter humbly aims to provide a contextually grounded but largely practical guide to using an interfaith service-learning methodology to build these types of positive relationships and environments between young people of diverse religious traditions. It begins with a brief exploration of some of the geopolitical and sociological trends that give this work particular urgency in the world today, and then we contrast this stark reality with a vision of what, in the Interfaith Youth Core's view, the end goal of interfaith work looks like: a global community, characterized by civil pluralism.

In a section on methodology, the Interfaith Youth Core's vision of civil pluralism is parsed into its different components; we see what it takes at a practical, programmatic level to build pluralism. Then, the chapter moves to the heart of the practice by unpacking the core elements of the Interfaith Youth Core's methodology, exploring how it interacts with or is distinct from others, and providing concrete suggestions for those readers who might be considering the possibility of organizing something along these lines themselves. The next section is devoted to presenting a case study of this methodology in action: the above story of the 2004–2005 Chicago Youth Council and Somali Bantu refugees. This is followed by an analysis of how the case study bears out both the methodology and the goals of pluralism. Finally, the chapter concludes with a discussion of the larger body of young people and institutions that are taking up this call to action, which will, perhaps, inspire a reader or two to get involved.

The Faith Line:
The "Clash of Civilizations" Meets the Pluralists

One hundred years ago, the great African American scholar W.E.B. Du Bois warned that the problem of the twentieth century would be what he called "the problem of the color line." The problems of the twenty-first century might well stem from a different line, no less divisive and no less violent: the faith line. From Northern Ireland to South Asia, from the Middle East to Middle America, people are condemning, coercing, and killing each other in purported defense of the sacred. The most pressing questions today may well be these: How will people who have different ideas of heaven interact together on earth? How will the steeple, the minaret, the synagogue, the temple, and the Sangha learn to share space in a world house whose walls are being knocked down at the speed of globalization?

Political scientist Samuel Huntington outlines one set of answers to these questions in his controversial "Clash of Civilizations" thesis, first published in *Foreign Affairs* in 1993 and later turned into a book of the same name in 1996. Huntington's argument, which unfortunately has become the leading paradigm for understanding the contemporary geopolitical situation, has three basic points.

1. The world is witnessing a rise in the saliency of religious and cultural identity as the primary way in which people understand themselves.
2. In the wake of the Cold War, the new dividing lines in international politics are between nations aligned by their religious and/or cultural affiliations, what he terms "civilizations."
3. These civilizations, and the religious traditions upon which they are based, are inherently and inevitably in conflict with each other.

Sadly, this argument served to reconfirm for many people what had long been the dominant public theory about cultural, particularly interreligious, interaction: We are too different to live together in peace, so we had better keep our distances from each other. Otherwise, violent coannihilation is inevitable.

It is not the premise but the conclusion of Huntington's argument that is so problematic and sells short the legacy of religious motivation in humanity. It is indeed true that religious identity has been and—contrary to the prevailing "secularization thesis" of the twentieth century—will continue to be the primary way through which most people in the world identify and understand themselves. It is also true that people who identify themselves in like manners have and will continue to associate with each other, forming communities, nations, and even civilizations. However, the faith line does not lie where these civilizations bump up against each other, but rather within and across all of them. As American philosopher Martha Nussbaum writes, "The real clash is not a civilizational one between 'Islam' and 'the West,' but instead a clash within virtually all modern nations—between people who are prepared to live with others who are different, on terms of equal respect, and those who seek the protection of homogeneity, achieved through the domination of a single religious or ethnic tradition."[1] It is not the faith line that divides Taoists from Buddhists, Muslims from Hindus, Orthodox Christians from Protestant Christians, or Catholics from Animists, as Huntington argues and many believe. Nor does it divide secular from religious people. What the faith line *does* divide are religious totalitarians and pluralists.

Religious Totalitarians

Those who hold with Huntington that a clash of religious civilizations is inevitable and actively work for its arrival are religious totalitarians. Frighteningly, there are many within all the world's religious traditions who not only share this view, but also delight in its implications: Osama bin Laden, strident followers of Pat Robertson and the legacy of Jerry Falwell, the Ku Klux Klan, extremist factions of the Hindu nationalist Bharatiya Janata Party in India, radical remnants of the Kach party in Israel, and far too many others. Though ostensibly opposed in their religious outlook, these extremist religious leaders in fact all stand on the same side of the faith line, which gives them the unique advantage of being able to oppose each other and work together at the same time.

Totalitarians are united in their opposition to the dream of a common life together and defined by two characteristics. A totalitarian is anybody (1) who believes that his or her way of being, believing, and belonging is the only legitimate way on earth, and (2) who will readily convert, condemn, cow, or kill anyone who is different. Both parts of this definition are equally important—belief and action—for what characterizes religious totalitarianism is not just belief but a specific type of belief paired with a specific type of action. There are plenty of people who believe that their way is the only way to salvation or of connecting to God but that other ways are tolerable or allowable. What characterizes religious totalitarianism is the willingness to act forcibly against those who do not fit into their restricted worldview. The question is not whether one evangelizes; the question is how one treats people if, after attempting to convert them, they remain committed to their original creed. Totalitarians are defined by their belief that our differences require both physical or ideological annihilation of the "other" and the actions they take to mobilize followers on that path.

Religious Pluralists

On the other side stand religious pluralists, people who believe that peaceful coexistence is possible as long as we are willing to invest the effort to get to know one another and come together around our common aspirations. Religious pluralists hold up the dream articulated in all traditions of a world as it might be and use their religious motivation to do acts of justice and love rather than bigotry and hatred. The Reverend Dr. Martin Luther King Jr. was one of the most visionary pluralists of modern times. During his Nobel Peace Prize lecture in 1964, King described his paramount vision not just as one of racial reconciliation, but as a call to religious, cultural, and racial coexistence:

> This is the great new problem of mankind. We have inherited a large house, a great "world house" in which we have to live together—black and white, Easterner and Westerner, Gentile and Jew, Catholic and Protestant, Moslem and Hindu—a family unduly separated in ideas, culture and interest, who, because we can never again live apart, must learn somehow to live with each other in peace.
>
> We are confronted with the fierce urgency of now. We may cry out desperately for time to pause in her passage, but time is deaf to every plea and rushes on. Over the bleached bones and jumbled residues of numerous civilizations are written the pathetic words: "Too late." We still have a choice today: nonviolent coexistence or violent co-annihilation.[2]

A devout Southern Baptist, King's dream was one of Christian love, inspired first by the gospel and Baptist teaching, reinforced by a bald, wrinkled, half-naked Indian Hindu's teaching of nonviolence, and practiced arm-in-arm with one of American Judaism's greatest theologians, Abraham Joshua Heschel. King's life exemplified interfaith cooperation and religious pluralism, the choice for nonviolent coexistence over the violent coannihilation of totalitarians. He encountered the Hindu concept of Satyagraha, or love force, in the work of Gandhi and put the idea into action in the civil rights movement. King's best-known interfaith friendship began in Chicago, where he met Rabbi Abraham Joshua Heschel at the Conference on Religion and Race in 1963. They discovered a mutual appreciation for the emphasis the Hebrew prophets placed on social justice, and made common cause against both segregation and the Vietnam War.

Civil Pluralism

King lived out what University of Chicago scholar of religion Martin Marty defines as "civil pluralism." King's focus was on working together with people of diverse traditions so they could make a greater difference on earth. This is different from "theological pluralism," which has to do with people of different faiths reaching a consensus about their beliefs about the nature of God and the validity of each other's religious paths. Theological pluralism is neither the focus of this chapter nor of this work. Many people are disdainful of interfaith work because they equate it with theological pluralism. They wonder, "Are these people out to dilute all of our religious identities, either into some universal spiritual mush or into areligious secularism?" Civil pluralism is not, however, remotely synonymous with syncretism or relativism. As King's life testified, believing we will all end up at the same place when we die is not a prerequisite for peaceful coexistence.

Civil pluralism is not merely the tolerance of diversity. Princeton sociologist of religion Robert Wuthnow was once asked how he thought faith communities were adapting to the reality of religious diversity. He used the analogy of an elevator: Christians, Muslims, Jews, and the rest of America's religious diversity are all riding in it together, we are increasingly aware of the other people around us, but we're doing just about everything we can to avoid real interaction. As Harvard scholar and head of the Pluralism Project Diana Eck discusses, this is "diversity," a merely descriptive term that refers to the fact of different people from different backgrounds living in close quarters. Diversity alone will not prevent the kind of ignorance, hostility, and violence we see expressed through discrimination, hate crimes, and war.

By asking us to go beyond merely acknowledging the fact of diversity toward making commitments to one another and the world that we share, civil pluralism can help combat these social ills. In his study of interreligious violence in India, *Ethnic Conflict and Civic Life* (Yale University Press), University of Michigan political economist Ashutosh Varshney discovered that the one significant difference between cities that remained relatively calm during times of interreligious tension and cities that exploded in sectarian violence—with comparable Muslim and Hindu populations—were what he calls "networks of engagement."[3] Essentially, these networks are civic organizations that bring people from different backgrounds together on a regular basis. When tensions flared, the preexisting public relationships those people had prevented them from killing each other. They also had basic tools—phone trees, for instance—to prevent tensions from escalating into violence. These cities, unlike their counterparts that had diversity but lacked networks of engagement, had succeeded in building civil pluralism.

At the same time that King was rising to national attention in the 1960s, historian of religion Wilfred Cantwell Smith wrote that "(the problem of our age) is for us all to learn to live together with our seriously different traditions not only in peace but in some sort of mutual trust and mutual loyalty."[4] He was talking about civil pluralism, in which we go beyond recognition and tolerance of diversity to make commitments to one another. Pluralism is neither mere coexistence nor forced consensus but the conviction that people believing in different creeds and belonging to different communities need to learn to live together in this "mutual trust and mutual loyalty." Civil pluralism is a form of proactive cooperation that affirms the identity of the constituent communities while emphasizing that the well-being of each and all depends on the health of the whole. It is the belief that the common good is best served when each community has a chance to make its unique contribution. It is, in the words of Rev. King, a "call for a worldwide fellowship that lifts neighborly concern beyond one's tribe, race, class, and nation."[5]

The Role of Young People

In the decades since his prophetic call, many religious and interfaith institutions have taken up King's mantle through tireless work to bring religious communities together around common causes. The Council for a Parliament of the World's Religions has been on the ground since 1993 and the United Religions Initiative catalyzed "circles of cooperation" around the world. Yet while young people are most often the ones at the front lines of religious conflict, only a few scattered and localized interfaith efforts have brought youth into the mix. Those organizations that have neglected young people have abandoned a key aspect of the legacy of the religious pluralists who came before them.

Rev. King was only twenty-six years old when he led the Montgomery bus boycott. Gandhi was even younger when he began organizing for South Asian civil rights in early-twentieth-century South Africa. His Holiness the Dalai Lama was younger still, just eighteen, when he was forced to lead his government into exile in India and began his campaign for a free Tibet. Indeed, young people have formed not just the leadership but also the body of the greatest social movements for human freedom and equality in the twentieth century, from King's encouragement of youth participation in the marches of the civil rights movement to the anti-Apartheid campaign in South Africa.

It was in recognition of this oversight that a group of religiously diverse young people founded the Interfaith Youth Core (IFYC) in 1998. From its outset, IFYC was dedicated to the mission of bringing religiously diverse young people together in cooperation characterized by "mutual trust and mutual loyalty." In the decade since, IFYC has established itself through empowering young people to build civil pluralism in their hometowns, college and university campuses, and faith institutions. The success of the organization rests largely on its implementation of a methodology that adequately translates the idealistic poetry of pluralism into the pragmatics of building local, grassroots programs.

Interfaith Service-Learning:
A Methodology for Building Civil Pluralism

The idea of religious pluralism and the unique role that young people have to play in furthering its cause—and the practical challenge of infusing this ideal into the everyday lives of ordinary young people—form the overarching goal of the work of the Interfaith Youth Core. Over time, multiple iterations, revisions, and rearticulations, the staff of the Interfaith Youth Core has developed a three-part bellwether for religious pluralism and an effective methodology for building it with young people.

A Practical Framework of Pluralism

Harvard scholar Diana Eck has written about the importance of making public commitments to one another; Ashutosh Varshney's observations of the power of "networks of engagement" to mitigate interreligious and intercultural strife highlight the need for us to develop formal social relationships. In his articulation of the need for "mutual trust and loyalty," Wilfred Cantwell Smith articulated the deep emotional bond that can develop between people of different communities. In the "Beyond Vietnam" speech delivered at Riverside Church in New York City in April 1964, Martin Luther King's call to "lift neighborly concern beyond one's tribe, race, class, and nation" reminds us that our social and emotional bonds should result in a commitment to a good that is greater than ourselves. Political philosopher Michael Walzer nicely draws these ideas together in his book *What It Means to Be an American* (Marsilio) in which he argues that the challenge of a diverse society is to embrace its differences while maintaining a common life together. The balance between a true embrace of difference and the sustained maintenance of a common life is difficult to attain and even harder to maintain.

A central part of the challenge of understanding pluralism practically is that it can only be understood in its gestalt; rarely is it described as the combination or interaction of different factors. In order to build programs that effect pluralism, the IFYC program staff felt it was important to break pluralism down into its composite factors so that an attempt could be made at teaching others how to construct it and also so that we could evaluate whether a program was successful at creating it. We isolated three factors or indicators, which are described below.

The thorny aspect of this endeavor is that those three indicators are not fully distinct nor are they intended to be linearly related. The sum remains greater than its parts and it is still the case that the most passionate parts of pluralism occur between the lines. While it may remain difficult to assess fully any indicator independent of the others, all three should be true of a pluralist society or of any set of pluralist relationships.

1. Respect for religious identity. Effective builders of religious pluralism are able to cultivate a respect for religious identity that makes room for both the difference and the common life. At the most superficial level, this respect requires that people feel that they do not need to hide or significantly compromise the daily public expressions of their religious identity: for example what they wear, how and what they eat, when they take their holidays. This level of respect indicates, at minimum, tolerance for public diversity. Pluralism, however, requires a deeper level of respect for religious identity, one that embraces difference and sets the stage for a common life together that is characterized by mutual trust and loyalty. All the world's religious and moral traditions have space for both. For example, Christianity holds a unique understanding of humanity's relationship to Jesus Christ (he is Lord and Savior), while also teaching that Christians must live in positive relationship with others who don't see Jesus the same way (numerous examples from the New Testament of Jesus's relationships with "sinners," as well as the commandment to love your neighbor as yourself).

People who are engaged in pluralist relationships hold deep respect for and knowledge of the particularities of their own tradition and similar appreciation and knowledge of the ways that their tradition equips them to live peaceably with others. They also develop similar esteem for the traditions of others, thereby allowing their relationship to create a space where they can find common ground and embrace the reality of their difference. It is important to note that while respect of religious identity in its most aspirational form calls on the devout to make room for respect of other traditions in the "world house" we must all inhabit, this house is purely an earthly one. Pluralism does not and cannot require that people make room for others' claims to truth or Truth in their temples of theology. The challenge lies in respecting others' commitments on earth without necessarily endorsing or condoning their understanding of the heavens and ultimate things.

2. Mutually inspiring relationships. It is clear from daily headlines that maintaining a peaceful common life together is not the easiest of tasks. The glue that binds us together must be strong enough to be resilient in the face of pressure from our communities (who may not agree with what we are doing), our political conflicts (the leaders of which may attempt to exploit our differences), and our internal conflicts (which may scare us into shutting the door on difference). We have to set the bar high and look toward long-term sustainability; this is why we cannot stop our relationship building at tolerance, which does not, by itself, elicit an emotional bond or even necessitate relationship or cooperation. Instead, we have to seek relationships that instinctively draw us closer together. These kinds of relationships make us feel better about who we are, and even make us feel that we can be better together, with our particular identities intact, than we can be on our own.

Our traditions each lay out for us a driving purpose, a higher aspiration for our lives: to bring good things into the world, to treat others well, to maintain our connection to the divine. The shared nature of these aspirations provides a common foundation for relationships that are mutually inspiring. We can get to know each other through the lenses of these shared values and find that through our relationships we are becoming better people, more faithful, more powerful in living out the call of our beliefs. When the rest of the real world comes calling and we find ourselves confronting difficult differences on political and lifestyle issues, we know that while these differences are strong, they do not have to tear us apart. We can acknowledge them and, while continuing to help one another, make the world a better place.

3. Common action for the common good. Notions of the common good, nuanced by our understanding of the religious values we share, can provide a guiding purpose for our relationships. We all feel called upon by our traditions to feed the hungry—a shared vision for the common good. We can inspire one another only so far by *talking* about how important this is to us. Not only can young Buddhists, Christians, Hindus, and so on talk about the inspirational values of their faith, they can actually *be* the best that their traditions call upon them to be. Doing something concrete collectively moves us to a new depth of relationship, of understanding, of mutual commitment, and, ultimately, of resilience. Common action toward the collaboratively defined vision makes our ideals reality and makes us partners in making the world a better place. Common action for the common good empowers young people involved in interfaith relationships to answer their traditions' callings to do the real work of the world, and to do it better by doing it together.

Methodology

Coincidentally, the methodology that the Interfaith Youth Core has developed to build pluralism also has three interlocking parts. No direct or linear connection is intended, nor should be inferred, between these three elements of the methodology and the three indicators of pluralism.

Due to the mutually reinforcing nature of the three components, the Interfaith Youth Core often represents its methodology visually with the image of a triangle (shown in figure 1), where each side of the triangle represents one of the three aspects: shared values, storytelling, and service-learning. The heart of the methodology lies in the middle, where all three components come together to form a gestalt that moves participants toward pluralism. Nonetheless, each component is broken down and explicated below.

Figure 1

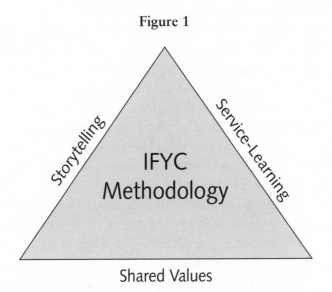

Shared Values

Shared Values

The concept of shared values forms the foundation of the IFYC methodology (and is thus visually represented at the bottom of the triangle). This concept is far from an Interfaith Youth Core innovation, however. The "shared values"/"common ground" approach to overcoming cultural and religious difference has long been established and many successful intercultural and interfaith initiatives have developed robust dialogue curricula and facilitation skills around it. The basic idea behind this approach is relatively simple. As multiple scholars have pointed out, the world's religious and moral traditions all articulate varieties of certain shared, universal values. These are grand values such as compassion, justice, and service, as well as more tangible values such as hospitality, stewardship of the environment, and charity. These "deeply held, widely shared" beliefs, to use Religions for Peace (RFP) terminology, provide a platform upon which people who may also hold many other widely disparate opinions can come together in agreement.

It is important to note that the concept of shared values is not a step toward relativism. Judaism is not Christianity and Hinduism is not Buddhism. It is a heresy to the world's traditions to suggest that they are all the same or to work for the establishment of some new, syncretistic religion that is devoid of all particularity and thus meaning. It is, however, equally blasphemous to suggest that our traditions are so disparate that they have nothing in common. What is precisely so interesting about the phenomenon of shared values is that they require the unique language of each of our religious and moral traditions to infuse them with true meaning and significance; in their general universal form, shared values like compassion appear almost vacuous and devoid of real consequence. It means something for someone to say she believes in compassion as an ideal, but it expresses a great deal more for her to say that she strives to live up to the example of Jesus and the compassion he showed everyone he met.

On a practical level, this is the challenge of facilitators of this methodology. They must be adept at pushing each participant to articulate how his/her community identifies, articulates, and embodies a given shared value. Some participants may respond in a vague or flippant manner, facilitators may also face an a priori rejection of a shared values–based encounter. As straightforward as it may seem, not only are many religious people not accustomed to this form of encounter but some are preprogrammed against it. For example, consider Jewish youth and Muslim youth, both of whom appear to be born knowing how to argue about Israel/Palestine. They are intentionally and unintentionally inculcated with enough claims and counterclaims that they can continue to argue throughout their entire lives. The indoctrination can be so intensive that it causes something akin to a mental rut, such that it becomes very difficult for Muslims and Jews to talk about anything else during encounters where their respective religious identities are the most salient.

One of the major obstacles facing an interfaith organizer walking into this setting is steering the young people into an encounter that does not fall prey to their previously constructed modes of engagement. The slogan of the interfaith organizer should be "There is another conversation we can have." This alternate conversation is one that, rather then focusing on the myriad differences and political struggles between traditions, encourages the participants to identify and examine their multiple shared values.

Storytelling

The most powerful tool a facilitator possesses for overcoming these obstacles is storytelling, which constitutes the second, equally crucial component of the methodology. Duke Univeristy professor and theologian Stanley Hauerwas describes religious communities as "narrative communities," for indeed, much of the enterprise of religious organization involves the telling and retelling of stories: about the creation of the world, about the prophets and their companions, about the origins of religious traditions, and about what is yet to come.[6] (It should be noted that when using the word *story* in this context, we in no way mean to imply that the narrative is fictive or in any way invented. A story might very well be entirely factual, though, of course, it may not.) It only seems natural, then, when working among people of faith, to engage in storytelling as a means of encounter. In every IFYC dialogue curricula, participants are called to relate stories both from their experience and from their tradition that speak to the issue at hand; the more specific and concrete the story is—that is, with a temporal beginning, middle, and end—the more fruitful it is for the encounter.

Especially when working with young people, stories are a matchless tool for interfaith sharing, and thus understanding. Storytelling provides a bridge for overcoming some of the previously articulated obstacles by opening the possibility for a different kind of conversation. Theology can be divisive, even when participants are honestly seeking to articulate shared values. If a Hindu speaks of justice stemming from the source of many gods, it can put an Abrahamic monotheist on edge, who not only understands justice as emanating from one God but also feels a compulsion to oppose polytheism. But if that same young Hindu tells a story about doing justice with her religious community, she is far less likely to push anyone else's buttons.

Personal storytelling moves the encounter from competing notions of truth to varied human experiences of life, which everyone already knows to be multiple. In other words, because we all already know that a billion people have lived a billion different lives, we are much less threatened when we hear stories that diverge from our own experiences. If a young Sikh speaks of covering his uncut hair with his turban and how that feels for him, it does not immediately force his Christian listeners to evaluate and judge whether the Divine does or does not demand such a practice. Other people's experiences are far less threatening than their opinions on ultimate reality.

The combination of shared values and storytelling thus allows for what the Interfaith Youth Core calls a "dialogue of life." Young people in IFYC programs spend a lot of time talking about what it is like to be a young person of faith growing up in a diverse world. They make connections between challenges they have in common—such as modesty, dating, dietary restrictions, and observance of holidays—and they share the ways they address those challenges without doing damage to the unique traditions of their specific religious community. More importantly, they make connections between the shared values they have in common—fighting racism and bigotry, eradicating poverty, caring for creation—and they share how their traditions have instilled those values in them.

Part of the power of the storytelling methodology is that it empowers young people to be teachers. When a young person is asked to tell a story from his or her own experience, it inherently promotes the value of that person's experience to something worthwhile enough that others can benefit from it. In asking the question, a facilitator is, in essence, saying, "Your life is so rich and so interesting that everyone else around the room will benefit simply by hearing you retell it." This sort of youth empowerment promotes young people to be what the IFYC calls "scholars of their own experience." When young people approach IFYC staff with the excuse that they cannot participate because they have not memorized the Qur'an, or did not pay attention in Sunday school, or never learned Hebrew, the response is simply that it does not matter. Young people in this methodology are not required to be scholars of their traditions; the expertise from which they speak is their own life experiences, of which they are the world's foremost experts. The line repeatedly is "No one in the world knows what it is like to be [the participant's name] better than you. Please tell us a story that will teach us a piece of what that has been like."

This "dialogue of life" approach differs significantly from two other modes of dialogue that are prominent in the interfaith field: dialogues of theology, where a priest, minister, rabbi, imam, and swami discuss the nature of the Divine, and dialogues of politics, where Jews and Muslims discuss Israel/Palestine, or Buddhists and Hindus discuss Sri Lanka. These two modes of dialogue are useful and necessary in the broader field, but the IFYC believes that such conversations are often more productive between people who already possess pluralist relationships with each other. The goal of this methodology is to build those relationships among young people.

Service-Learning

The original and continuing capstone shared value identified by the Interfaith Youth Core is the value of service. Not only is service a universal value expressed across and throughout all of the world's religious and moral traditions—thus providing solid common ground upon which to forge mutual appreciation—it is also something that one can do. More than anything else, young people want to make a difference in the world; they want to leave their footprint on earth. Sometimes that desire is so great that if not given the channels for productive outlet, some young people, in the words of the poet Gwendolyn Brooks, will create "if not a note, a hole; if not a symphony, a desecration." By zeroing in on the common value of service and coupling dialogue with action, the Interfaith Youth Core methodology taps into the preexisting desire on the part of many young people to simply do something in a world gone profoundly astray. Many young people are drawn to IFYC programs not out of a desire for religious reconciliation but because of the excellent opportunities they provide for productive service in their communities.

"Service" is the catchall for what is in fact a multitude of what the Interfaith Youth Core calls "actionable" shared values, including hospitality, stewardship of creation, teaching, and caring for the sick and elderly. The service-learning component of the IFYC methodology helps make the connection of shared values between the world's diverse traditions real on an experiential level. It responds immediately and directly to the cynical teenage crack that "talk is cheap." It also provides another opportunity for young people to share their traditions, not simply through words but by putting their faith into action. It proves that pluralism is possible when a young Jew is doing *tikkun olam* (repairing the world), a young Christian is building the kingdom of God, and a young Buddhist is performing acts of love and kindness, all of them together, through the same activity.

This element of the methodology should follow the best practices of the service-learning field, which pushes institutions to move beyond the outdated model of community service. If community service is one community bringing its assets to meet another's deficits, service-learning is a true partnership between two communities to discover how their mutual gifts can work to overcome mutual challenges. If community service is where young people feed soup to the hungry without asking why they are living on the street, service-learning is feeding the hungry while engaging in an analysis of the socioeconomic forces at work in the community. If community service is a one-time event, service-learning is ongoing.

Case Study: The Chicago Youth Council and Somali Bantu Refugees

The reading party described at the opening of this chapter took place at the culmination of a nine-month intensive interfaith leadership program called the Chicago Youth Council (CYC), which the Interfaith Youth Core has run every year since 2002.[7] What follows is a case study of the 2004–2005 year of this program, selected because of the particular depth and richness it achieved in IFYC's interfaith service-learning methodology.

Composition

The composition of the CYC was based on a theory of mentorship that proposed that the people that high school students most look up to and emulate are college students. Therefore, the CYC was comprised of an equal number of high school and college students, with the intention being that the latter play a mentorship role to the former. This dynamic is further reinforced in religious settings, where the transition out of one's home community into college life presents a serious test of faith for many students. As the high school seniors prepared for this transition, they benefited from the experience of college sophomores and juniors who had come through on the other side with their faith commitments intact.

In the fall of 2004, Mariah Neuroth, then Chicago Action program director for the Interfaith Youth Core, solicited, reviewed, and selected applications from college students at DePaul University in Chicago to become CYC facilitators. The Interfaith Youth Core had a longstanding relationship with the university, which provided space for the dialogue meetings and hosted the midyear day of interfaith youth service on Martin Luther King Jr. Day. The facilitators were selected based on their religious diversity, their prior involvement and experience of leadership in their respective religious communities, and their interest in interfaith work. In addition to the college students, one high school student, Ayala, who had served with the CYC in previous years, also was selected as a facilitator. Following the MLK day of service in January, an equal number of high school students, recruited through IFYC workshops at faith communities around the city, joined the CYC as participants, also representing diverse religious backgrounds and a prior commitment to leadership in their faith communities.

Process

On the alternate weeks that the facilitators were not volunteering at Interfaith Refugee and Immigration Ministries (IRIM), they engaged in interfaith, shared values–based storytelling, following IFYC's three-part methodology. The intention behind these sessions at first was to build relationships among the CYC members and between them and their service partners, the Bantu children. The meetings would commence with check-ins, an opportunity for everyone to go around the room and say how their week had been and what was on their mind.

These check-ins provided an opportunity for everyone to get to know each other and were allowed to be open-ended. Following check-ins, Mariah facilitated the group in structured storytelling. At the outset, the curricula focused on all members sharing stories that illustrated the value of hospitality in their respective religious traditions. When asked to tell a story of a time they or their community had welcomed the stranger, participants shared stories about their families welcoming visitors during Shabbat, iftar, or Christmas with large meals and warm homes. They talked about their favorites foods their mothers cooked and what it smelled like at the dinner table. They also related stories from their traditions: Jewish students spoke of the hospitality Abraham showed the visitors in his tent (who turned out to be angels); Christian students spoke of the hospitality Jesus showed his followers; and Muslim students related the story of the second caliph, Umar, who made daily rounds of Medina to make sure all were well in his community.

Some of the remaining time was devoted to discussing what activities they would plan for the Bantu children on their next visit. Ayala recalls, "After one visit in the middle of January, we noticed that they were still dressing their kids in tank tops, so we planned the next visit to go over winter clothing. Really basic stuff, like, 'This is a scarf. It keeps your neck warm.' They had never seen winter clothing before." As much as possible, they strived to match a pair of CYC members with the same two or three children week after week. At the close of each visit to IRIM, the Bantu children would put on a musical performance for the CYC featuring drumming and dancing.

Through the process of shared values–based storytelling and service-learning, the CYC members came to see each other as living out many of the same values and ideals in their nonetheless disparate traditions. These connections through storytelling were viscerally reinforced by their visits to the Bantu community, where all the CYC members felt mutually inspired by each other and the children in the work they were doing. Nathan, a Jewish participant in the group, comments, "Now that I'm in college, you realize that there are people who are involved in something and there are people who are really involved in something, who jazz you up just by talking to them. Everyone in CYC was like that second group. I didn't get a lot of that in high school and it felt great to be with people who were where I was. It was great to be at that level and all to be at that level together."

Usman, a Muslim participant, recalls, "I don't think the whole thing could have happened unless we had connected with each other the way we did. It wouldn't have had the same meaning. If there was someone who wasn't there one week, everyone immediately knew, like a group of friends where you always know who to look for and who to go to for what. People felt so comfortable that everyone always talked. It felt weird if someone wasn't there." Jen, a Christian student, says, "From the get-go it went crazy fast in a good direction. We were all tutoring the refugees or playing a game with them and even if the ultimate purpose wasn't clear at every moment, we seemed to be all going in the same direction toward the common good."

After this period of cohesive group building, Mariah transitioned the conversation to really beginning to think about what project the CYC could do for this community that would draw on the Bantus' as well as their own gifts and resources. The CYC members had grown to respect and cherish their relationships with the Bantu community and thus felt strongly that while they wanted their project to meet a core community need, it was crucially important that they do so in a way that was empowering to and affirming of the Bantu community's dignity. They did not want to repeat the typical pattern in community service where an outside group comes in to save the day, and treating the community served as lucky recipients of other people's privileges.

Mariah led the CYC in a process of assessing the Bantu children's challenges and resources, tying the assessment back to the theme by asking the CYC members, "What are the hard parts about welcoming the stranger? Are there times when your needs and their needs don't match up?" In addition to different dietary restrictions for both the Bantus and the CYC members, the language barrier also formed a challenge for the two groups. The CYC's conversation moved to the children's struggles around English proficiency and literacy. The Bantu children were almost completely illiterate, for even their native language was solely an oral language. Consequently, the children were feeling ostracized in their schools.

Alternately, Mariah asked, "What do strangers bring? How do you benefit from being hospitable? As we welcome this new community of refugees into Chicago, what gifts and assets do they bring?" The CYC members discussed the Bantu kids' amazingly rich musical tradition—as witnessed in the musical performance each visit—and the way they had lived for generations in community with one another and their attempt to do the same here. The final, central asset the CYC members identified was the Bantus' rich oral tradition. Though without a written language, the Bantu used storytelling, often accompanied by drumming, to pass on knowledge from one generation to the next.

In keeping with service-learning and positive youth development best practices, Mariah helped the CYC members think about ways of addressing the challenges of the Bantu children that relied on enhancing their strengths, rather than coming to them with the idea that the CYC members had something new that the Bantus were "missing." The CYC members felt strongly that they wanted the Bantu community to see themselves as an asset to the greater Chicago community, so they focused on the concept of using the Bantu's rich oral tradition to help address the challenge they faced around literacy. The group brainstormed several different ways of implementing the idea and hashed them out together.

Finally, the group decided on the idea of writing a children's book for and about the Bantu kids. The CYC felt that the experience of working with the children had opened their eyes to the story of the Bantus, a story that was not getting a lot of attention or press, and they wanted to help tell that story. But rather than just writing the book for them, however, they wanted the children to be centrally involved in it, so that the CYC's skills in literacy would be matched and complemented by the Bantus' skills in oral storytelling.

The CYC members created a detailed questionnaire that took account of language, trust, and cultural barriers. Some of the questions they included were "What happened in your country? What is your favorite memory? What is one thing you would want your children to remember from Somalia? What is it like living here? How did you get here?" As they designed the questionnaire, they realized that the core question was "Why are you here?" Then the CYC members split into pairs and visited with the Bantu children's families at their homes. With the help of local translators, they interviewed the families and explained their idea for the book.

Nathan remembered that he visited Siyad's house. Just three years old, Siyad was the youngest of the Bantu children. At his house, his older brother, who was seventeen, told Nathan about how, when he went to school in Somalia, he was not allowed inside the classroom because he was Bantu. He had to stand outside a window and listen as best he could. "I remember him saying that every day was a struggle," Nathan said, "Teachers would hit him and people would make fun of him. Nonetheless, he went to school every day until he left. His parents left Somalia before him and he had to cross the border in the middle of the night by himself and with his one-year-old brother, Siyad. When he finished, Mariah and I were just sitting on the couch and didn't know what to say."

Following the interviews, the CYC reconvened to retell and write down the stories they had collected from the families. Mariah then led a discussion on the importance of including the CYC members' stories in the book as well. Jen recalls, "The idea was that we didn't just want to collect the Bantu kids' stories; part of welcoming the stranger was weaving them into our culture and our city. We wanted this to be about how the Bantus were a part of our communities too and we thought we could welcome them by interweaving our own stories of identity into the book." Ayala remembers discussing the parallels between how the Bantu families got to America and how the CYC got to each other. "We also felt that the values in children's books are values we want instilled in society. Children's books offer distilled versions of our highest societal values, so we wanted this book to talk about the value of what we were doing together, across our differences."

In order to get the CYC members' stories of what brought them to each other, they spent the session asking each other, "Why are you here?" This proved to be one of the most intense sessions of the whole year. The CYC members discussed their inspiration to do service work, their faith inspiration, their heroes, their local faith communities, and families. As Mariah pushed them to talk about why they chose to do this work in an interfaith setting, some members began to have a difficult time articulating how they felt. "I remember feeling frustrated," Nathan says. "We were each there because of our own personal journey and that is often traumatic; it often involves problems you've had with others along the way. Especially when it gets hard, you start to ask yourself, 'Why am I here? Why am I giving up every Monday afternoon of my spring semester of my senior year? What does this really mean in the larger scheme of things?' Then when you can't answer it clearly for yourself, it gets really frustrating."

Usman grew especially frustrated and said that he was not sure why he was there and that sometimes he did not think there was a point to this work. Ayala recalls that the room was filled with more tension than there had ever been before. Jen says she remembers being under an incredible amount of stress and that it was a "very emotionally charged environment" as they ventured into territory that they had not fully engaged before. Listening to everyone's story of how hard it was for each of them to be there, Ayala broke down and began to cry. "Somehow it was the link to the outside world," she says in retrospect. "Sometimes it feels as though there is only space for similarities. As people talked about what had brought them to the group from before, it was like we met the outside world with a thud." Jen walked across the room and gave her a hug. Then she made a comment that no one there ever forgot. "We're all supposed to hate each other," she said, "but here we are, working together. There's something really divine and beautiful about that." After watching Jen comfort Ayala, Usman turned to Ayala and said, "I guess I am here because of you. I am here because I am inspired by you, by your faith, by your commitment. That's it. That is why I am here." In looking back at that moment a few years later, Jen comments:

> I grew up in a really small town before moving to Chicago. I hadn't really interacted with anyone of any different faiths. The most different you got was if you were Catholic or if you were Protestant and it wasn't that big of a deal. So I was thinking about what I'd heard about other faiths and, even to some extent, what my faith tradition had been teaching me about "Jesus is the only way or else you're going to hell" and all these other really powerful things that had been ingrained in me. It was a moment of reflection, looking at all these people that I had come to know and love and accepted on this level of being a family almost. I was thinking to myself that there are so many forces out there in the world that would have us hate each other and would want us to be torn apart in some way because we are different. But the fact that we were able to join together in one accord, there's something really special about that and really divine about that. I was just thinking how God must be smiling on all of us right now and there's something so beautiful about this experience and so much of him is in it. Maybe it's my own personal faith thing, but I think there is something so beautiful

about cooperation and functioning in your faith for the betterment of mankind in a way. I know that sounds really grandiose, but I feel like in our own small way what we were doing was making a really large impact that will impact generations to come.

"I don't think that conversation could have happened if we hadn't been working together for so long," Ayala says in hindsight. "It couldn't have been session three, it had to be session thirteen, or whatever it actually was."

While the CYC members shared their most intense dialogue to date, Mariah and the other IFYC staff furiously scribbled down notes of the stories they had related. Together with the stories of the Bantu children they had collected, they edited a first draft of the narrative of the book and brought it back to the CYC at their following meeting. The members wanted each of the faith communities present at CYC to be clearly reflected in the book, so they split into groups with their coreligionists and worked on their traditions' subsection of the story.

Once the narrative of the book came together, the CYC discussed how they wanted the book to really feel like a children's book. They realized that the best way to make a child comfortable was to make the book look like it was something that a child had created. They decided on some of the kinds of images they wanted and then organized a painting day with the Bantu children, in the course of which they drew and painted all the illustrations for the book. A local graphic designer scanned the paintings and laid out a proof of the book. Once again, Mariah brought these images back to the CYC for discussion, prompting another pivotal moment in the evolution of the CYC's relationships with each other.

The CYC members did not immediately agree on which pieces of artwork they should use. Even though it was a relatively trivial issue, it started to put everyone on edge as they allowed themselves to really disagree for the first time. Ayala remembers, "There was something about that space that stopped us from disagreeing. Once we broke that invisible barrier, it was as though it opened the floodgates of emotions. We were disagreeing about the pictures and then suddenly about everything." The disconsonance shocked them. "I think we were unsure whether it jeopardized things or not," Ayala continues. "We felt so tense because we weren't sure we could make it through and it seemed to bring the whole concept of dialogue into question."

"That moment was terrifying," recalls Jen. "Our whole program was built on the idea of commonality. If that is at risk, then what do we have?" Just as suddenly as the tension mounted, it diffused as everyone realized that no matter what pictures they selected, the book would be excellent. More importantly, they realized that their relationships were resilient enough to withstand disagreement. Jen remembers, "I didn't know that there was room to disagree with anyone until that moment. After all the crying, we did still have relationships. Even when we disagree we still have relationships." Nathan says of the incident, "We finally got to a point where we knew it would be OK to get a little upset and get a little angry. We had figured out a way to still be friends and have very different viewpoints, not just about the pictures, but about more fundamental issues too."

After weathering and bouncing back from these intense moments of relationship testing, the CYC had built the resiliency they needed to finish the book on time. The CYC had discovered that literacy was not just something that the Bantu children struggled with, but their parents did as well. The hope became that when they learned to read, the first story they would read would be about themselves, about how they integrated with the people in this country, who wanted to welcome them. When the book was finally completed, they printed one hundred copies, one for each Bantu child, plus fifty extra for IRIM. The CYC planned the big reading party described at the chapter's opening.

Mariah sat on the floor and called up the Bantu children one at a time to receive their own copy of the book with their name inscribed in it. Once everyone had a copy, the children sat with their CYC partners to read it aloud or to have it read to them. Ayala recalls, "It was clear it made them feel so important that there was a book about them. I think it was really empowering for them. There was their story published; there was their artwork published." All the children laughed, giggled, and squealed as they heard their own stories read back to them from a real book.

Conclusion: Shoring Up the Sides of Pluralism

While this chapter has offered three measures by which to evaluate the effectiveness of interfaith youth programming—the development of respect for religious identity, mutually inspiring relationships, and common action for the common good—ultimately one of the best indicators of success is the longitudinal tracking of participants. IFYC staff interviewed several members of the 2004–2005 Chicago Youth Council about their experience on the Youth Council that year. It is noteworthy that these members, two years later, are still actively involved in the Interfaith Youth Movement through local and national efforts to build religious pluralism.

Ayala spent the year immediately following her graduation from high school and the CYC on a Jewish youth program in Israel. "In terms of IFYC strengthening my religious identity," she says, "there was a clear link between my interfaith work and my choice to take a year off to further study Judaism in Israel. Israel gave me another context in which to discover ways of being a pluralist Jew in relation to others." Upon returning to the United States and starting college at a prestigious New England liberal arts school, she immediately joined her campus Interfaith Justice League and pushed the group toward more action-based programming. Through the connections she made there, she has begun to work on developing an interfaith service-learning alternative spring break program. The program will bring college students from diverse faith backgrounds and campuses to spend their spring break volunteering in Central America and engaging in regular IFYC-style interfaith dialogues.

Nathan assumed a leadership position in administering his university's multiyear grant to increase interfaith awareness on campus. He too pushed his peers toward adopting a service-learning methodology based on his experience at CYC. Nathan coordinated an IFYC training on his campus as part of a weeklong interfaith awareness program. Their program culminated in a daylong interfaith service-learning project as part of IFYC's Days of Interfaith Youth Service global campaign. Reflecting on the service project, which involved making no-stitch baby blankets for a local women's shelter, Nathan comments, "We were all there from different religious communities getting to know each other while tying these knots of felt and I remember thinking that it was such an apt metaphor for what was happening interpersonally and intercommunally." Both Nathan and Ayala have spent a summer interning at the Interfaith Youth Core.

Usman continued on the CYC as a college student for two years and participated in the IFYC's international interfaith exchange with an interfaith youth council in Amman, Jordan. Jen, a classmate of Nathan's at the same university, has designed and implemented several service-learning programs for her peers to get involved in their city's communities. "The reason I started the high school outreach programs was because of what I had done at CYC. I knew how powerful it would be and I knew what it was like and I wanted to give that to other people," Jen says. "I wanted to give back because of my experience on CYC."

This is exactly the type of social entrepreneurship IFYC aims to nurture in emerging young leaders and eager institutions that are committed to the pluralist side of the faith line. With 6 billion people in the world, over half of whom are under age thirty, there is simply no way a single organization can effectively reach a critical mass working with twenty youth at a time. We need a movement led by powerful agents of change who build religious pluralism wherever they go and train others to become its architects as well. It is our hope that some such architects are reading this chapter. For those who are interested in making a commitment to this dream and believe that the methods we have described are a reasonably effective way to get there, we invite you to step fully into leadership. Tell us what you want to make happen and how we can help you get there. Come to our annual Interfaith Youth Work Conference and get with others who care as much as you do. Catalyze something where you are through your own creativity. Join the thousands of others in eight countries who are creating and practicing religious pluralism through the Days of Interfaith Youth Service campaign. With your help, we can build more cathedrals of pluralism than totalitarian bombs can ever take down.

5

Action through Advocacy— Many Faiths, Common Purpose

by Rev. Dr. C. Welton Gaddy

True peace is not merely the absence of tension: it is the presence of justice.

—MARTIN LUTHER KING JR.

"**W**e need help!" The voice on the phone was resonant with alarm and urgency. "A group in our city is trying to trample on the religious freedom of everybody. They have announced plans to construct a huge monument of the Ten Commandments on the lawn of the county courthouse, promising that this giant stone tablet will help improve the morality of the entire area. Can you help us?"

A similar call came on a different occasion. "The religious right is disrupting a special election in our congressional district and confusing voters about the proper role of religion and politics in government. Will you help us counter their strident words, manipulation of religion, and unfair tactics?"

Such calls are common in the organizations in which I work—the Interfaith Alliance and the Interfaith Alliance Foundation. As much as possible, we seek to respond positively to such inquiries regarding help. However, we always accompany our responses with a contingency, a condition that must be met by groups with whom we work. Toward that end, we ask, "Are you willing to bring together an interreligious group to address this issue?" Interreligious cooperation has become a virtual necessity for any religious group that embraces an agenda for advocacy, whatever the issue. There are two reasons why religiously oriented groups seeking social change must engage in inter-religious organizing. One has to do with credibility and the other has to do with effectiveness.

First, in the United States, the most religiously pluralistic nation in the world, influential advocacy requires words and actions from members of diverse religious communities. The absence of diversity in a religious group devoted to advocacy raises red flags about the group's legitimacy. No longer is it sufficient to plan advocacy pro-grams in a community (or nationally) that do not involve words and actions from a breadth of persons sufficient to reflect the religious and cultural diversity that characterize the community. In a multireligious setting, the best strategies for challenging an issue, supporting an ini-tiative, and facilitating change involve participants from multiple reli-gions working with secular, civil, and social organizations. Without a diverse constituency, a movement claiming motivation from or interest in religion faces a lack of credibility.

Second, only when all religions have a place at the table in a move-ment will all voices be heard and all efforts at advocacy enlightened and empowered. Not surprisingly, the most credible way to organize for advocacy is also the most effective way to do advocacy. There are always major differences that can divide the group. However, differ-ences between various religious traditions fade as individuals from those respective traditions devote their attention to the kind of coopera-tion needed to accomplish a particular goal that will improve the com-munity. When that happens, what's distinct about each tradition contributes to rather than complicates the group's shared work. Through meaningful interreligious dialogue, members of the group become better informed and increasingly well-equipped for facilitating social change. Interreligious relationships that are formed and fed by broad-based cooperation can be as meaningful and lasting as those formed specifically for the purposes of interfaith study and dialogue.

Whether described by the old cliché "killing two birds with one stone" or framed as a tactic by which two important goals can be real-ized simultaneously, the truth is that both interreligious relationships within groups and effective advocacy can be strengthened and sus-tained by the advocacy work of interreligious groups. Interreligious understanding and community action reciprocally strengthen each other. Shared actions for the purpose of advocacy informed by shared values for the purpose of mutual understanding and relational bonding will nurture interreligious appreciation and cooperation within a community and may lead to the solution of inequities, injustices, and other social and political problems. Think about it: an activity that serves well the strengthening of good interreligious fellowships in a particular area also contributes to the enhancement of the greater good in the social, cultural, and governmental life of that area and beyond. What is not to like about that?

A word of warning is in order, however. While interreligious advocacy offers all sorts of positive possibilities, those benefits will never be claimed accidentally or realized fully without making a significant, often frustrating effort. Basic organizing skills are a prerequisite to success. Other prerequisites include strong leadership and a group's willingness to exercise courage and take risks in relation to both words and actions involving a wide variety of persons. Hard work usually pays off in these efforts and pressing problems get solved, but there is no guarantee. Even if a group's work on the particular issue or concern that brought it together proves unsuccessful, vital interreligious camaraderie likely has developed among participants. And that in itself counts as a major success.

Getting Started

Not uncommonly, interreligious activist groups take form in the face of a crisis that demands advocacy-oriented actions. An effort to prevent the construction of a ten-foot-high stone with the Ten Commandments chiseled into it brought interreligious activists together in Green Bay, Wisconsin. A diverse group of religious people came together in Santa Barbara, California, to counter unfair election practices. Incidentally, both of these groups successfully eradicated the injustices they were organized to defeat. Other recent issues that have prompted the formation of interreligious advocacy groups include an outbreak of hate crimes in a community in Iowa, a sudden economic downturn that affected a particular neighborhood and ethnic group in Louisiana, the discovery of several episodes of police brutality in Fresno, California, urban sprawl in Rochester, New York, and an investigative reporter's series of newspaper and television presentations on injustices in a small town in upstate New York.

Not every such group has to be reactive in nature. Some groups form out of a shared dedication to a proactive agenda of activities. As soon as the water level was lowered and communications were reestablished after the Gulf Coast was pummeled by Hurricane Katrina, interreligious groups that had formed to address post-hurricane needs went into action raising money, offering assistance to the newly homeless, and appearing before national congressional committees in Washington, D.C., requesting support. Had it not been for the compassionate work of already-in-place religious organizations, many of which were interreligious in nature, the snail-paced cleanup and recovery in that devastated region would have been even slower.

Numerous interreligious advocacy groups take form when a critical mass of people learn that they share a common concern and come together to reach out to a state or national organization for partnership and assistance. Such has been the case with the organizations in which I work, as well as with agencies such as the Industrial Areas Foundation and Religions for Peace-USA. Not uncommonly, originators of the group gather because of their associations with each other through less advocacy-oriented agencies.

In recent years, interreligious advocacy groups have multiplied as a result of Internet organizing. Several permanent multireligious advocacy groups have developed from occasional Meetup groups* that have formed as a result of an individual, an agency, or a loose-knit group of activists in a community posting an announcement on a popular website. Often the web announcement has been duplicated in a local newspaper or as a public service announcement on a radio station. Attracted to a posting such as "Anyone interested in talking about how to improve the public school system in our community is invited to meet for coffee on Thursday, September 12 at 7 p.m. in the house of John Doe who lives at 1212 Activist Avenue," people gather in a Meetup group, feed off of each other's enthusiasm for an advocacy campaign, form an entity, and turn discussion into action. Invariably organizers are surprised at how many people are excited to learn that others in their community share their concern about a matter and are willing to put together an action plan to work on it.

---

*See www.meetup.com to understand this phenomenon.

The manner in which a group comes together substantially impacts the manner in which the group develops and how long it stays together. All too frequently groups formed to address a local crisis dissolve once the crisis has been resolved. Exceptions are local groups that affiliate with state or national agencies that provide them with encouragement, resources, and counsel sufficient to keep their interest in a particular issue alive, continue to energize their activities and, thus, sustain the groups' existence. Ideally, people from diverse religious traditions who came together to address a specific local crisis related to environmental issues, handgun control, censorship in public libraries, public money dedicated to private schools, attempts to replace scientific education with indoctrination, or religious discrimination develop relationships with larger organizations related to these respective issues and nurture interpersonal relationships that cause them to continue meeting and learning together so as to be ready for the next crisis.

Generally speaking, however, interreligious advocacy groups formed for the joint purposes of interreligious dialogue and community, state, or national advocacy tend to enjoy a much longer life than those that take shape around a particular crisis. One interest feeds and encourages the other. An interest in advocacy recognizes the need for mutual understanding and respect among those involved, thus supporting interreligious discussions. Conversely, conversations focused on tenets of faith, values, and beliefs almost invariably prod a shared concern that brings about cooperative advocacy spawned by mutually held convictions. Once the members have gone through trials together and shared either victory or defeat, bonds have been established that endure even if the group chooses to cease meeting.

Clarifying the Focus

It is crucial to clarify hopes and intentions, preferably at the very first meeting. Ideally, the temporary (or permanent) leader of the group welcomes all present and explains that this is a different kind of group—a group that focuses on interreligious dialogue through actions of advocacy. The leader should give every person present an opportunity to introduce herself or himself and state briefly her or his interest in being a part of this group. Should the number of people in attendance be too large for such introductions, personal information on each participant can be secured on paper, copied, and distributed to the group later. These introductions present an opportunity for stressing the importance of religious diversity. If religious segments of the community are not represented, specific persons in attendance should pledge to take responsibility for making contacts with certain religious groups so as to broaden the religious diversity among members of the group.

If the group did not gather because of a specific issue, participants should agree on a process to choose an issue on which to focus their advocacy. This process provides an opportunity to begin the kind of interreligious conversations that will be helpful to all involved, even when the group is not specifically organized as an interfaith group. As participants share ideas about various needs in the community, state, or nation, they will reveal some of their religious convictions, values, and vision. Even participants who care little about discussing religious values will be drawn into this conversation because of its importance in moving the group toward focused activism.

If one particular issue does not rise to the top, hearings on a variety of issues may need to be held in order for the group to make a wise decision regarding the object of its interest and expenditure of energy. This process, too, can yield valuable insights into participants' openness to public demonstrations or acts of civil disobedience, their understandings of various religious traditions' views about the proper relationship between houses of worship and government agencies, and how social change best happens.

A clear understanding of the bifocal purpose of the group—interreligious dialogue through actions for advocacy—is indispensable in the formation and development of the group. Persons who favor a different type of organization can feel free to move away from the interreligious group just as persons committed to this distinctive kind of activism can solidify their relationships and resolve to work together.

Keep Out!

There are subjects that can and should be discussed in other venues, but should be strictly avoided during the initial stages of the formation of an interreligious advocacy group. Specifically, these are topics that needlessly splinter the group and blunt interest in cooperation for advocacy rather than nurture cohesion within the group and inspire meaningful action.

For many reasons, interreligious advocacy groups should stay away from partisan politics. First, ideologically—to protect the integrity of religion—no religious group should wed itself to one political party alone. Even to infer that a singular political party represents the best interests of the Buddhist Church of America, Orthodox Judaism, or the Council on American-Islamic Relations, is to taint the religious tradition involved and to stereotype unjustly all adherents to that tradition. Second, pragmatically—to benefit from the power of diversity—mutual concern about an issue does not guarantee agreement on how best to deal with it politically. If group conversations become preoccupied with advancing partisan politics, the issue chosen for advocacy will fade in importance rather rapidly as members of the group argue the pros and cons of political partisanship.

Having a common interest in one issue does not assure likemindedness among the members of an interreligious group when it comes to other issues. When a group has formed for the distinctive dual purposes of doing advocacy and exchanging insights into different religions' identity, the group has an obligation to reach a consensus on the issue to be addressed and to set aside issues that will prove disruptive. No need exists for an interreligious advocacy group to fragment over divisive issues when there are so many important issues on which its members can agree. A group's decision not to deal with a particular issue is not an indication of the group's inability to see the importance of that issue or the group's lack of courage; it is only an indication that the issue under consideration is not right for that particular group.

Threats to Religion

The two religious liberty clauses in the First Amendment to the Constitution—"Congress shall make no law respecting an establishment of religion, or prohibiting the free exercise thereof"—are among the best friends that religion has in this country. As long as these clauses govern the relationship between the state and religion, no person has to worry about the government endorsing one religion over others as the official religion of the nation or requiring that religion be present in people's lives. Here reside two inalienable freedoms—freedom *for* religion and freedom *from* religion. Individuals in this nation are free to practice their respective religions up to the point that they do not impinge upon, restrict, or destroy another person's freedom. Enforcement of these constitutional guarantees protects the integrity of religion generally, promotes freedom for all religions, protects the rights of those who do not embrace any specific religion, and assures the continuing vitality of democracy as a secular form of government.

As I look back on the vision of government cherished by the founders of our nation, I am astounded by the prescience with which they crafted an almost perfect formula to promote America's then unimaginable, now expansive religious diversity and pluralism. The vitality of religion in America, the comity of different religions' relations with one another, and the continuing strength of our secular democracy are all testaments to the wisdom of the First Amendment. Even so, an expanding number of critical issues have emerged that pose significant challenges to the preservation of religious liberty and the corollary separation of church and state, among them the imposition of prayers and scripture readings in public schools, the mandatory use of the words "under God" when reciting the pledge of allegiance to the American flag, and the use of government money to support pervasively sectarian agencies, including houses of worship. Interreligious action groups should steer away from advocacy for any initiative, any piece of legislation or community action that threatens to weaken religious liberty generally or to do harm to any one religion.

Currently, a strong emphasis on majoritarianism has surfaced in many discussions about the role of religion and religious practices in many communities. Proponents of this philosophy argue that since Christianity is the religion that claims the most adherents in this nation, deference should be given to the positions, beliefs, celebrations, and institutions of the Christian tradition. Caution! Even the slightest hint of such thinking can destroy mutual trust, terminate interreligious conversations, and disrupt unified efforts in advocacy in an interreligious group.

On the other hand, an action group characterized by religious diversity is the perfect public body in which people can demonstrate an unwavering commitment to democracy's promise to protect the rights of minorities and to demonstrate each religion's respect for other religions with which it may disagree. Make no mistake about it, such a group should never devote its time and efforts to any cause that elevates one religion over another or even implicitly suggests that such an elevation could ever be acceptable or appropriate. No advocacy that threatens the constitutional guarantee of religious liberty, or impinges upon the equal treatment due every religion, has any place in a group that derives its strength, at least in part, from the religious diversity of its members.

Core Religious Values

Interreligious advocacy groups often make a surprising discovery—theology aside, we are much more alike than we are different. This realization, which is important beyond measure, can offer indispensable guidance to a group's decision making about its priorities for advocacy. The group will tap the greatest amount of energy when it focuses on issues that the core values of virtually every religious tradition deem critical.

For example, I know of no religion that does not affirm the dignity and worth of every person; the importance of compassion; the necessity of justice, of care for the poorest and weakest among us; and reverence and respect for the earth. Think about how many different social and political issues escalate in importance when viewed from the perspective of these shared values! There is simply no reason for an interreligious advocacy group to fixate on an issue that stands outside a broad-based commitment to those values.

Proselytizing

Though it should go without saying, I must point out that the quickest way to break up an otherwise effective interreligious group dedicated to dialogue or advocacy or both is to permit its members to proselytize among themselves. Groups have distinctive purposes. If a member of one religion wishes to convince another member of the group to become an adherent to his or her religion, there is a time and a place for such a discussion, if both members are interested in having it, but not in the group and not amid the advocacy work the group is doing! A failure to protect the unique purpose of a group—its dedication to interreligious discussion and to cooperation in advocacy—will result in the quick disruption and ultimate disbandment of the group.

Issues for Advocacy

Enough of what not to do. What issues should be embraced and supported by advocacy? Which religious values ought to be advanced by national and state legislation or local government policies?

Much has been written about the role of so-called values in American politics. The mass media exaggerated their influence on the last presidential election; the dominance of a particular set of values among the religious right has further muddled an already confused public's understanding of the actual and the desirable relationship between politics, religion, and values in our government.

First, we need to set the record straight about the role of religion and religious values in the politics of recent elections. The religion that was most influential was not any one of the numerous religions of the world that call our nation home. The religion in question did not seek to make its followers better Muslims, better Buddhists, better Jews, or better Christians; it didn't even care whether the public was more or less religious. The religion that has been most influential in recent national elections is the religion of *real politick*, practiced by political strategists whose motivations are strictly partisan and whose sole goal is to elect particular candidates to public offices. Similarly, the most prominent values in these elections were not drawn from the classic literature of moral philosophy or even from sacred pages of various scriptures but ripped from the polling data of political strategists in search of wedge issues that could help their clients/candidates win an election.

Already, polling data is documenting a serious backlash to such blatant manipulation of religion for political purposes and to values that are more sectarian and partisan than religious and democratic. Even numerous members of the religious right are paying more attention to quality-of-life issues now, such as the necessity of quality public education, affordable gas prices and other forms of energy, access to health care, and a more peaceful strategy for lessening global tensions. Yes, some values ought to be legislated, but not narrow sectarian ones. The religious values that should be legislated are those core religious values that overlay basic democratic values, thus contributing to the general welfare without seeking to establish any particular religion.

The values that are worthy of embodiment in legislation advance the common good; they don't establish the narrowly defined moral conceptions of one particular religious or political group in the nation. Those universal values allow all citizens, not just a few, to experience the blessings of democracy, and they strengthen rather than threaten our national commitment to religious freedom—the free exercise of religion for all people up to the point that one person's free exercise infringes on or denies another person's freedom, and the assurance that there will be no establishment of religion in appearance as well as in law, subtly or explicitly.

The political arena is packed with people who are calling for the government to be more "Christian." But when individuals from religious traditions that are as different as they are numerous speak as if with one voice, when they advocate for laws that strengthen liberty and democracy for everyone, not just for a few, the entire nation is aided beyond measure.

A Strategy for Interreligious Dialogue

A group that has come together to engage in interreligious dialogue and advocacy usually functions best if its earliest discussions revolve around the question of what issues on which to focus its interests and actions and why. Immediately, advocacy and interreligious concerns should all take center stage. Of course, distinctive religious interests will emerge as members of the group explain their respective reasons for becoming a part of the group. In the process of choosing an issue for advocacy, participants will reflect as well as reference specific beliefs and values within their respective religious traditions. That is the point at which interreligious dialogue begins, not for purposes of argumentation and disagreement but for enlightening discussion and mutual understanding.

Most activist groups have little tolerance for abstract discussions; they want to move quickly into actions. But that very eagerness creates teachable moments for learning about different religions. Listening to other people talk about their religious motivations for membership in the group and hearing how, for some, religious values compel their actions, helpfully deepens mutual understanding and forges cooperation. A strong leader can do much to facilitate meaningful interreligious dialogue, help guide discussions in the process of choosing an issue for action, and encourage beneficial strategizing for ways to combine interreligious education with effective social and political action. Sadly, I have seen numerous groups with great potential slowly stagnate and then disintegrate because of lack of such leadership. Any interreligious group interested in action through advocacy will do well to affirm leadership by a person with group skills, patience, vision, a passion for advocacy, and expertise in knowing how to nudge members of a group toward consensus. Such dialogues and the strategic decisions they give birth to go far to provide a learning experience for those involved and aid in the development of a compelling strategy for social change.

Strategies for Advocacy

Good intentions and noble objectives are no substitutes for effective planning and strategizing. The principles of social change and political action are the same for everybody, whether the motivation is religious or secular. Failure to acknowledge this truth virtually assures failure in advocacy.

A group is strengthened considerably by the thoughtful development of a sound strategy. As pointed out above, a strong leader is an invaluable asset in this process. From my personal perspective, honed by various organizational experiences, at a minimum a strategy must incorporate some of the following ingredients:

Do Something in Which You Can Succeed

A fledgling group needs to get its "sea legs," to develop confidence, to see that it can make a difference. Biting off more than it can chew can be a fatal downer. Sometimes the challenges are such that it is impossible to assure even a small victory. But if victory is in reach, by all means go for it.

Plan Actions and Debrief on Actions

Developing a sound strategy for action is every bit as important as engaging in action. Likewise, once undertaken it is also essential to evaluate an action. Planning and evaluating are excellent processes for brainstorming future, more effective actions and for drawing from the wisdom and values of the religious traditions present in the group. Values may emerge at this point with more power than had been anticipated. The entire group will have an opportunity to see the resourcefulness of religion as a positive, just, and healing force in public life.

Choose Carefully Which Tools to Use

Certain tools are staples in advocacy work. Learn to use them wisely and skillfully. Often difficult choices have to be made after considering the group's finances, strategic relationships, and human resources as well as the nature of prevailing public opinion on the issue being advocated.

Among the most important tools in advocacy work are press conferences, direct mail, high-profile endorsements, media appearances, petitions, door-to-door neighborhood visits, letters to the editors of local newspapers, consultations with primary decision makers, e-mail lists, a web presence, and opportunities for online advocacy.

Here is an example of an effective use of tools. After failing to persuade civic officials to host a city prayer breakfast that included all of the city's religious communities, the Interfaith Alliance in Fresno, California, developed a proactive plan to advance their concern. At the time of the civic event, with the assistance of earned media coverage, they called attention to the exclusionary nature of the mayor's prayer breakfast. Then, a few months later, they hosted a well-organized Fourth of July picnic celebrating religious pluralism. Hundreds of people from a variety of religious traditions attended the event, interacted, sang, danced, and demonstrated that Fresno is not a "one-religion city."

A similar experience occurred in Lexington, Kentucky. Following a series of negative, disruptive public meetings led by an outside "evangelist" who was condemnatory of interfaith cooperation, the Interfaith Alliance of the Bluegrass invited members of the community into a series of events as a part of a festival of diverse faiths. The event was educational, enjoyable, and a civic incentive to encourage better understanding between local religious communities.

Celebrate Successes and Ritualize Losses

A conversation with Sen. Mark Hatfield many years ago remains fresh in my memory. In response to my question of what difference religion had made in his life, the senator from Oregon explained, "My faith gives me permission to fail." As the distinguished lawmaker continued his reflection, he pointed out that in the realm of public affairs, some issues are worth losing. Of course, he did not mean that he would intentionally lose on an important vote, but that his religion placed failure in proper perspective.

In the realm of public advocacy and social action, a loss is not always a failure. Moral responsibility has never been defined by a vote count. Do not ever forget how many losses and setbacks occurred in the earliest days of the struggle for civil rights in our nation. More often than not, those meaningful losses were marks of courageous faithfulness among the groups that ultimately helped bring about the passage of civil rights legislation. An interreligious advocacy group should set each of its losses in perspective, learn from it, and consider it a stepping stone on the way to success.

Celebrate victories by all means—but not as personal accomplishments to be bragged about as opponents are put down, but as advances of social justice that help this nation move closer to the fulfillment of its founding vision. Each religious tradition represented in the group should be able to make an important contribution to a celebration.

Best Practices

A brief summary of interreligious organizations that have experienced success in their advocacy work can be inspiring as well as enlightening. The Interfaith Alliance of Middle Tennessee has done exemplary work to build support for hate crimes legislation. The Interfaith Alliance of Hawaii has integrated all the members of the former Council of Churches with a wide variety of other religious congregations from other religious traditions to engage in a variety of advocacy projects throughout the islands. The Interfaith Alliance of Idaho courageously stood by Muslims who are longtime citizens of their community, forcefully advocating for their liberty in the face of governmental pressures to intrude into their mosques and to round them up for questioning related to terrorism.

Three examples of best practices merit more discussion:

1. The Interfaith Alliance in Des Moines, Iowa, has long advocated for substantive voter education aimed at increased voter participation in elections. The group conducts an afternoon-long training session prior to the Iowa caucuses in presidential election years and, using media, direct mail, and cooperation from houses of worship, distributes issue-oriented briefing materials well in advance of every major election. The group has also provided transportation for voters on election day.

2. Shortly after September 11, 2001, when the Muslim and the Sikh Faith communities were targeted by vicious hate talk and even murderous acts, the Interfaith Alliance of Colorado organized an event to demonstrate appreciation and support for members of minority religions in Denver. In a dramatic twilight event that was widely covered by the media, this group brought together enough people to completely encircle a huge mosque in Denver. As people held hands, lit candles, and meditated, they symbolically embraced the Muslim community at a time when it was under harsh attack, and laid a foundation for better interreligious relations.

3. The Interfaith Alliance of Wake County, North Carolina, chose to work on a shelter for homeless people to be located near the center of the city of Raleigh. This particular group had agreed that it did not want to be involved in political activities, but stressed its desire to engage in a form of ministry or social service. Interestingly, however, the group immediately encountered resistance from city officials who did not want a shelter located anywhere near the city center. Eventually the group was forced to engage in political advocacy if it was to have a chance at fulfilling its vision for its ministry. Zoning laws had to be changed. The mayor had to be lobbied and convinced that it was in his best interest to support this endeavor. Local media were approached to publicize this project. This interreligious advocacy group worked steadily for a period of at least two years, engaging in public relations, political activities, strategizing on how to gain more broad-based support, and planning the shelter itself. Advocacy for these dedicated people took on numerous unexpected ramifications. Though they only wanted to minister to

homeless people they found that they had to engage in a level of politics they had hoped to avoid. However, their insights from this effort enabled them to understand even better how difficult it can be to do "good works" and how pervasive politics is in accomplishing social change. I am pleased to report that in addition to a transforming learning experience, this group's work happily ended with the construction of a homeless shelter in the area of the city that they had targeted.

What happened in these communities can happen anywhere. A group does not have to be an Interfaith Alliance or even affiliated with any national organization to do similar work.

A Win-Win Initiative

Seldom do people associate strenuous advocacy with the nurturance of stronger and more cooperative interreligious communities. However, this is the promise of a group that comes together to engage in interreligious dialogue while also pledging to adopt an issue for actions in advocacy that will contribute to justice and/or a better quality of life for everyone.

First, durable relationships are formed across lines of religious differences. These relationships carry within them a refutation of religion-based prejudice and discrimination and an affirmation of cooperation that transcends religious or political tensions. Second, the community itself is made more stable and life in the community is enhanced as members of the community advocate for the realization of the liberty and justice for all that is the birthright of every person in this nation.

PART III

Interfaith Resources

6

Brief Overview
of Faith Traditions

*If you have two religions in your land, the two
will cut each other's throats; but if you have thirty
religions, they will dwell in peace.*

—VOLTAIRE

If we are going to work with our neighbors, we need to know a little bit
about them and their sacred texts. *Our Religions*, created at the time of
the 1993 Parliament of the World's Religions and edited by Arvind
Sharma, offers relevant extracts from the scriptures of major religions as
well as in-depth background, as does my colleague Ian Markham's *A
World Religions Reader*. Look ahead in this section for recommendations of more books and other resources both for the featured traditions
and those beyond. However, to get you started, this chapter offers
thumbnail sketches of the history and beliefs of some of the world's religions. While the sections have been reviewed by leaders from each tradition, they are not meant to take the place of a personal encounter with
each religion's original texts and present-day practitioners.

Bahá'í Faith

Nomenclature: *Bahá'í* derives from an Arabic word meaning "glory."
The religion practiced by Bahá'ís is known as the Bahá'í Faith.

History: The Bahá'í Faith originated with Sayyid 'Ali Muhammad,
who was born in Persia in 1819. He called himself the Báb, which
means "gate" in Arabic. Proclaiming himself a messenger of God, the
Báb attempted to pave the way for a greater Messenger who would

follow him. His claims were not well received, and the Báb and his followers were heavily persecuted before he was executed in 1850. One of the Báb's followers, Mirza Husayn 'Ali Nuri, adopted the name Bahá'u'lláh ("the glory of God") and became the founder of the Bahá'í Faith.

During a life of exile, Bahá'u'lláh expanded on the teachings of the previous world religions, stressing unity of all the world's peoples. When he died in 1892, his son 'Abdu'l-Bahá succeeded him. 'Abdu'l-Bahá was in turn succeeded by his grandson, Shoghi Effendi, who expanded the Bahá'í administrative system. When Shoghi Effendi died, the Universal House of Justice was established. The Universal House of Justice has authoritative decision-making and interpretive powers, but so far has left decisions to individual Bahá'í followers and communities.

Scripture: Bahá'í scriptures are predominantly composed of the writings of Bahá'u'lláh. The most important of his writings is the *Kitáb-i-Aqdas*, "the Most Holy Book," which expounds laws and social regulations for the Bahá'í community. He also wrote the *Kitáb-i-Íqán*, "the Book of Certitude," which discusses theological matters, including the prophecies of the Bible and the Qur'an. His other writings include spiritual and mystical books and numerous letters, called Tablets, written as answers to his followers' questions. The writings of the Báb and 'Abdu'l-Bahá are also regarded as scripture and include philosophical discussions and interpretations of other religious scriptures. Shoghi Effendi also wrote many interpretations of Bahá'u'lláh and 'Abdu'l-Bahá's writings, but while these are considered authoritative, they are not classified as scripture.

Beliefs: Bahá'ís believe the world is a place for human beings to advance their spiritual lives. The best way to achieve advancement is by following the teachings of the founders of the world's religions. They believe that there exists one God, whom different religions call by different names and recognize in different forms. Bahá'ís see their lives as journeys toward God accomplished through fairness, compassion, honesty, wisdom, and love. While human beings can never fully comprehend God's nature, Bahá'ís believe that listening to the wisdom of the world's religious leaders will help them understand God. They refer to the founders of these faiths as Manifestations of God and recognize Abraham, Krishna, Zarathustra, Buddha, Jesus, Muhammad, Bahá'u'lláh, and the Báb as Manifestations. Bahá'ís believe that the messages of these Manifestations are specific to the era in which they are preaching, that they reflect the needs of their specific communities and expand on the teachings of previous manifestations. Bahá'u'lláh is considered the most recent Manifestation.

Bahá'ís believe that after they die, their souls survive and continue on their journeys toward God. They believe that the concepts of heaven and hell that exist in many of the world religions are metaphors to express nearness to or distance from God. For this reason, an individual can be in heaven or hell while alive or after dying.

Practices: The Bahá'í Faith has very few formal rituals or practices, and Bahá'u'lláh left strict instructions not to institute them. Consequently, many Bahá'í practices and traditions assume the local or cultural elements of a specific community.

Since the biggest emphasis in the Bahá'í Faith is unity, Bahá'ís do not have any form of priesthood or clerical hierarchy. No one has the power to make an authoritative interpretation of scripture, and all Bahá'ís are encouraged to read and interpret scripture for themselves. For this reason, education is highly valued within the Bahá'í Faith community, as Bahá'ís must be able to read, write, and think critically in order to interpret scripture. Men and women are treated equally in the Bahá'í Faith, and girls and boys receive equal educational opportunities.

While there are few formal rituals, Bahá'ís are expected to pray at least once a day using one of the three obligatory prayers written by Bahá'u'lláh or 'Abdu'l-Bahá. There is also a mandated funeral prayer as well as other optional prayers designed for weddings, funerals, or times of illness. Since there is no formal clergy, prayer services generally take place in someone's home, where scripture is read and prayers are recited. There are currently seven Houses of Worship worldwide. Eventually the goal is to establish a House of Worship in the center of each Bahá'í community.

There are nine Bahá'í Faith holidays, including the Bahá'í New Year, the Báb's birthday, Bahá'u'lláh's birthday, the anniversary of the day Bahá'u'lláh proclaimed his mission, and the day the Báb was martyred. The Bahá'í Faith calendar has nineteen months of nineteen days each, and one of these months is a month of fasting. Bahá'ís also meet once a month for the Nineteen Day Feast, which has devotional, consultative, and social components.

Symbols: The symbol of the Bahá'í Faith is a nine-pointed star. In Arabic, every letter has a numeric value. The total numeric value of the letters in the word *Bahá'í* is nine.

Common Misunderstandings: There is a widespread misconception that the Bahá'í Faith is a branch of Islam. While the Bahá'í Faith developed out of the Shi'a branch of Islam, it is now an entirely separate religion.

It might seem that since the Bahá'í Faith emphasizes world unity, the religion preaches the elimination of cultural and religious difference and diversity. This is not true, however; Bahá'ís desire the people of the world to come together *despite* their differences, embracing the diversity of their fellow human beings.

Buddhism

Nomenclature: Buddhism comes from the name *Buddha*, "awakened one," given to its founder Siddhartha Gautama.

History: Siddhartha Gautama was born into a royal family over 2,500 years ago in modern-day Nepal. During his ventures from his palace, Siddhartha saw three sights that disturbed him greatly: sickness, old age, and death. Realizing that these three fates awaited all beings, he left his family and took up an ascetic life.

During his asceticism, Gautama traveled to modern-day Bodh Gaya and sat under a great peepul tree called the Bodhi tree, vowing not to move until he attained Enlightenment. After numerous hardships and temptations, he touched his hand to the earth, calling it as his witness to his Enlightenment. From this point onward, Siddhartha Gautama was known as Buddha Shakyamuni, "sage of the Shakyas." He traveled to modern-day Sarnath, India, where he taught his first five followers, and continued teaching until he died in his eighties. Buddhism quickly spread throughout Asia via trade routes, migrations, and pilgrimages.

Scripture: Buddhism has no one scripture, but rather a multiplicity of sutras, or strands, that inform its practitioners. The Buddha's teachings were first compiled into a collection called the Pali Canon, but there are many additional, later texts important to one or more of the three major subgroups of Buddhism. These include scriptures like the Diamond Sutra, the Heart Sutra, the Lotus Sutra, the Pure Land Sutra, and the Tantric Sutras. While the sutras and other Buddhist scriptures are important, the Buddha did not consider written teachings as important as lessons gained through experiential knowledge.

Beliefs: The Buddha's teachings are called the Dharma; their primary focus is on the nature of suffering. The Four Noble Truths outline the Buddhist understanding: all of life is suffering; desire is the origin of suffering; the end of suffering is obtainable; and the Noble Eightfold Path is the path to end suffering. The Noble Eightfold Path is a guide for living correctly via right views, intention, speech, action, livelihood, effort, mindfulness, and concentration. By recognizing the Four Noble Truths and practicing the Noble Eightfold Path, a Buddhist can experience Enlightenment and obtain Nirvana, a state that is separate from the cycles of reincarnation.

Buddhism has no single deity; the Buddha is a teacher and inspirational figure who, although revered, is not universally worshipped. Other revered figures are the many bodhisattvas, beings who have attained Enlightenment but choose to remain on earth to help other people end their suffering. In addition to the Dharma and Buddha, Buddhists also recognize the importance of the Sangha, the community of practitioners.

Though defined differently, Buddhism liberally borrows concepts from Hindu traditions, especially reincarnation. Buddhism, however, rejects some of the characteristics of Hinduism, including the hierarchies of caste, Brahman, and the concept of an eternal soul, or atman.

Practices: A principle practice of Buddhism is meditation, which calms the mind and brings the senses under control. Although many types of meditation exist, some groups choose to focus on a single form. For example, the Nichiren school uses a sacred phrase "*Namu myoho renge kyo*" or the Pure Land Buddhists say, "*Namu amida butsu*," which they believe embodies the Buddha's teachings in one phrase: "I yield to the Buddha of Compassionate Light." Other Buddhist groups will make use of mantras (sacred phrases and chants), mandalas (mappings of the cosmos), and prayer wheels. Essential to

Buddhist practice are good deeds, which yield positive karmic effects. Karma is the notion that every action has an inevitable consequence for good or ill, in this life or another. By practicing good deeds, a Buddhist can obtain a positive rebirth even if he or she does not attain Enlightenment.

Subtraditions: Three major subgroups exist within Buddhism—Theravada, Mahayana, and Vajrayana. Theravada is sometimes called Hinayana ("lesser vehicle"), a derogatory term used by some Mahayanists (which itself means "greater vehicle"). Theravada Buddhism dominates Buddhist practice in parts of Southeast Asia. Practitioners of Theravada Buddhism generally believe that only the monastic community can attain Nirvana, and thus, lay practitioners focus on maintaining good karma.

This tradition contrasts with the Mahayana tradition. Mahayana Buddhism was founded around the first century BCE and teaches that all humans should strive for Enlightenment in order to be bodhisattvas. One of the most important bodhisattvas of this tradition is Avalokiteshvara, the bodhisattva of compassion. For Mahayana Buddhists of the Tibetan School, the Dalai Lama is the living presence of the bodhisattva of compassion. Mahayana Buddhism is the dominant Buddhist practice of many parts of Asia as well as the United States.

The third group is the Vajrayana, or the "diamond vehicle," which includes many esoteric practices designed to obtain Enlightenment in one lifetime. Many sources now place this as a subset of Mahayana. Around 500 CE, new texts called Tantras emerged that outlined new intensive rituals. Mandalas, tutelary deities, mudras (hand gestures), and religious implements like the bell, scepter, dagger, and hand drum are all essential items of Tantric practice.

Symbols: Buddhism's most commonly recognized symbol is the chakra, or wheel. The chakra represents, among other things, the dissemination of the Buddha's teachings.

Common Misunderstandings: Some people mistakenly believe that all Buddhists are nonviolent, vegetarian celibates. Buddhists, however, emphasize different aspects of the Buddha's teaching depending on their location, culture, and personal choice. For instance, vegetarianism is difficult to practice in the harsh climate of Tibet.

In another misconception, many believe that the Laughing Buddha is the primary depiction of the Buddha. This fat, jolly figure is a favorite of children in China and Japan and is actually Maitreya, who personifies the Buddha's compassion, rather than a representation of the historical Buddha.

Christianity

Nomenclature: Christianity is a religion whose adherents believe in one God and accept Jesus Christ as the Messiah, both the Son of God and God himself. *Messiah* and *Christ* translate from Hebrew and Greek respectively to "the anointed one," and refer to Jesus's role as the savior of his people. Some Christians identify more specifically with their particular subtraditions than with Christianity as a whole, and therefore call themselves by those names.

History: Jesus, a Jew, was born in approximately the year 4 BCE in Roman-controlled Judea. He spent his adult life as a traveling preacher, speaking of the "kingdom of God" and the necessity of repentance in order to enter that kingdom. Seen as a threat by some Jewish religious leaders, Jesus was eventually arrested, convicted on a charge of blasphemy, and sentenced by the Roman government to death by crucifixion. Christians believe that after Jesus was crucified, he was bodily resurrected, a miracle witnessed by his followers.

Some of these followers, Jesus's disciples, began traveling throughout the world to preach his teachings. Among these disciples were twelve of Jesus's original followers, known as the apostles, or the "ones who are sent." Though its followers were initially persecuted, by the fourth century CE Christianity had become the official religion of the Roman Empire.

In 1054, the Great Schism divided Eastern and Western Christianity into what are known today as the Orthodox and Catholic churches. A second division occurred in the sixteenth century, when some Christians demanded moral, theological, ritual, and institutional reform. The ensuing multistreamed split that followed is known as the Protestant Reformation, and members of the resulting forms of Christianity are known as Protestants. There are also many groups of Christians who do not fit neatly under any of these headings.

Scripture: Since Christianity is an outgrowth of Judaism, Christians consider the Hebrew Bible, which they call the Old Testament, sacred scripture. In addition to the Old Testament, Christians also recognize the New Testament, which focuses on the teachings of Jesus and his followers. The New Testament comprises twenty-seven books, including four Gospels (Matthew, Mark, Luke, and John) that relate different experiences of Jesus's birth, life, death, and resurrection. The Old and New Testaments are referred to collectively as the Bible.

Beliefs: Traditionally, Christians insist that God—who is righteous, omnipotent, omnipresent, and omniscient—is Triune. That is, they understand the One and Only God to be Relationship Itself—at one and the same time Father, Son, and Holy Spirit. They believe that Jesus is the Messiah, the Christ (which are Hebrew and Greek titles meaning "God's anointed one"), by which they mean Jesus is God Incarnate, simultaneously fully human and fully divine. They believe that Jesus was born of Mary, a virgin who became pregnant by the power of God's Holy Spirit; that Jesus died willingly on the cross for the forgiveness of the sins of all humanity; that he was raised from the dead, ascended into heaven, and will come again on the Day of Judgment.

Practices: While certain practices differ among Christian traditions, almost all Christians practice some form of a purification ritual, or baptism. Baptism cleanses an individual from sin and marks his or her entry into the Christian community. Another important practice involves the consumption of bread and wine, which, depending on tradition, either represent or are considered literal manifestations of the body and blood of Jesus Christ. This ritual is variously called the Lord's Supper, Holy Communion, or the Eucharist.

Some Christians observe Sunday as the Sabbath, traditionally refraining from work; others emphasize that Sunday is the first day of the week—the Eighth Day of Creation. In either case, participation in community worship is an important practice. These services generally include reading from scripture and singing hymns praising God, and preaching lessons from scripture. Birth, marriage, and funeral services are also traditionally celebrated in churches.

Christians observe a multitude of holidays and corresponding seasons, the two most important being Christmas and Easter. Christmas commemorates Jesus's birth and Easter celebrates his resurrection.

Subtraditions: There are a multitude of Christian subtraditions, most of which fall into three major categories—Orthodox, Catholic, and Protestant. Orthodox Christians are sometimes referred to as Eastern Orthodox. The various Orthodox churches are often affiliated with a specific nationality, such as Greek Orthodox or Russian Orthodox. The Catholic Church is centered at the Vatican in Rome. The pope, who is believed to be the spiritual link between Christ and his people, leads Catholicism. Protestants generally place more emphasis on the Bible and personal prayer than Catholics, who tend to place more emphasis on the role of the clergy.

Symbol: The main symbol of Christianity is a cross, which symbolizes the cross on which Jesus was crucified. This symbol of Jesus's death is a reminder of his ultimate victory over death.

Common Misunderstandings: Some evangelical and fundamentalist Christians often refer to their initiations into Christianity as "born-again" experiences. However, many people identify themselves as Christian without having had these experiences. Another misunderstanding associated with Christianity concerns the Virgin Mary. Many believe that Catholics worship Jesus's mother, Mary, as if she were a deity herself. While Mary is Catholicism's most important saint, she is not worshipped as one would worship God.

Many people also misunderstand the role of the pope in Catholicism, believing him to be infallible. While the pope has the authority to speak as an infallible figure (*ex cathedra*), this privilege is only invoked under very specific circumstances and is exceedingly rare. Many non-Christians have the impression that the pope speaks for (and has authority over) all Christians. He does not.

Confucianism

Nomenclature: Jesuit missionaries in China during the seventeenth century assigned the name Confucianism to a body of ritual practices. The Chinese term for Confucianism is *Ju*, meaning "scholars," which is indicative of the fundamental rationality of Confucius's teachings. In China, Confucianism is generally understood to be both a philosophy (*chia*) and a religion (*chiao*, which literally means "doctrine").

History: Confucius was born in the Chinese state of Lu circa 551 BCE. Early writings in the *Analects* suggest he was of humble status, though it cannot be stated for certain. Since the eighth century, China had been experiencing instability and a steady decline in the social order. Seeing his nation thus reduced, Confucius, along with many philosophers, became preoccupied with restoring the social order by reviving the ancient traditions of the Chou dynasty.

Scripture: The Five Classics are a substantial collection of books that span a range of genres. The *Classic of History* includes reports and writings from early Chou rulers. The *Classic of Odes* contains a multitude of Chou poems that evoke the virtues of the ancients. The *Classic of Changes*, also known as the *I-Ching*, is concerned with divination, ontology, and the nature and principles of change. The *Classic of Ritual* includes three texts, the most popular of which is the *Book of Rites,* describing the model welfare state. The fifth classic is the *Spring and Autumn Annals*, which gives an edifying account of the Lu state from 722–481 BCE. These classics provided the foundation for the Chinese civil service examination, which began in 125 BCE, and served to transform individuals into educated, righteous men.

The Four Books, including the *Analects*, the *Doctrine of the Mean*, the *Great Learning*, and the *Book of Mencius,* contain lessons of moral philosophy. In later years they replaced the Five Classics as the heart of the examination syllabus. Primarily a collection of Confucius's aphorisms, the *Analects* emphasizes the value of ritual and its relevance for maintaining order. Scholars consider it to be the cornerstone of Confucianism. The *Doctrine of Mean* became increasingly more important over time; it describes the individual, family, and social obligations of the gentleman and the sage.

Beliefs: Confucianism is understood today to comprise a system of philosophy, religion, and ethics. One could say that Confucianism, in essence, is humanism, though it was certainly rooted in an acceptance and appreciation of heaven's will. Although heaven is inherent in Confucius's original moral philosophy, it was not its primary focus. Its emphasis was on the human sphere and on achieving harmony in personal conduct and beliefs.

Confucius said that individuals must cultivate an understanding of the Tao, the way things really are. People should then aspire to act in harmony with the Tao by constructing a society that mirrored its nature. In ascribing to the Tao, one ascribed to goodness and earned the title "sage." Confucius taught a disciplined practice of personal moral conduct in the hopes that individual transformation would lead to wider social transformation, curing the social disorders that were plaguing China.

Practices: Hsun-tzu (310–238 BCE), the third founding father of Confucianism after Confucius and then Mencius (372–289 BCE), was responsible for prescribing a life of daily ritual (*li*) as central to the achievement of Confucian ideals. According to Hsun-tzu, one must engage in correct ritual action in order to discipline the mind, transform the heart, and live the life of a sage. Unlike his predecessors, Hsun-tzu did not believe that humans were inherently motivated to be good. He believed humanity was essentially selfish and thus in need of a strict code of conduct. Central to this code of conduct were the ideals of filial piety, humaneness, and loyalty. Though all three fathers of Confucianism supported this type of conduct, Hsun-tzu, possibly due to his innate mistrust of human nature, codified it into an explicit set of rules.

Subtraditions: Confucianism evolved over time. In its later years it absorbed divination practices and cosmological teachings that were not present in Confucius's original teachings. Neo-Confucianism, a more pantheistic approach to understanding the human condition, emerged during the Sung dynasty (960–1279 CE). The new focus on mysticism was precipitated by contact with Buddhism and Taoism during the eleventh century. Some people today consider the Neo-Confucianism of Japan and Korea to be separate schools from the Confucianism of China.

Symbols: The primary symbol for Confucianism today is the bust of Confucius.

Common Misunderstandings: Most Americans do not realize how significant an impact Confucianism's model for ethical living had on all East Asian cultures, not just the Chinese. Confucianism's emphasis on education has also led people to believe that people from traditionally Confucian societies are disproportionately gifted academically.

Hinduism

Nomenclature: Adherents of Hinduism usually refer to their religion by one of two names—Sanatana Dharma, the "universal religion," or Vedic Dharma, the "religion of the Vedas." *Hinduism* is actually a European umbrella term for a number of different traditions that share some beliefs and practices.

History: Although generally considered the world's oldest religion, the exact origins of Hinduism remain unclear. Its beginnings are generally, although not exclusively, associated with the Indus Valley civilization. This civilization, located in the northwestern portion of the Indian subcontinent, flourished from around 2500–1500 BCE. Because of its ancient and undetermined association with this culture, Hinduism has come to denote not only a religion but also an entire civilization.

Scripture: Hindus generally recognize two categories of scripture, the Sruti and Smrti. The Sruti, or "revealed scriptures," are divinely inspired and focus especially on the four Vedas, the Rig, Yajur, Sama, and Atharva. These works were composed in Sanskrit sometime after the decline of the Indus Valley civilization. Remarkable continuity exists between modern Hinduism and the religion described in the Vedas. The Vedas are particularly concerned with achieving a good life in the present world. The Upanishads are writings that continue the Vedic tradition and are concerned with achieving eternal liberation, or Moksha. They were written between 900 and 400 BCE and form the basis for much of Hindu philosophy.

Smrti, or "remembered scriptures," contain Hindu laws and stories passed through antiquity. Its two major components are the *Ramayana* and *Mahabharata*, both epic stories of Hindu mythology. The Bhagavad Gita, one of the most famous Hindu scriptures worldwide, forms a portion of the *Mahabharata*. The Bhagavad Gita, "song of God," was written later than most of the *Mahabharata* and is often viewed by both Hindus and non-Hindus alike as an altogether separate work.

Beliefs: Hinduism recognizes many gods and goddesses, all of whom are considered aspects of Brahman. Brahman, the "one Supreme Being," is manifest in every being as atman, the personal self. Hinduism recognizes various forms of Brahman, particularly in the form of the Trimurti, which consists of Brahma the Creator, Vishnu the Sustainer, and Shiva the Destroyer. Brahman can also become incarnate as a human. Hindus often worship these human forms, known as avatars; particular favorites are Rama and Krishna, heroes of the *Ramayana* and *Mahabharata*, respectively.

An overarching element of the religion is Dharma, the ideology of righteous duty that governs both everyday and eternal life. Karma, the consequence of every action, can be good or bad in accordance with the law of Dharma. Accordingly, each person will be held accountable for his or her individual and collective actions, whether in this life or the next. Generally, Hindus believe that four life goals must be achieved by all practitioners in accordance with Dharma. These goals are worldly success, the pursuit of pleasure, morality, and Moksha, spiritual liberation. Moksha occurs when an individual's soul becomes one with Brahman and is freed from the cycle of reincarnation. Sometimes, an individual achieves Moksha during his or her life on earth and becomes recognized as a guru, a teacher to help others on their path to Moksha.

Hindus recognize many paths to spiritual liberation. These paths are known as yogas. The three general categories of yogas described by the Bhagavad Gita are: jnana, the yoga of knowledge; karma, the yoga of action; and bhakti, the yoga of devotion. Even more ancient is raja, the yoga of mental discipline, which is described in the Yoga Sutras of Patanjali. Hindus may practice one yoga exclusively or all three simultaneously. In keeping with their tradition of diversity and tolerance, Hindus generally believe that all religious paths are valid.

Practices: Hindus invoke the presence of Brahman through many sacred symbols, images, and mantras, or sacred sounds. One of the most important of these mantras is the syllable *om*, the cosmic sound. Puja, the ceremonial offering of praise and hospitality to a deity, is perhaps the most common ritual for Hindus today. Hindus also observe numerous festivals with dancing, music, fasting, feasting, and processions in honor of the deity. Both historically and in modernity, marriage has been one of the most important Hindu occasions for worship and traditional rituals.

Pilgrimage is also an important aspect of Hinduism. Many devout Hindus visit the ancient city of Varanasi, which is located on the banks of the Ganges River. Bathing in the Ganges, or drinking from it before death, is considered a ritual act. Because Hindus believe that all life is an emanation of Brahman, many adhere to the ethic of nonviolence. This is often expressed through vegetarianism.

Subtraditions: Differences in these forms of worship gave rise to numerous Hindu subgroups that represent much of the diversity present in the religion today. Three of the largest subgroups are Shaiva Hinduism, Vaishnava Hinduism, and Shakta Hinduism. Shaivites worship Shiva, his consort Parvati, and their children, Ganesha and Skanda. Vaishnavites instead worship Vishnu or his incarnations as Krishna and Rama. Shaktas worship the Mother goddess Devi, or one of her many forms. Rather than worship specific deities, many Hindus, particularly Vaishnavites and some Shaivites, choose to follow the teachings of particular gurus, especially the guru Shankara who lived from 788–820 CE. Shankara taught that all of the deities are pointers to Brahman.

Symbols: The most common symbol of Hinduism is the syllable *om* (also spelled *aum*). It is a sacred sound comprised of three curves (visually) and sounds (linguistically)—a-u-m.

Common Misunderstandings: Hinduism is sometimes mistakenly associated with cow worshipping. Most Hindus venerate the cow as a symbol of fertility that honors their agricultural past; one way they honor cows is by abstaining from beef. The caste system is also frequently misunderstood. While historically Hindus have recognized a hierarchical and hereditary caste system, and while abuses based on caste still persist, the system is in decline. "Untouchability" as a legal category was abolished in 1948.

Islam

Nomenclature: The Arabic word Islam means "to be in peace" and "to be integral, whole," however, it is widely translated as "submission to God," implying that a person becomes whole when he submits himself to God. Followers of Islam are called Muslims, and Arabic is the sacred language of Islam.

History: Muhammad, the prophet of Islam, was born in Mecca around 570 CE. Muhammad received his first message from God in 610 CE. This message, and the many that were to follow, were relayed through the angel Gabriel. Among these messages was the central teaching that there exists only one God, or Allah in Arabic. Muhammad and his followers were persecuted by the majority of Meccans, whose beliefs Muhammad contradicted. In 622 CE, Muhammad's small group emigrated to Medina in a migration called the Hijrah. The Hijrah signified the beginning of the Islamic era.

Many people in Medina accepted Muhammad and his teachings, and the original ummah, or Muslim community, was formed. Around 630 CE, Muhammad returned to Mecca and seized control of the city. After his victory, Muhammad treated the Meccans well and many embraced Islam. Muhammad became both head of state and spiritual leader, and soon gained converts throughout the Arabian peninsula.

Scripture: There are two major bodies of scripture in Islam. The most important is the Qur'an, a collection of the revelations that Muhammad received from God. The Qur'an is believed to be the word of God, and its contents are handled with great care and reverence. It is divided into 114 chapters, called suras, which contain varying numbers of verses, or ayas. A universal version of the Qur'an was compiled in the late seventh century and remains in use today. The other body of scripture in Islam is the Hadith, a collection of the sayings and actions of the prophet Muhammad as recorded by his companions; these words and deeds are called *sunnah* (example). Muhammad is considered the ultimate role model in Islam; the Hadith are read to inspire the faithful to emulate his *sunnah*, his example.

Beliefs: Islam is a monotheistic religion centered on the idea of Tawhid, the oneness of God. While Muhammad is viewed as the final and greatest prophet, Muslims also recognize all of the prophets of the Jewish and Christian traditions.

Muslims believe in a day of judgment on which everyone will be judged according to their repentance, good deeds, and obedience to God's law.

Practices: For most Muslims, ritual life revolves around the Five Pillars. These pillars consist of:

1. Reciting the Shahada, the declaration (in Arabic) that "There is no God except Allah; Muhammad is his messenger"
2. Praying five times a day while facing Mecca
3. Fasting from dawn until sunset during the month of Ramadan
4. Charitable giving
5. Making the Hajj, the pilgrimage to Mecca

Islam draws a distinction between what God has allowed, called *halal,* and what he has forbidden, known as *haram.* Shari'ah (Islamic law) is the path given by God. It has been interpreted and codified over the centuries by drawing upon the Qur'an and Muhammad's example, and by making use of analogy or turning to the consensus of the Muslim community. Some modern countries, such as Saudi Arabia, claim that their legal code is in accord with Shari'ah. Muslim opinion about the legitimacy of such claims varies widely.

Important holidays include the festival 'Id al-Fitr, which marks the end of Ramadan and is characterized by gift giving and feasts, and 'Id al-Adha, the Feast of Sacrifice, which is the more important of the two. It begins on the tenth day of the month in which Hajj (pilgrimage) is made to Mecca, about two-and-a-half months after Eid al-Fitr, and extends over four days. It is associated with Abraham's willingness to fulfill God's request to sacrifice his son. Muslims may also observe *Laylat al-Qadr,* the "Night of Power," the anniversary of Muhammad's first revelation and the beginning of his prophecy.

Subtraditions: The two largest groups in Islam are the Sunni and Shi'a traditions. The separation between these streams began in the late sixth century over issues of leadership. Sunnis derive from those early Muslims who preferred the selection of a caliph by community consensus; Shi'as preferred to keep leadership within the family of the Prophet. The two streams have developed certain distinctive differences in theology and practice and the sources by which they interpret Islamic law. Approximately 85 percent of Muslims are Sunnis.

Shi'a Muslims believe in the authority of a series of infallible Imams (leaders) who guided the community during the early centuries. All Shi'as agree that 'Ali (the Prophet's son-in-law), Hasan and Husayn (the Prophet's grandsons), and 'Ali ibn al-Husayn (the Prophet's great-grandson) are the first four of these divinely inspired leaders. There are several Shi'a sects, which differ from each other in the number of

Imams that they recognize in total. Some believe that the last Imam in the series never died, but is "in hiding" and will return to help usher in the Day of Judgment. Shi'as give deep devotion to all of Muhammad's family, especially 'Ali, the first infallible Imam. All Muslims also use the term *imam* simply to refer to the leader of their congregation. Sunni Muslims use the term only in this sense.

Symbols: The most common symbol of Islam is a crescent moon with a star. Originally a symbol for the Fertile Crescent, it has come to represent the beginning of Ramadan, which commences at the first sighting of the new crescent moon.

Common Misunderstandings: Islam is sometimes inaccurately called "Mohammedanism." Referring to Islam as such suggests that the religion is centered on Muhammad, while in reality the oneness of God and submission to God are its central beliefs. Many also believe that Islam is innately oppressive to women. This is ironic because at one time Islamic law was considered revolutionary for its progressive treatment of women, guaranteeing them as it did the right to inherit and own property and to initiate divorce. Islam teaches that the best Muslim is the most pious Muslim, regardless of gender.

Jainism

Nomenclature: Jinas, also called Tirthankaras, or conquerors, are religious teachers or ford founders who have attained Enlightenment and can impart perfect wisdom to help others reach spiritual liberation, or Moksha. Jains are the followers of Jinas.

History: With prehistoric roots dating before 3,000 BCE, Jainism is one of the world's oldest religions. The twenty-four Jinas of the present era guided the religion's evolution through their teachings and spiritual guidance. All Jinas began their lives as historical figures who enjoyed both political power and high social status. However, at the peak of their success, each of them renounced their materiality and set out on a path of spiritual Enlightenment. Jainism in its current form is popularized and spread by the teachings of Vardhamana Mahavira, the last of the twenty-four teachers approximately 2,600 years ago.

Followers of the Jinas began migrating throughout India. Some traveled as ascetics, having taken the vow of itinerancy, while the majority, who were lay followers, pursued mercantile opportunities. By the sixth century CE, the Jains had greatly diversified by geography and sect. Jainism also benefited from periods of royal patronage, which allowed it to develop wealth and political influence. By the thirteenth century, as both Islam and the Hindu *bhakti* movement became more dominant in India, Jainism retreated politically and geographically, but remained vibrant in certain areas, e.g., Gujarat and Kerala. Since the nineteenth century, Jainism has been experiencing a revival and is now enjoying increased social and political recognition as a distinct tradition with global reach.

Scripture: The Jain scriptures are the historical records of the lives and teachings of the Jinas. The Jain canon consisted of about sixty books. It was divided into three sections, the first being the *Purva* (meaning "previous" or "ancient"), which contained fourteen texts that are mostly lost but are referred to in later works. The *Purva* dealt with astrology and other methods of attaining esoteric powers. The other two sections of the Jain scriptures are called the *Angas* ("limbs") and the *Angabahya* ("outer limb"). Ancient Jain literature was composed in poetry, prose, and dramatic form, and written in Prakrit, Ardha-Maghdhi, and Sanskrit. In recent centuries, the scriptures have been translated into many Indian regional languages, including Hindi, Gujarati, and Marathi, as well as into English.

Beliefs: Jains believe that individuals are trapped in a cycle of birth and death based on one's own karma. The highest goal of existence is to be free of this cycle and become *siddhas*, free beings without physical bodies that exist eternally in bliss. Jains attain siddha-hood by unburdening themselves of karma. Karma consists of physical particles that stick to and obscure an individual's soul, which is fundamentally pure. Karma particles adhere to the soul when people indulge their passions, such as anger or greed. The way to avoid gathering karma is to remain nonviolent and nonattached; to succumb to neither attachment nor aversion.

Jains believe that every living thing can become a siddha, though not necessarily within its current lifetime. For Jains, all living things are in possession of a soul. This includes humans and animals, but also plants and small insects. Because all souls are equal, alive, and capable of suffering, Jains strive to do the least harm possible, and thus cause the least pain.

The three basic tenets of Jainism are: *ahimsa* (nonharming), *anekantwad* (relativity of viewpoint), and *aparigraha* (nonattachment).

Practices: As explained above, Jains believe that anything in possession of a soul has the ability to attain Moksha. They do not believe, however, that Moksha can be spontaneously attained by anyone at any time. Generally, it is only the ascetics who are considered capable of imminent liberation; thus, the worship of the lay community is generally aimed toward becoming like them, while the ascetics themselves worship the Jinas.

When Jain ascetics are initiated they renounce worldly possessions and pledge to keep five great vows (*mahavratas*): nonviolence, truthfulness, not stealing, celibacy, and nonattachment. They eat only what is given to them and are expected to uphold a spiritual ideal for the lay community. Lay Jains may also take vows, but these are generally less stringent. They may, for example, pledge fidelity instead of celibacy. As in all traditions, commitment to practice varies among individuals; all Jains, however, are expected to be vegetarians, and many also abstain from root vegetables like potatoes, whose cultivation involves the destruction of a habitat for microorganisms.

Subtraditions: Early in their history, Jains divided into two major sects—the Shvetambara (those who wear white color clothes), who predominately live in Western and Northwest India, and the Digambara (those who consider skin as their clothes), who are predominant in South India. The traditions differ mostly in outward appearance and ascetic practice. For instance, Digambara male ascetics do not wear any coverings, considering them to be a form of attachment. Shvetambara ascetics wear white clothing. Although both groups allow women to enter mendicant orders, Digambaras place female ascetics on a lower level than male ascetics. Digambaras also believe that all twenty-four of the original Jinas of the last cosmic cycle were men, while Shvetambaras believe that the nineteenth Jina was a woman. Another distinction between the two groups concerns the interpretation of the Jinas. Digambaras consider the Jinas to be omniscient in a manner that requires constant meditation and the inability to teach by voice or example. Shvetambaras believe that Jinas can be omniscient while still engaged in human activities. Today, Jainism has a handful of sects, most of which grew out of these two primary branches.

Symbols: A contemporary symbol of Jainism is that of a wheel on the palm of the hand. The wheel's twenty-four spokes represent the twenty-four Jinas, while the five fingers signify the five ascetic vows. In the center of the wheel is the word *ahimsa*, which means nonviolence. The open hand signifies the friendly assurances.

Common Misunderstandings: Some expect all Jains to be ascetic, other-worldly, nonviolent vegetarians. However, the degree of observance varies markedly between laypersons, as well as between lay and mendicant Jains. Historically, Jains have been merchants, a profession they believed caused others a minimum of pain. Today, this business focus remains strong, with many Jains entering financial professions, becoming quite successful, and expressing the tenets of their faith by donating liberally to charity.

Judaism

Nomenclature: Judaism is a monotheistic religion practiced by Jews based on teachings and ethics culled from the Hebrew Bible (*Tanakh*) and further explored in the Talmud and later rabbinic writings. The term *Judaism* derives from the name of the biblical kingdom Judea, which was inhabited by their ancestors. Jews have also been known as Hebrews, Israelites, or the Children of Israel, the latter two referring to the patriarch Jacob, who was also called Israel. Consequentially, the terms *Hebrew, Jew*, and *Israelite* are often used interchangeably in a historical context.

History: Although the *Tanakh* begins with the story of the Creation and Adam and Eve, Jews trace their heritage to Abraham, who is believed to be the first monotheist. Judaism teaches that Abraham entered into a covenant with God, which was reaffirmed with Abraham's son Isaac, and grandson Jacob (Israel).

The Children of Israel are first recognized as a nation after the Exodus from their slavery in Egypt and, shortly thereafter, the theo-phany ("appearance" of God) at Mount Sinai at which point the entire Jewish people entered into a covenant with God. The Jews then settled in the land of Israel, a highly volatile region in the Middle East coveted by the Egyptian, Assyrian, Babylonian, Persian, Greek, and Roman empires. In 70 CE, the Jews were exiled from the land. In the diaspora, the focus of the religion turned to a more portable form of worship, centered around holy texts, ritual, and community prayer.

Scripture: Judaism has a number of important texts. The central text is the *Tanakh*, a Hebrew acronym that refers to the Torah (also called the Pentateuch or Five Books of Moses), the books of the Prophets, and the books of Writings. The word *torah* can be used to refer narrowly to the Pentateuch or more broadly to the *Tanakh* in full, or even to the entire corpus of Jewish learning.

Although the *Tanakh* shares books with the Christian Bible, the *Tanakh* has a different arrangement and, depending on the denomination of Christianity, may not share all of the books. It is therefore erroneous to refer to the *Tanakh* as the "Old Testament." A preferable synonym for the *Tanakh* is the "Hebrew Bible" or "Hebrew Scriptures."

This written tradition is supplemented by an oral tradition that was passed on by the scholarly and religious leaders of each generation. In the diaspora, some of these oral traditions were canonized as the Talmud. Jews also recognize the authority of later medieval and modern rabbinic texts.

Beliefs: Judaism stresses conduct rather than doctrine or creed. While there is a diversity of belief within the Jewish tradition, traditionally Jews have believed in a single omniscient, omnipresent God. It is believed that God entered a covenant with the Jews at Mount Sinai, and therefore Jews are to set an example for humankind by obeying and serving God and being "a light unto the nations."

Practices: Jewish practices include individual and communal rites. All Jews are expected to live ethically and within certain guidelines, although individual practices vary. As an example, some Jews abstain from eating certain foods governed by Jewish dietary laws, known as *kashrut*. As a community, Jews celebrate holidays commemorating periods in their history, their relationship with God, and seasons of the agricultural year in Israel. One of the most well known holidays is Passover, in which Jews recreate the Exodus from Egypt. Additionally, each week Jews celebrate Shabbat (the Sabbath), a day of rest, recalling the creation of the universe. There are also practices that correspond to certain periods in a Jew's life, such as the bar mitzvah or bat mitzvah, which is the coming of age ceremony for a boy or girl, respectively.

Subtraditions: Judaism has four principal movements. Orthodox Jews understand Jewish tradition as given explicitly by God and therefore unchangeable. Reform Jews regard Judaism as an ongoing process resulting from the relationship between God and the Jewish people over its history. Reform Judaism considers Torah divinely inspired and subject to individual interpretations based on study, and emphasizes the ethical and moral messages of the prophets to help create a just society.

Conservative Jews believe that while Torah as a whole is binding and that much of Jewish law remains authoritative, nonetheless new ideas and practices have always influenced Jewish beliefs and rituals and this should continue today as well.

Reconstructionist Jews represent the most recently developed Jewish subgroup. This tradition understands the Jewish religion as but one element in Jewish identity.

Christianity, which began as a Jewish subgroup, is now considered an independent religion. Likewise, Messianic Judaism, a new religious movement whose adherents believe that Jesus is the messiah, is rejected by every Jewish denomination as a legitimate form of Judaism.

Symbols: Judaism frequently uses two symbols: the menorah, or seven-branched candelabrum, and the six-pointed Star of David. The menorah—and light in general—has been traditionally used in Judaism to represent eternity and redemption. The Star of David, known in Hebrew as the *Magen David,* is an ancient symbol that now adorns the flag of the State of Israel.

Common Misunderstandings: A common visual stereotype of Jews portrays men with long beards and ringlets by their ears, donning black coats and fur hats. Although there are some Jews who can be recognized by this dress, most Jews enjoy wearing the popular styles of the communities in which they reside. Another misunderstanding is that the term *Jew* is a derogatory word. This word is not inherently negative and is only offensive when used in an inappropriate context. Most Jewish people today take no offense to being identified as "a Jew."

Shinto

Nomenclature: The Chinese coined the word *Shinto* by combining the words *shen* ("divine being") and *tao* ("way"). It means "the way of the deities." Shinto-followers call their religion *kami-no-michi.*

History: While some believe that Shinto began around 2,500 to 3,000 years ago in Japan, the origins of the tradition are shrouded in prehistory. It has much overlap with Buddhism and is often called the indigenous religious tradition of Japan. No one founder is recognized; the thirteen ancient sects, however, claims a founder of its own. Shinto has been connected to the imperial system of Japan, and gained ascendancy when the Tenno clan came into power in the seventh century CE.

Scripture: Shinto does not have a sacred canon per se. It does, however, look to the eighth century CE texts of the *Kojiki* and the *Nihongi* (also known as *Nihonshoki*) for its mythology and cosmology. Also, a collection of ritual hymns and prayers can be found in the *Yengishki*.

Beliefs: At the center of Shinto belief are kami—the innumerable life-creating and life-sustaining powers that are venerated and worshipped as often personal or clan-centered divine beings. Kami can be heavenly or earthly, divine beings (gods and goddesses), or forces of nature (e.g., fertility). A major goal of Shinto practice is to gain a proper relationship with kami.

Impurity of body and spirit are religious transgressions, and the natural and beautiful things of this world interpenetrate the divine supernatural world of kami. The use of ceremony and ritual are emphasized, especially in the Shrine Shinto subgroup. Today, an estimated 30 million Japanese perform Shinto practices and rites in over one hundred thousand shrines spread across the nation.

Practices: Important to Shinto-followers are shrine worship, observance of taboos, and avoidance of impurity. Approaching the shrine of a specific kami, practitioners wash their hands and rinse their mouths with water; make offerings of food, water, and incense; call on the kami; and make a silent prayer. Shinto rites are especially important for marriage, birth, a first visit to the shrine, anniversaries, the New Year, rice planting, and the coming of spring, midsummer, and harvest time. Over the lifetime of a Japanese individual, well over forty personal rituals and events signify important Shinto observances. Every shrine is devoted to different kami and exists as a separate, geographically distinct entity. Some shrines, however, hold special importance. For example, the Grand Shrine of Ise is important to Amaterasu Omikami, the sun goddess and mother of the imperial family.

Shinto beliefs and practices are not limited to shrines; homes are also considered sanctified places and are used as sites of worship. Altars located centrally in the household (the spiritual residence of the ancestors) are used for prayers of thanks and peace. Families pray together in the mornings and the evenings. During the New Year, each family returns a divine emblem to the deity of a neighborhood shrine, receiving a new emblem to bring freshness and life into the coming year. The introduction of Buddhism to Japan altered Shinto practices, making them more systematized. Additionally, a Shinto belief that purification of "dust" will reveal one's true and divine nature found a counterpart in Buddhism, which teaches that removing defilements from one's mind will reveal one's essential Buddha nature.

Subtraditions: Shinto is roughly grouped into State (*Kokka*) Shinto, Shrine (*Jinja*) Shinto, Sect (*Kyoha*) Shinto, and Folk (*Minzoku*) Shinto. State Shinto was a strange aberration of Shinto beliefs that used totalitarian and nonpluralist views of spirituality to coerce the Japanese population into loyalty, especially during World War II. Under this system, Buddhist influences were purged from Shinto, and many popular local shrines were destroyed and replaced by shrines chosen by the emperor. Shrine Shinto is the most common strain of Shinto practiced today. Its major practices are visiting and paying homage at the plethora of shrines located throughout Japan. Sectarian Shinto comprises the aforementioned thirteen ancient sects, which originated around the nineteenth century. Folk Shinto is not very organized nor does it hold any generally defined doctrinal beliefs. Instead, it connects with local areas' agricultural and familial rites.

Symbols: Shinto's primary symbol is the torii, a wooden gate that stands at the entrance to Shinto temples. The gate consists of two vertical posts connected by a third horizontal post. The pillars represent those that support the sky, and the horizontal bar represents the earth.

Common Misunderstandings: Due to its lack of a founder, an official canon, a doctrinal system, and a central deity, the strength and legitimacy of Shinto are sometimes doubted. However, the strong feelings of reverence toward various kami evidenced by its followers, their continuing worship at the multitude of Shinto temples, and the presence of shamans and seminaries suggests that Shinto is alive and well, even if loosely bound.

Shinto is often thought of as the religion that caused Japan to enter World War II. Only, however, when Shinto practices were co-opted and manipulated to serve the state during World War II did they serve a negative purpose. Shinto is in essence a peaceful faith that respects nature first and foremost.

Sikh Faith

Nomenclature: The Sikh Faith is the name of the religion practiced by Sikhs. A Sikh is any person who demonstrates faith in one God, the Ten Sikh Gurus, *Siri Guru Granth Sahib* (scripture), and written teachings of the Ten Sikh Gurus, and who has faith in the Amrit (formal initiation) of Tenth Sikh Guru.

History: The Sikh Faith is one of the youngest major religions of the world. It was founded by Siri Guru Nanak Sahib (1469–1539 CE) in the South Asian region of Punjab. A succession of Gurus followed, each taking the name "Nanak." Before his passing away in 1708 CE, the tenth Guru declared that after him the Word of God revealed through the Gurus, the *Siri Guru Granth Sahib*, shall be the Eternal Guru. The Sikh Gurus were believed to be perfect beings sent by God for the benefit of all humankind, in complete union with God, and not in the cycle of birth and death. Sikh Faith is the fifth largest religion in the world. Sikhs number about 25 million worldwide.

Scripture: Before passing away in 1708 CE, the Tenth Sikh Guru, Siri Guru Gobind Singh Sahib, instructed the Sikhs to regard the *Granth Sahib* as their eternal Guru. The *Granth Sahib* consists of verses given by six of the ten Gurus as well as selections from the works of several Hindu and Muslim saints and holy men. It is the Sikh scripture, referred to as *Siri Guru Granth Sahib*. Sikhs regard it as the Word of God, and most revere it as the only living Guru.

Beliefs: Sikhs believe in one God, revealed to humankind through the Guru. The Sikh Faith view of God is summarized in the opening verse of *Siri Guru Granth Sahib*: "One God, Eternal, The Reality, The Name, Creator and Doer, All-pervading, Without fear, Without rancor, Transcending time, Unincarnate, Self-existent, (understood) through the Guru's Grace." Sikhs view human life as an opportunity to meet God. Lust, anger, greed, attachment, and self-will are impediments to understanding God. One has to cleanse one's mind of the dirt of self-will and in humility seek the True Guru's help in understanding the purpose of life. The True Guru instructs the Sikh about God, warns a Sikh of the impediments, and instructs a Sikh in a lifestyle that would prepare oneself for the ultimate union with God and for eternal joy. Meeting the True Guru is possible only through God's Mercy. The Sikh prays to God for that.

The faith denounces idolatry and hypocrisy, and holds that ultimate joy is obtained through constant remembrance of God, enabling one to see God in everyone and in all of God's creation. The relationship between God and creation is analogous to that between the ocean and the wave. Sikhs believe that once this is understood, there can be no inequality among people, and no intolerance. One sees God in everything.

Practices: A Sikh follows the Gurus' teachings and tries to live by them to achieve liberation while leading the life of an ordinary householder. A Sikh's motto is, "Remember God, engage in honest labor, and share the fruits of that labor."

Formal initiation into the Sikh Faith is referred to as *Khande da Pahul* (initiation with the double-edged sword), which has come to be called the *Amrit* ceremony. The initiates are called *khalsa,* meaning the "chosen ones" (of the Guru). The *khalsa* lifestyle is to be that of "saint-soldiers" exemplified by the Gurus during their own lifetimes. The *khalsa* are to be a brotherhood and sisterhood of equals, regardless of caste. They are to bear arms, to be trained in their use, and to be prepared to fight as soldiers whenever the occasion arises. The *khalsa* (men and women) are required to wear the five k's. The most visible of these is uncut hair (*kes* in Punjabi). The others are *kachch* (special type of shorts), *kara* (an iron bangle), *kirpaan* (a sword), and *kangha* (a small wooden comb). Any Sikh who after taking *Pahul* violates the commandments is a *patit* or "fallen" one. Repentance and implementation of advice, given by five *amritdhari* (those who have taken the Pahul) Sikhs, in the presence of *Siri Guru Granth Sahib*, would make the person eligible for forgiveness or re-initiation. The assembly of all *amritdharis,* the *Guru Panth*, was invested with Guruship by the Tenth Guru and is the ultimate authority in all matters affecting the faith.

The Sikhs have no priests. Any Sikh, man or woman, can officiate at any religious ceremony. Their common link is allegiance to *Guru Panth* and the *Sikh Rehit Maryada* (Sikh Principles of Living).

Subtraditions: Orthodox Sikhs believe in *Siri Guru Granth Sahib* as the only living Guru. Other sectarian groups have formed historically from differences in caste distinctions, ritual practices, and Guru succession. Therefore, there are some cultural divisions visible in the Sikh community, especially in the United States. Most Sikh Americans are immigrants of South Asian origin, speak Punjabi, and have distinct customs and dress. Since the 1960s, however, a new group of American Sikhs, the Sikh Dharma movement, has evolved. These particular American Sikhs, who follow the teachings of Harbhajan Singh (also known as Yogi Bhajan), are distinguishable by their all-white attire and turbans, worn by both men and women. Their 3HO Foundation (Healthy, Happy, Holy Organization) is also well known.

Symbols: The Sikh symbol, called *khanda,* consists of two side swords, a circular shield, and a double-edged sword in the middle. The two swords on the side represent *Miri* (worldly power) and *Piri* (spiritual power). The circular shield indicates that God has no beginning or end. The double-edged sword in the middle represents the one used in the formal initiation ceremony of the Sikh faith. It also emphasizes that a Sikh is committed to peace with justice, and that when all peaceful means are exhausted and the tyranny over the weak and oppressed continues, it is rightful for a Sikh to become a soldier striving for justice in pursuit of peace.

Common Misunderstandings: There is a significant theological misconception that the Sikh Faith is an offshoot of Hinduism or Islam or a combination thereof. Since 9/11, many Sikhs have been victims of hate crimes because of their distinctive appearance and attire.

Taoism

Nomenclature: *Tao* means "the way" and refers to a metaphysical absolute—an infinite, cosmic whole that governs the order of nature and the world.

History: The first philosopher associated with Taoist thought (philosophical Taoism) was Lao Tzu (the "Old Master"). Though little is known of his life, he is believed to have lived in the sixth century BCE. Lao Tzu has been identified as the author of the *Tao Te Ching*, a compilation of Taoist sayings. A second philosopher, Chuang Tzu, is considered to have written a book of the same name but more complex and mystical than the writings of Lao Tzu.

Popular Taoism grew from the influence of shamans, individuals who acted as mediums between the visible and spirit worlds. Known either as *wu* (meaning "wizard," "witch," or "magic") or *fang-shih* (meaning "magician and scholar of magical recipes"), male and female shamans in China were typically associated with the expulsion of evil spirits through magical healing.

After philosophical Taoism and popular Taoism each expanded on their own, they became subsumed into religious Taoism, which developed its own mystical tradition. The connection between Taoism's two sources was maintained in the religion's primary objectives: longevity, vitality, and harmonious life.

During the first century BCE, a popular movement arose that was dedicated to the cultural hero Huang Ti (or "Yellow Emperor") and Lao Tzu. Known as the Huang-Lao philosophy, the movement divinized Lao Tzu and raised many of Taoism's practices into prominence. In the second century CE, Chang Tao Ling formally organized this movement and has since been recognized as the historical founder of Taoism.

Scripture: The *Tao Te Ching* is considered a political treatise for a ruler, but its philosophy pertains to all basic facets of Taoism. Scholars have concluded that it was most likely not the product of one person but rather a compilation of sayings by several teachers that were gathered under the pen name Lao Tzu. About five thousand words in length, it was intended as both a guide to the cultivation of the self and a political manual for social transformation. The *Chuang Tzu* is another important sacred book, a more individually geared work compiled in the third century CE by the commentator Kuo Hsiang. Taoism also encompasses a number of other sacred books specifically associated with the various Taoist movements or sects.

Beliefs: The premise of Taoist belief is that the Tao is the fundamental underlying form, substance, and being of the cosmos. Tao is an infinite whole that cannot be measured by human standards. Tao is described throughout the *Tao Te Ching* as being empty, invisible, and formless yet complete, eternal, mysterious, spontaneous, simple, natural, and in existence prior to heaven and earth. The highest embodiment of Tao is *Te*, which is the natural indwelling of Tao that gives objects and people their essence. Since Taoism is a corrective to excessive activity, complexity, passion, and artificiality, the highest state of living is nonaction (*wu-wei*). To achieve this state, one must conform to the Tao by embracing simplicity, plainness, and nature.

The complementary yet opposing principles of yin and yang combine to form an illustration of wholeness in Taoism. This symbol was adopted in the *Tao Te Ching* to represent the harmonious duality in the universe. Everything has both a yin and yang principle within it, and maintaining harmony between the yin and yang is essential to physical and mental health.

Practices: Taoism emphasizes practices designed to promote health and longevity, such as alchemical practices, breathing exercises, movement exercises designed to circulate the *ch'i* ("vital breath"), and meditation. Taoists also strive to enhance their health and life span by minimizing their desires and centering themselves on stillness.

Underlying Taoist practice is a quest for freedom. Seeking immortality, the religion pursues oneness with the Tao itself, a liberating concept for the Taoists that allowed them to escape social confines and live in a spontaneous fashion. Taoism also advocates the nonviolent coexistence of states, and Taoists repudiate the use of weapons and renounce warfare.

Subtraditions: Taoism encompassed several sects, some still surviving today. The first sect came about under Chang Tao Ling, the "Heavenly Master" and founder of the religion, a sect still prominent in Taiwan. A second sect, founded by Chang Chiao, was millenarian and dissident in nature. He taught that 184 CE was to be the beginning of a new era. Followers, called Yellow Turbans for their distinctive garb, participated in an insurrection that was brutally overthrown.

Buddhist influence initiated the development of sects and religious communities that included priests and monks. As a result of this influence, many Taoists added ritual practices to celebrate the birthdays of gods, ward off misfortune, attain or maintain peace, and ordain priests. In the fourth century, the Mao Shan sect was established. In reaction to the Buddhist monastic organizations, it formed its own community, which practiced Taoist meditation and alchemies.

The fifth century witnessed the advent of the Ling Pao sect, which introduced the worship of T'ien Tsun, the eternal force that transcends the creation and destruction of universes, and the keeper of knowledge of the Tao. Finally, in the twelfth century, the Ch'uan-chen sect was founded by Wang Che. It advocated a syncretistic amalgam of Taoism, Confucianism, and Buddhism.

Symbols: The yin and yang symbol, a circle with equal, opposing, complementary components of black and white, signifies how opposites interact and complement each other, creating a dynamic tension that results in a perpetual process of change—production, reproduction, and the transformation of energy.

Common Misunderstandings: Those unfamiliar with Taoism might consider it superstitious or magical, but magic does not apply to the religion as a whole.

Zoroastrianism

Nomenclature: Zoroastrians are the followers of the prophet Zarathushtra, who the Western world often calls Zoroaster. There are two main groups of Zoroastrians. Zoroastrians on the Indian sub-continent are known as *Parsis* and *Iranis*. Another group of Zoroastrians is in present day Iran. Their beliefs and practices are very similar.

History: The Indo-Iranian Aryans who settled in Persia and India between 3000 and 1500 BCE were pastoral, worshiping many gods of nature, fire being the main one around which they performed their rituals. This polytheistic religion was the precursor to Zoroastrianism, which Zarathushtra, by the divine revelation from *Ahura Mazda* (God), the Wise Lord, propagated in Iran around 1500 BCE. Zoroastrianism is credited to be the oldest monotheistic religion. Though many scholars fix Zoroastrianism's date of inception around 1500 BCE, some believe Zarathushtra was born as early as 6000 BCE or as late as 700 to 600 BCE.

Due to a lack of reliable sources, it is unknown what happened to the religion after Zarathushtra's death. By the seventh century

BCE, however, Zoroastrianism was present in the court of the Medes, a dynasty that ruled Persia. In 559 BCE, Cyrus the Great emerged as the sole king of Persia and founded the Achaemenian Dynasty. He liberated Jews from Babylon, allowed them to go to Jerusalem, and helped them build their Temple. Celebrated for his tolerance of different religions and ethnicities, Zoroastrianism flourished under his reign and that of his successors, Darius the Great and Xerxes.

After the conquest of Iran by Alexander the Great in 331 BCE, Iran was in turmoil under the Greek rule until 224 BCE, when the Parthian Dynasty was founded and Zoroastrianism flourished again sporadically. Parthians were defeated by the Sasanian King Ardeshir in 226 CE and established the powerful Sasanian Dynasty, during which Zoroastrianism became the state's most powerful religion. After the fall of the Sasanian Empire at the hands of the Arabs in 651 CE, an era of persecution began. Zoroastrians were prohibited from worshipping freely and relegated to rural villages. By the tenth century, these conditions had prompted many Zoroastrians to move to India, where their community thrived. Modern Parsi Zoroastrians in India and Pakistan continue to enjoy economic and social success. Iranian Zoroastrians, however, still suffer from conditions of inequality that leads in some cases to poverty.

Scripture: The revelations Zarathushtra received from *Ahura Mazda* are contained in a collection of hymns called the *Gathas*. These seventeen hymns are all that survive of Zarathushtra's teachings, and are an integral part of the Zoroastrian worship ceremony called the *Yasna*. There is also religious literature in a later form of the *Avesta* language and redaction of the *Avesta* literature and commentary and prayers in *Pahalevi*, which was the language of the later Parthian and Sasanian dynasties. Because the majority of the religious literature is in the *Avesta* language, the word *Avesta* often refers to the holy book(s) of Zoroastrianism.

After the fall of the Achaemenian Dynasty, it is generally believed that the *Avesta* was destroyed and scattered by the Greeks. A first restoration of *Avesta* was made by the Parthian king Vologases I (51–77 CE), who had collected the scattered *Avesta,* including the *Yasna* containing seventy-two chapters. The collection and restoration of the *Avesta* continued vigorously under the Sasanian Dynasty (226–651 CE). The writing and canonization of the texts was under Shapur II (309–379 CE) by his prime minister and high priest, Aturpat Marespandan. The Sasanian *Avesta* was written in the specially invented alphabets in order to render with extreme precision the slightest nuance of the liturgical recitation. After the fall of the Sasanian Dynasty at the hands of the Arabs, much of the *Avesta* once again was destroyed and scattered, with a few fragments surviving. Numerous religious texts were written by various authors in the Pahalvi and Pazand languages in the ninth century CE. During this time, many Zoroastrians from Iran migrated to the west coast of India and thrived there as Parsis. They have preserved most of the *Avesta* fragments from the Sasanian time.

Beliefs: Zoroastrians believe in the Wise Lord, called *Ahura Mazda* or *Ohrmazd* (Pahlavi form). *Ahura Mazda* has the attributes of Good Mind, Righteousness, Dominion, Devotion, Wholeness, and Immortality. These are also known as the Holy Immortals and are the virtues to which each Zoroastrian should aspire. Creation in the material state is good and is destined to move toward perfection. This is opposed by the destructive acts of evildoers and deceivers, inspired by *Angre Mainyu* (the evil mentality). Human beings are required to choose and act so that they move creation toward the goal of perfection by fighting evil and working for the triumph of good.

Zoroastrians see all aspects of nature as *Ahura Mazda*'s creation and are required to maintain an ecological balance and strive to take care of their bodies as instruments for the good.

Zoroastrians also believe in two moments of judgment. Individual judgment occurs immediately after death and the soul suffers or benefits from its actions before death. There is a final judgment when good ultimately triumphs over evil, at which time all souls are purified.

Practices: One of the earliest and most basic Zoroastrian practices is worshiping at fire temples. The fire, a symbol of purity, burns in the spiritual center of Zoroastrian temples. Worshipers purify themselves before entering the temple, which is devoid of all decoration, and then pray individually around the fire.

Another important Zoroastrian ritual is *navjote*, in which Zoroastrian priests initiate boys and girls into their religious community. During the ceremony, the children receive a *sudreh* (white cotton undervest) and *kusti* (a white wool cord) which they will wear their entire lives.

The final Zoroastrian rite of passage is the funeral ceremony. In order to avoid polluting the environment, bodies are not buried, burned, or drowned. Traditionally, they are left on top of a circular stone tower, where carrion birds devour the flesh. This practice is now followed only in India and Pakistan.

Symbol: The Zoroastrian symbol is the *farohar*, sometimes considered an image of the Wise Lord, *Ahura Mazda*, who is depicted as a man from the waist up with the wings and tail feathers of an eagle.

Common Misunderstandings: Many believe Zoroastrians are fire-worshipers. Zoroastrians believe that fire promotes their connection with God, but they never pray directly to it. Fire is used as a symbol of the divine energy of God that permeates his creation, and in Zoroastrian rituals and Zoroastrian temples it represents the presence of God. Since Zoroastrians strongly emphasize the battle between good and evil, many have considered Zoroastrianism a dualistic religion that places equal emphasis on good and evil. Zoroastrianism, however, is a monotheistic religion that worships one God who is perfectly good.

Other Traditions

Depending on a tradition's footprint in the microcosm of your own community, you may not find a representative of some of these traditions above, for example, a Bahá'í or a Zoroastrian. Modern forms of transportation and communication, however, make it quite possible to have encounters with them. It is important to think of the impact of one degree of separation on members of your own community. They may have a relative or an online pal that reflect the religious diversity beyond that evidenced in your own community. Therefore, this diversity may take on a significance not immediately obvious in your local interfaith work.

What you are more likely to find is difficulty in dealing with the great diversity within the predominant or larger religions within your community, such as for people of other faiths trying to comprehend intra-Christian diversity. If you are struggling to understand the difference between Catholics and Protestants or between Methodists and Baptists, you are not alone. Take comfort in knowing that many Christians themselves do not understand appreciably the differences. Yet knowing something of the differences helps guide local interfaith organization and work.

For a closer look at intra-Christian diversity, take a look at Eileen Lindner's *Yearbook of American and Canadian Churches* and the *Handbook of Denominations in the United States* by Frank Mead and colleagues.

In my experience, much tension in local interfaith organizations emanates from the struggle to define how to accommodate newer or smaller traditions with those that are older or larger. Many interfaith organizations develop structural and operating conventions for weighting the size and diversity of traditions proportionally, for example, in matters of voting or representation.

A commonly agreed upon set of expectations about participation and membership can avoid later tensions. Such expectations usually speak to what constitutes a faith tradition, how a tradition should interact with other traditions, and different levels and means of participation. A very common example that I have seen in the United States is local interfaith groups that receive a request for participation from members of the Church of Scientology, the Unificationist Movement, or one of the pagan traditions. For more detailed information on one of these new religions, sects, or alternative spiritualities, I recommend Christopher Partridge's *New Religions: A Guide*. Having some advance knowledge of the diversity in your own community and a clear policy about the parameters of your membership help in dealing with these matters as they arise. Unfortunately, having an open policy of everyone being welcome to the table does not mean that everyone will be. Because of the tensions that exist between some religious communities, including all without discretion means that some simply will not come to the table. It is a frustrating reality of interfaith work.

7

Interfaith Organizations and the Web

I believe that if we really want human brotherhood to spread and increase until it makes life safe and sane, we must also be certain that there is no one true faith or path by which it may spread.

—ADLAI E. STEVENSON

Where are some of the best places to turn for information about individual religions and interfaith work? Hundreds of interfaith websites have turned up on the Internet in recent years. Even more interfaith organizations have taken root. A broad sampling of exemplary ones are listed below.

Again, there are many, many excellent organizations throughout North America and beyond working to promote interfaith understanding. All of them could not be included here. This section concentrates on organizations with significant web presences, helpful networks or resources, noted histories in interfaith work, or broad reach, for example, umbrella or national organizations that can redirect to a local presence. This section includes interfaith-savvy examples of: research centers; academic centers; religious community and interreligious resource centers; media outlets; local, regional, and national interfaith organizations; web-based clearinghouses; and museums.

If you have a favorite resource, we want to hear from you! The editors and contributors to this book welcome feedback and tips at www.interreligious.org/InterActiveFaith. Your contributions may be included in future editions of this book. In the meantime, additional resources and updates will be available on this site.

If you work in interfaith relations on an ongoing basis, it is also advisable to consider signing up for Google alerts on subjects such as "interfaith," "religion," "multifaith," and similar topics to stay abreast of a broad assortment of web and news stories about these topics.

9/11 Unity Walk
4000 Cathedral Ave., NW
Ste. 313
Washington, D.C. 20016
Tel: (202) 234-6300
Fax: (202) 234-6303
Website: www.911UnityWalk.org
The 9/11 Unity Walk formed in Washington, D.C., in 2005 and expanded to other cities, including New York City, in subsequent years. It offers an excellent model and resources for persons interested in a public witness interfaith event.

Adherents.com
Website: www.adherents.com
This is a great website to get statistics on world religions. Statistical information is available on 4,200 "subreligions" of the world, as well as links to hundreds of other facts about religious communities and people.

American Academy of Religion
825 Houston Mill Rd. NE
Ste. 300
Atlanta, GA 30329
Tel: (404) 727-3049
Fax: (404) 727-7959
Website: www.aarweb.org
The members of AAR are teachers and professors of religion and its related topics. The aim of the Academy is to foster excellence in the understanding of religion. Its website includes a nifty database for journalists called ReligionSource.

American Jewish Committee
Department of Interreligious Affairs
165 E. 56th St.
7th Fl.
New York, NY 10022
Tel: (212) 891-6761
Fax: (212) 891-1415
Website: www.engagingamerica.org

Since 1906, the American Jewish Committee has worked to safeguard and strengthen Jews and Jewish life worldwide by promoting democratic and pluralistic societies that respect the dignity of all peoples. In a new century of rapid demographic change and a widening cultural and socioeconomic divide, they continue striving to strengthen a democratic America.

Arts & Spirituality Center
3723 Chestnut St.
Philadelphia, PA 19104
Tel: (215) 386-7705
Fax: (215) 222-1015
Website: www.artsandspirituality.org

Founded in 2000, the Arts & Spirituality Center empowers and transforms individuals and communities through spiritual and creative expression, in partnership with a broad range of multicultural groups in the Philadelphia area. As a nonsectarian organization, the Arts & Spirituality Center serves people of all faiths as well as those not religiously affiliated, nurturing the life-giving resources and values that strengthen the human spirit and build the capacity for change. Activities integrate spiritual expression with poetry and creative writing, visual arts, music, dance, and other artistic media. Through programs such as MasterPeace, We the Poets, Drums for Peace, and other workshops, the Arts & Spirituality Center builds bridges and deepens relationships across cultural and racial divides. The work enables individuals and communities to draw on their intrinsic strengths to overcome alienation, to impact the revitalization of neighborhoods, and to heal the wounds of injustice.

Association of Religion Data Archives
Department of Sociology
Pennsylvania State University
211 Oswald Tower
University Park, PA 16802
Tel: (814) 865-6258
Fax: (814) 863-7216
Website: www.thearda.com
Located at Penn State University, this archive contains religious data
and research from a number of sources across the United States. It
contains, to give just one example, a handy guide to religious diversity
in every county, state, and metro area in the United States, based on
the Religious Congregations and Membership Study collected by the
Association of Statisticians of American Religious Bodies, the most
complete census of its kind ever compiled. An interactive feature of the
site allows you to compare your religious views and practices to those
of the nation, as measured by the Baylor 2005 Religion Survey.

Auburn Theological Seminary
3041 Broadway
New York, NY 10027
Tel: (212) 662-4315
Website: www.auburnsem.org
Auburn Theological Seminary has been educating and motivating peo-
ple to learn since 1818. A special emphasis is placed on interfaith
understanding in its continuing education programs and its Center for
Multifaith Education. Auburn also has a special focus on multifaith
media.

BBC Religion & Ethics
Tel: 44 (0)11-3-244-2131
Fax: 44 (0)11-3-242-0652
Website: www.bbc.co.uk/religion
The BBC offers religious news as seen from a British perspective,
including many stories with interfaith implications. One useful feature
of the site is a searchable interfaith calendar that covers holy days and
festivals in every corner of the world.

Beliefnet
115 E. 23rd St.
New York, NY 10010
Tel: (212) 533-1400
Website: www.beliefnet.com
The largest and certainly the liveliest interfaith website, Beliefnet documents various facts regarding religious groups and offers blogs, articles, personal testimony, resources, and even whimsical quizzes that are geared to the interests of every faith.

Center for Global Ethics at Temple University
Department of Philosophy
Anderson Hall
Temple University
1114 W. Berks St.,
Ste. 511
Philadelphia, PA 19122
Tel: (215) 204-0122
Fax: (215) 204-6266
Webstie: http://astro.temple.edu/~dialogue/geth.htm
What does it mean to be a reasonable citizen of the world? Through the lens of the scholarship of Hans Küng and Leonard Swidler, the Center for Global Ethics brings together the philosophies of people from different religious disciplines.

Center for Interfaith Relations
415 W. Muhammad Ali Blvd.
Louisville, KY 40202
Tel: (502) 583-3100
Website: www.interfaithrelations.org
Previously the Cathedral Heritage Foundation, this Louisville-based organization is widely recognized for its annual Festival of Faiths week of events.

Children of Abraham
307 W. 38th St.,
Ste. 1805
New York, NY 10018
Tel: (212) 375-2620
Fax: (212) 375-2629
Website: www.children-of-abraham.org
Children of Abraham works to build more comprehensive relationships between Jews and Muslims while honoring their common heritage and reaffirming the essential principles that lie at the heart of both faiths.

Committee of Religious Non-Governmental Organizations at the United Nations
Church Center for the United Nations
777 United Nations Plaza
9th Fl.
New York, NY 10017
Tel: (212) 661-1762
Fax: (212) 983-0566
Website: www.rngo.org
The Committee of Religious NGOs at the United Nations is composed of representatives of national and international organizations that define their work as religious, spiritual, or ethical in nature. They monitor and instigate interreligious efforts at the United Nations.

Common Tables
PO Box 4010
Parker, CO 80134
Tel: (303) 690-3900
Fax: (303) 253-9822
Website: www.commontables.org
The interfaith organization Common Tables seeks to establish 750,000 small dinner groups that overcome barriers, misconceptions, and fear-based thinking about diversity and inclusion to recognize one single truth: we have much more in common than we do in difference.

Council for a Parliament of the World's Religions
70 E. Lake St.,
Ste. 205
Chicago, IL 60601
Tel: (312) 629-2990
Fax: (312) 629-2991
Website: www.cpwr.org

Fostering harmony and spiritual healing in a world plagued with unnecessary war, the modern Council for a Parliament of the World's Religions encourages dialogue between people of distinct faiths. Its primary vehicle is an international forum held approximately every five years.

The Dialogue Project
123 Seventh Ave., #234
Brooklyn, NY 11215
Tel: (718) 768-2175
Fax: (718) 768-2094
Website: www.thedialogueproject.org

This Brooklyn-based outfit focuses on facilitating education and modeling dialogue between Christians, Jews, and Muslims in schools and community organizations. It hosts monthly conversations and has interesting sets of audio samples of spoken dialogues on its website, particularly framed around the Middle East.

Faith & Values Media
475 Riverside Dr.,
Ste. 530
New York, NY 10115
Tel: (212) 870-1030
Fax: (212) 870-1040
Website: www.faithandvaluesmedia.org

Faith & Values Media uses electronic media—video and the Internet—to enrich spiritual life, heal wounds by advocating religious tolerance, and build bridges of understanding among people of faith. Its programming includes music, worship, magazine shows, talk shows, movies of the week, documentaries, and specials. Faith & Values Media is a service of the National Interfaith Cable Coalition, and both have made recent efforts to broaden their religious table.

Faith in Public Life
1101 Vermont Ave., NW
Ste. 900
Washington, DC 20005
Tel: (202) 481-8165
Fax: (202) 962-7201
Website: www.faithinpubliclife.org
Faith in Public Life is a new player on Capitol Hill, founded by a diverse group of America's religious leaders to strengthen the effectiveness, collaboration, and reach of faith movements that are engaged in political and social advocacy. Its website features an evolving National Directory of Faith Groups for Justice and the Common Good that includes an interactive state-by-state map.

Faith Quilts Project
PO Box 256
Scituate, MA 02066
Tel: (781) 545-5707
Fax: (781) 545-5710
The Faith Quilts Project is a collaborative effort among people of various faith communities in the Greater Boston area to "visually express deeply held beliefs" in the form of interfaith quilts. The project has resulted in the creation of dozens of quilts, which have been displayed in a series of public exhibitions.

Family Promise (formerly known as Interfaith Hospitality Network)
71 Summit Ave.
Summit, NJ 07901
Tel: (908) 273-1100
Fax: (908) 273-0030
Website: www.familypromise.org
Family Promise is committed to helping low-income families nationwide to achieve lasting independence. They do this by helping communities mobilize to provide safe shelter, meals, and support services for homeless families through the cooperation of local faith communities and through programs designed to redress the underlying causes of homelessness. Local affiliates retain the historic name, Interfaith Hospitality Network.

Fellowship of Reconciliation
PO Box 271
521 N. Broadway
Nyack, NY 10960
Tel: (845) 358-4601
Fax: (845) 358-4924
Website: www.forusa.org

Since 1915, the Fellowship of Reconcilation has carried on programs and educational projects concerned with domestic and international peace and justice, nonviolent alternatives to conflict, and the rights of conscience. Participants are committed to active nonviolence as a transforming way of life and as a means of radical change.

Glenmary Research Center
1312 Fifth Ave., North
Nashville, TN 37208
Tel: (615) 256-1905
Fax: (615) 256-1902
Website: www.glenmary.org/grc

Affiliated with a Catholic society of priests, brothers, and nuns who are dedicated to assuring a Catholic presence in traditionally non-Catholic, rural regions of the United States, the Glenmary Research Center provides research to support their efforts. Every ten years, they produce *Religious Congregations & Membership in the United States*, which gives an invaluable snapshot of religious diversity in local communities.

Hartford Institute for Religion Research
Hartford Seminary
77 Sherman St.
Hartford, CT 06105
Tel: (860) 509-9543
Fax: (860) 509-9551
Website: www.hirr.hartsem.edu

The HIRR conducts research and offers consultation on matters related to the sociological study of religion in the United States. It produces several helpful products and scholarly resources for anyone interested in interfaith dialogue, including *Faith Communities Today*, the Cooperative Congregational Studies Partnership, and the U.S.

Congregational Life Survey. See especially the *Meet Your Neighbors: Interfaith FACTs* booklet at http://fact.hartsem.edu.

Hartley Film Foundation
49 Richmondville Ave.
Ste. 204
Westport, CT 06880
Tel: (800) 937-1819
Fax: (203) 227-6938
Website: www.hartleyfoundation.org
The Hartley Film Foundation produces and distributes documentary film, video, and audio programs about world religions, spirituality, ethics, and well-being. It also actively supports, through fiscal sponsorship and seed grants, award-winning filmmakers who direct and produce compelling documentary films that illuminate and illustrate the Foundation's mission.

Institute on Culture, Religion and World Affairs
Boston University
10 Lenox St.
Brookline, MA 02446
Tel: (617) 353-9050
Fax: (617) 353-6408
Website: www.bu.edu/cura
As a research-centered organization, CURA deals with a variety of concerns, but its main focus of research is the role of religion in shaping society. Exemplary of the cross-disciplinary centers forming at universities, it produces resources that are useful to interfaith efforts, such as "The Toleration Project: A Cross-National Study of Interreligious Tolerance."

Institute for Interreligious, Intercultural Dialogue
Temple University (022-38)
1114 W. Berks St.
Ste. 511
Philadelphia, PA 19122
Tel: (215) 204-7251
Fax: (215) 204-4569
Website: http://astro.temple.edu/~dialogue
Founded as an outreach instrument of the *Journal of Ecumenical Studies*, the IIID promotes dialogue in the broadest sense among indi-

viduals and groups of different religions and cultures, focusing especially, though not exclusively, on the opinion shapers of society, such as scholars, professionals, and institutional and business leaders.

Institute on Religion and Public Policy
1620 I St., NW
Ste. LL10
Washington, DC 20006
Tel: (202) 835-8760
Fax: (202) 835-8764
Website: www.religionandpolicy.org
The IRPP is an interreligious organization that works globally with government policymakers, religious leaders, business executives, academics, international and regional organizations, nongovernmental organizations, and others in order to develop, protect, and promote religious freedom.

The Interfaith Alliance
1212 New York Ave. NW
7th Fl.
Washington, DC 20005
Tel: (202) 238-3300
Fax: (202) 238-3301
Website: www.interfaithalliance.org
Founded in 1994 to challenge the radical religious right, the Interfaith Alliance's 185,000 members, drawn from seventy-five different religions and belief systems, promote the positive and healing role of religion in public life by encouraging civic participation, facilitating community activism, and challenging religious bigotry where they find it.

Interfaith Association of Central Ohio
57 Jefferson Ave.
Columbus, OH 43209
Tel: (614) 849-0290
Fax: (614) 849-0290
Website: www.iaco.org
The Interfaith Association of Central Ohio is unique for the partnerships it has developed in the Greater Columbus community on a variety of issues and for the publication of a landmark book, *Religion in*

Ohio: Profiles of Faith Communities (Ohio University Press), for Ohio's bicentennial celebrations.

Interfaith Center at the Presidio
PO Box 29055
San Francisco, CA 94129
Tel: (415) 775-4635
Website: www.interfaith-presidio.org
The Interfaith Center at the Presidio was created to welcome, serve, and celebrate the diverse spiritual wisdom and faith traditions of the Bay Area in California. Through the United Religions Initiative, the Center is networked globally with hundreds of interfaith groups in fifty countries that share a common commitment "to promote daily, enduring interfaith cooperation, to end religiously motivated violence, and to create cultures of peace, justice, and healing for the Earth and all living beings."

Interfaith Center of New York
475 Riverside Dr.
Ste. 540
New York, NY 10115
Tel: (212) 870-3510
Fax: (212) 870-3499
Website: www.interfaithcenter.org
This organization, which has launched some of the more innovative and effective programs of any local interfaith organization, was founded in 1997. Its network of more than one thousand religious community leaders from twenty traditions and denominations works together to solve common community problems through education, civic connections, and arts and culture.

Interfaith Center on Corporate Responsibility
475 Riverside Dr.
Rm. 1842
New York, NY 10115
Tel: (212) 870-2295
Fax: (212) 870-2023
Website: www.iccr.org
ICCR is an association of 275 faith-based institutional investors, including national denominations, religious communities, pension funds, founda-

tions, hospital corporations, economic development funds, asset management companies, colleges, and unions. ICCR and its members press companies to be socially and environmentally responsible. Each year ICCR-member religious institutional investors sponsor more than two hundred shareholder resolutions on major social and environmental issues.

InterFaith Conference of Metropolitan Washington
1426 Ninth St. NW
2nd Fl.
Washington, DC 20001
Tel: (202) 234-6300
Fax: (202) 234-6303
Website: www.ifcmw.org
Founded in 1978, the IFCMW brings together the Bahá'í, Buddhist, Hindu, Islamic, Jain, Jewish, Latter-day Saint, Protestant, Roman Catholic, Sikh, and Zoroastrian faith communities to promote dialogue, understanding, and a sense of community among persons of different faiths and to work cooperatively for social and economic justice.

Interfaith Marketplace
PO Box 1298
Ashland, OR 97520
Tel: (877) 525-8883
Website: www.interfaithmarketplace.com
The Interfaith Marketplace provides tools that will guide you in experiencing the beauty in all the world's religions. Started as a U.S. distribution point for the Multifaith Action Society's Multifaith Calendar, this company now provides a range of products of interest.

Inter-Faith Ministries
829 North Market
Wichita, KS 67214
Tel: (316) 264-9303
Fax: (316) 264-2233
Website: www.ifmnet.org
For more than 120 years, Inter-Faith Ministries of Wichita has been calling people of all faiths together to build interreligious understanding, promote justice, relieve misery, and reconcile the estranged. With everything from a TV studio where they produce a cable show to blocks of housing and social care facilities, they are arguably the

largest, best-equipped, and perhaps the oldest local interfaith operation in the United States.

Interfaith Voices for Peace and Justice
PO Box 270214
St. Louis, MO 63127
Tel: (314) 892-1192
Fax: (314) 892-1255
Website: www.interspirit.net/ifv.cfm
A communications network for faith-based activist groups, Interfaith Voices for Peace and Justice provides a number of valuable resources, including a searchable database of hundreds of other religious organizations and people dedicated to your cause.

Interfaith Worker Justice
1020 W. Bryn Mawr Ave.
4th Fl.
Chicago, IL 60660
Tel: (773) 728-8400
Fax: (773) 728-8409
Website: www.iwj.org
Interfaith Worker Justice calls upon our religious values in order to educate, organize, and mobilize the religious community in the United States on issues and campaigns that will improve wages, benefits, and working conditions, especially for low-wage workers.

Interfaith Youth Core
1111 N. Wells St.
Ste. 501
Chicago, IL 60610
Tel: (312) 573-8825
Fax: (312) 573-1542
Website: www.ifyc.org
Interfaith Youth Core (note that it is not Corps!) builds mutual respect and pluralism among young people from different religious traditions by empowering them to work together to serve others.

International Association for Religious Freedom
2 Market St.
Oxford OX1 3ET, United Kingdom
Tel: 44 (0)1865 202-744
Fax: 44 (0)1865 202-746
Website: www.iarf.net
With more than ninety affiliated member groups in approximately twenty-five countries, from a wide range of faith traditions, the IARF works at a global level to assure religious freedom. At one hundred-plus years old, it is one of the oldest and still one of the most effective organizations of its kind.

International Committee for the Peace Council
1112 Grant St.
Madison, WI 53711
Website: www.peacecouncil.org
This eclectic international and interfaith group brings together prominent faith leaders for private retreat and collaboration. Together they seek to show how it is possible to live together in peace.

International Interfaith Centre
PO Box 750
Oxford, OX3 3BR, United Kingdom
Tel: 44 (0)1 865-202745
Fax: 44 (0)1 865-202746
Website: www.interfaith-centre.org
The International Interfaith Centre conducts research, organizes projects, and enables a safe space for international interfaith organizations to meet together in a yearly gathering. The IIC has conducted surveys on people's perceptions of and attitudes toward interfaith dialogue.

Michigan Roundtable for Diversity & Inclusion
525 New Center One
3031 W. Grand Blvd.
Detroit, MI 48202
Tel: (313) 870-1500
Fax: (313) 870-1501
Website: www.miroundtable.org
The Michigan Roundtable for Diversity & Inclusion seeks to eliminate discrimination and racism by working proactively across racial, religious,

ethnic, and cultural boundaries. The Michigan Roundtable assists in building more inclusive communities, businesses, and institutions through diversity training, advocacy, conflict resolution, interfaith collaboration, youth leadership training, and community dialogue. They have an exemplary interfaith play called *The Children of Abraham*, which has been staged throughout the country.

Multifaith Action Society
#5-305 West 41st Ave.
Vancouver, BC V5Y 2S5, Canada
Tel: (604) 321-1302
Fax: (604) 321-1370
Website: www.multifaithaction.org
Renowned for its colorful multifaith calendar, the Multifaith Action Society brings together the many faith groups that characterize Vancouver. It sponsors socially responsible and relevant initiatives relating to the common good, including starting the first food bank in Vancouver.

Museum of World Religions
7th Fl., No. 236
Chungshan Rd. Section 1
Yunghe City, Taipei County, Taiwan
Tel: 886-2-8231-6118
Fax: 886-2-8231-5966
Website: www.mwr.org.tw
This massive Taiwanese institution, the realization of the vision of Master Hsin Tao, exhibits collections of artifacts from various world religions and features interactive educational displays.

North American Interfaith Network
1426 9th St. NW
2nd Fl.
Washington, DC 20001
Tel: (202) 234-6300
Fax: (202) 234-6303
Website: www.nain.org
Through annual meetings and newsletters, this organization encourages networking between interfaith organizations. It is where local interfaith leaders come for professional development and collaboration.

Ontario Consultants on Religious Tolerance
Box 27026
Kingston, ON K7M 8W5, Canada
Tel: (613) 547-6600
Fax: (613) 547-9015
Website: www.religioustolerance.org

The mandate of this website is to promote religious tolerance and freedom; objectively describe religious faiths in all their diversity; and objectively describe controversial topics from all viewpoints. It is a cornucopia of resources and information.

PBS Religion & Ethics Newsweekly
1333 H St. NW
6th Fl.
Washington, DC 20005
Tel: (202) 216-2380
Website: www.pbs.org/wnet/religionandethics

This is an online companion to the weekly PBS television show that covers religion and ethics issues as they play out in the public sphere.

Pluralism Project
Harvard University
1531 Cambridge St.
Cambridge, MA 02139
Tel: (617) 496-2481
Fax: (617) 496-2428
Website: www.pluralism.org

The Pluralism Project at Harvard University provides plenty of resources for interfaith activists who are seeking to learn about other-than-Christian-or-Jewish faith communities in the United States. An army of scholars and interns record data, including interesting case studies, that document America's growing religious diversity. Many local interfaith organizations use the Pluralism Project's electronic data feeds of news about religious diversity and its catalog of religious communities and interfaith organizations.

Religion Communicators Council
475 Riverside Dr. #1355
New York, NY 10115
Tel: (212) 870-2985
Fax: (212) 870-2171
Website: www.religioncommunicators.org
Religion Communicators Council, founded in 1929, is an interfaith association of religion communicators at work in print and electronic communication, marketing, and public relations. Together, RCC members promote excellence in the communication of religious faith and values in the public arena and encourage understanding among religious and faith groups. RCC might be best known for its work in producing a handbook for religion communicators.

Religions for Peace
777 United Nations Plaza
9th Fl.
New York, NY 10017
Tel: (212) 687-2163
Fax: (212) 983-0098
Website: www.religionsforpeace.org
Historically known as the World Conference of Religions for Peace (WCRP), RFP is the largest global coalition of representatives from the world's religious traditions dedicated to an enduring mission: stop war, end poverty, and protect the earth. There are more than seventy RFP affiliates worldwide.

Religions for Peace-USA
777 United Nations Plaza
9th Fl.
New York, NY 10017
Tel: (212) 338-9140
Fax: (212) 983-0098
Website: www.rfpusa.org
The U.S. affiliate of Religions for Peace is a coalition for senior religious leaders to work together for peace. This chapter produces podcasts and study guides and distributes mini grants and movie kits. In addition, it produces a monthly newsletter filled with resources and ideas for interfaith dialogue and action.

Religion News Service
1101 Connecticut Ave. NW
Ste. 350
Washington, DC 20036
Tel: (202) 463-8777
Fax: (202) 463-0033
Website: www.religionnews.com
RNS is a secular news and photo service devoted exclusively to unbiased coverage of religion and ethics issues. Headlines and summaries are available for nonsubscribers; full stories are available for subscribers.

Sacred Spaces
PO Box 29055
San Francisco, CA 94129
Tel: (415) 775-4635
Fax: (415) 771-8681
Website: www.interfaithdesign.org
Is it possible to design a physical space that can be welcoming to more than one religion? All religions? Some California interfaith leaders asked this question and got 160 answers from architects from seventeen countries. Anyone who has ever struggled to figure out how to make a prayer room that is inviting to more than one faith will want to explore this website.

Spirit Break
3470 Blazer Pkwy.
Ste. 150
Lexington, KY 40509
Tel: (859) 422-0455
Fax: (859) 422-1167
Website: www.spiritbreak.com
Sporting the tagline "Take a moment to feed your spirit," this website offers short streaming videos with spiritual and uplifting content from Faith & Values Media. See also www.faithstreams.com.

Tanenbaum Center for Interreligious Understanding
254 W. 31st St.
7th Fl.
New York, NY 10001
Tel: (212) 967-7707
Fax: (212) 967-9001
Website: www.tanenbaum.org

Created to diffuse religious antipathy, this organization provides targeted resources for dealing with religious diversity in the workplace, schools, and in war zones around the world. It also develops special programs that address conflict and explore the religious roots of prejudice.

Temple of Understanding
211 E. 43rd St.
Ste. 1600
New York, NY 10017
Tel: (212) 573-9224
Fax: (212) 573-9225
Website: www.templeofunderstanding.org

Envisioned originally as a catalyst for a spiritual United Nations, this UN-based nongovernmental organization supports interfaith cooperation through education and community outreach. In recent years it has developed a specialty in multifaith religious education.

United Communities of Spirit
PO Box 23346
Santa Barbara, CA 93121
Tel: (805) 966-9515
Website: www.origin.org

Built by Bruce Shulman, who provides support to several web-based interfaith networks, this virtual interfaith organization brings together people of diverse faiths and beliefs who want to work with others to build a better world.

United Nations Educational, Scientific and Cultural Organization
New York Field Office
2 United Nations Plaza
Rm. 900
New York, NY 10017
Tel: (212) 963-5995
Fax: (212) 963-8014
Website: www.unesco.org
From protecting World Heritage Sites to sponsoring global forums on intercultural and interreligious relations, UNESCO serves as a laboratory of ideas and a forger of agreements, helping member states to build their capacities to build peace. Its website features dozens of useful links.

United Religions Initiative
1009 General Kennedy Ave.
San Francisco, CA 94129
Tel: (415) 561-2300
Fax: (415) 561-2313
Website: www.uri.org
This rapidly growing grassroots organization works toward interfaith understanding, with a special emphasis on using the model of appreciative inquiry and on ending religiously motivated violence.

United States Conference of the World Council of Churches
475 Riverside Dr.
Ste. 1371
New York, NY 10115
Tel: (212) 870-2533
Fax: (212) 870-2528
Website: usa.wcc-coe.org
A Christian ecumenical organization, this conference brings together thirty-four U.S. churches and friends of ecumenical work and the World Council of Churches. Resources and initiatives are often so broadly framed that they can be useful for interfaith as well as their intended ecumenical efforts.

United States Institute of Peace
1200 17th St. NW
Washington, DC 20036
Tel: (202) 457-1700
Fax: (202) 429-6063
Website: www.usip.org
The United States Institute of Peace is an independent, nonpartisan, national institution established and funded by Congress. Its goals are to help prevent and resolve violent conflicts, promote post-conflict stability and development, and increase peacebuilding capacity, tools, and intellectual capital worldwide. The Religion and Peacemaking Program of the Centers of Innovation produces study documents and hosts special programs that explore interfaith issues.

Virtual Religion Network
Dept. of Religion
Loree 140
Rutgers University
70 Lipman Dr.
New Brunswick, NJ 08901
Tel: (732) 932-9641
Fax: (732) 932-1271
Website: www.virtualreligion.net
A comprehensive trove of information on religious, cultural, and philosophical studies. One of its most useful features is the Virtual Religion Index, which analyzes and highlights the content of religion-related websites.

VisionTV
Liberty Market Building
171 E. Liberty St.
Ste. 230
Toronto, Ontario M6K 3P6, Canada
Tel: (416) 368-3194
Fax: (416) 368-9774
Website: www.visiontv.ca
Available through Canadian cable and satellite services, this may be the world's first multifaith television network. VisionTV presents inspirational, insightful, and original programming that celebrates diversity and promotes understanding among people of different faiths

and cultures. No programs are allowed that would violate the company's stance on religious tolerance and respect.

World Congress of Faiths
London Inter Faith Centre
125 Salusbury Rd.
London NW6 6RG, United Kingdom
Tel: 44 (0) 20 8959 3129
Fax: 44 (0) 20-7604-3052
Website: www.worldfaiths.org
This group publishes a very important journal in the field of interfaith studies, *Interreligious Insight*. Its educational work encourages interfaith understanding and cooperation at all levels of society.

8

Suggestions for Other Resources

You must be the change you wish to see in the world.

—Mahatma Gandhi

Here are some of our other favorite resources—many of which can't be found on the Web—from old-fashioned books and journals to podcasts, posters, interactive games, and more. These are the resources from which this book's editors and contributors have learned and, in turn, taught about interfaith work. You will find more valuable interfaith resources from SkyLight Paths at the back of this book. Again, if you have a favorite resource to recommend, please tell us online at www.interreligious.org/InterActiveFaith. Your contribution may find its way into the next edition of this work.

Books and Articles

Following are a few publications that we believe belong on the bookshelves of anyone who is seriously engaged in interfaith work.

Albanese, Catherine L. *America: Religions and Religion*, 4th ed. Belmont, CA: Wadsworth, 2007.
Banchoff, Thomas, ed. *Democracy and the New Religious Pluralism*. New York: Oxford, 2007.
Barrows, John Henry, ed. *The World's Parliament of Religions*. 2 vols. Chicago: Parliament Publishing Company, 1893.
Berthrong, John H. *The Divine Deli: Religious Identity in the North American Cultural Mosaic*. Maryknoll, NY: Orbis Books, 1999.

Beversluis, Joel D., ed. *Sourcebook of the World's Religions: An Interfaith Guide to Religion and Spirituality.* Novato, CA: New World Library, 2000.

Bojer, Marianne, Marianne Knuth, and Collen Magner. *Mapping Dialogue: A Research Project Profiling Dialogue Tools and Processes for Social Change,* Version 2.0. Johannesburg, South Africa: Pioneers of Change Associates, 2006. (Available for free at www.pioneersofchange.net).

Coppola, David L, ed. *What Do We Want the Other to Teach about Us? Jewish, Christian, and Muslim Dialogues.* Fairfield, CT: Sacred Heart University Press, 2006.

Eck, Diana L. *A New Religious America: How a "Christian Country" Has Become the World's Most Religiously Diverse Nation.* San Francisco: HarperCollins, 2001.

Fisher, Mary Pat. *Living Religions,* 7th ed. Upper Saddle River, NJ: Prentice Hall, 2007.

Frew, Donald H., ed. *Sacred Spaces: 2004 Interfaith Sacred Space Design Competition.* San Francisco: Interfaith Center at the Presidio, 2004.

Halvorson, Peter L., and William M. Newman, eds. *Atlas of Religious Change in America, 1952–1990.* Glenmary, AL: Glenmary Research Center, 1994.

Idliby, Ranya, Suzanne Oliver, and Priscilla Warner. *The Faith Club: A Muslim, a Christian, a Jew—Three Women Search for Understanding.* New York: Free Press, 2006.

Jones, Dale E., et. al., eds. *Religious Congregations & Membership in the United States 2000.* Glenmary, AL: Glenmary Research Center, 2002.

Knitter, Paul F. *Introducing Theologies of Religions.* Maryknoll, NY: Orbis Books, 2002.

———. *No Other Name? A Critical Survey of Christian Attitudes Toward the World Religions.* Maryknoll, NY: Orbis Books, 1985.

Knitter, Paul F., ed. *The Myth of Religious Superiority: Multifaith Explorations of Religious Pluralism.* Maryknoll, NY: Orbis Books, 2005.

Küng, Hans. *Christians and World Religions: Paths to Dialogue.* Maryknoll, NY: Orbis Books, 1993.

Lindner, Eileen W. *Yearbook of American and Canadian Churches 2007*. Nashville: Abingdon, 2007.

Lundin, Jack W., ed. *One World, Many Voices: An Interfaith Songbook*. San Francisco: Interfaith Center at the Presidio, 2002.

Magonet, Jonathan. *Talking to the Other: Jewish Interfaith Dialogue with Christians and Muslims*. London: I.B. Taviris, 2003.

Markham, Ian S. *A World Religions Reader*, 2nd ed. Oxford: Blackwell Publishers, 2000.

Markham, Ian S., and Tinu Ruparell, eds. *Encountering Religion: An Introduction to the Religions of the World*. Oxford: Blackwell Publishers, 2001.

Marty, Martin E. *The One and the Many: America's Struggle for the Common Good*. Cambridge, MA: Harvard University Press, 1997.

Matlins, Stuart M., and Arthur J. Magida. *How to Be a Perfect Stranger: The Essential Religious Etiquette Handbook*, 4th ed. Woodstock, VT: SkyLight Paths Publishing, 2006.

McCarthy, Kate. *Interfaith Encounters in America*. New Brunswick, NJ: Rutgers, 2007.

Mead, Frank S., Samuel S. Hill, and Craig D. Atwood, eds. *Handbook of Denominations in the United States*, 12th ed. Nashville: Abingdon, 2005.

Melton, J. Gordon. *Encyclopedia of American Religions*, 7th ed. Detroit: Gale Group, 2007.

Mosher, Lucinda. *Faith in the Neighborhood: Understanding America's Religious Diversity*. New York: Seabury. An ongoing series: *Belonging* (2005), *Praying* (2006), *Loss* (2007).

Novak, Philip. *The World's Wisdom: Sacred Texts of the World's Religions*. San Francisco: HarperCollins, 1994.

O'Donnell, Kevin. *Inside World Religions: An Illustrated Guide*. Minneapolis: Fortress, 2007.

Ontario Multifaith Council on Spiritual and Religious Care. *Multifaith Information Manual: An Authoritative Guide to Religious Rights and Accommodations*, 4th ed. Toronto: OMCSRC, 2006.

Partridge, Christopher, ed. *New Religions: A Guide—New Religious Movements, Sects and Alternative Spiritualities*. New York: Oxford University Press, 2004.

Patel, Eboo. *Acts of Faith: The Story of an American Muslim, the Struggle for the Soul of a Generation.* Boston: Beacon Press, 2007.

Patel, Eboo, and Patrice Brodeur, eds. *Building the Interfaith Youth Movement: Beyond Dialogue to Action.* Lanham, MD: Rowman & Littlefield, 2006.

Peck, J. Richard. *Speaking Faith: The Essential Handbook for Religion Communicators,* 7th ed. New York: Religion Communicators Council, 2004.

Prothero, Stephen. *Religious Literacy: What Every American Needs to Know—and Doesn't.* San Francisco: HarperSanFrancisco, 2007.

Shafiq, Muhammed, and Mohammed Abu-Nimer. *Interfaith Dialogue: A Guide for Muslims.* Herndon, VA: International Institute of Islamic Thought, 2007.

Sharma, Arvind, ed. *Our Religions.* San Francisco: HarperCollins, 1993.

Smith, Huston. *The Illustrated World's Religions: A Guide to Our Wisdom Traditions.* San Francisco: HarperCollins, 1958.

_____. *The World's Religions: Our Great Wisdom Traditions.* San Francisco: HarperCollins, 1961.

Swidler, Leonard, Khalid Duran, and Reuven Firestone. *Trialogue: Jews, Christians, and Muslims in Dialogue.* New London, CT: Twenty-third Publications, 2007.

Thangaraj, M. Thomas. *Relating to People of Other Religions: What Every Christian Needs to Know.* Nashville: Abingdon, 1997.

Calendars

Interfaith calendars are available from many sources, which is all to the good since they are essential for anyone planning events and activities that will involve more than one faith. Every interfaith leader seems to have his or her own story about a scheduling goof that caused embarrassment. Learn to plan ahead—always consult interfaith calendars and then confirm with an actual community leader as to how a holiday is honored.

The oldest and one of the most respected print calendars is produced by the Multifaith Action Society in Vancouver, Canada. See www.multifaithaction.org for more information on the Multifaith Calendar. This resource was crafted for many years by David Spence. David now produces another calendar that includes both cultural and ecological holiday information. This Plurality Calendar is available through www.festaviva.ca.

Online alternatives also exist. For more than a dozen years, Delton Krueger has been producing an interfaith calendar online. See www.interfaithcalendar.org. The volunteers at Religions for Peace-USA and the Interfaith Center at the Presidio have produced an online multifaith calendar that pulls from a wide variety of sources. See www.rfpusa.org/links.

A final word about cross-honoring and shared days needs to be said. Americans should avail themselves of opportunities to experience another faith tradition through its outward, public forms, perhaps a ritual dinner like a Jewish seder or the Islamic iftar dinner that breaks the Ramadan fast, or at a religious festival, for example Diwali, Hinduism's festival of lights.

Interfaith organizations have increasingly come to utilize three holidays—Martin Luther King Jr. Day (January 15), the International Day of Peace (September 21), and Thanksgiving (the fourth Thursday in November)—as unique opportunities to host and honor interfaith activities that transcend framing by one tradition. Also many local interfaith community organizations have marked the anniversary of 9/11 with an interfaith prayer service, a peace/unity walk, a community service day, or a fundraising concert or gala.

CD-ROM

On Common Ground: World Religions in America, 2nd ed. Diana L. Eck and the Pluralism Project. New York: Columbia, 2002.

This interactive CD-ROM contains audio and visual clips, many case studies, and other fascinating features. It brings the reality of local religious diversity in the American context into sharp relief.

Etiquette Guides

By what title do you properly address an Episcopal, Shinto, or Muslim leader? Reverend Canon or Father? Sensei or Reverend? Imam or Sheikh? Confused? You are not alone. And it is awkward, because the very first step in interfaith encounters can be how to properly address the individual whom you are encountering. Here are a few resources that can help you navigate the waters:

- The online *Guide to Religious Etiquette* from the Tanenbaum Center for Interreligious Understanding can be found at www.tanenbaum.org/resources/ReligiousEtiquette.aspx.
- The chapter "Summary of Proper Forms for Addressing Leaders of Various Faiths" in Stuart M. Matlins and Arthur J. Magida's *How to Be a Perfect Stranger: The Essential Religious Etiquette Handbook* (listed above).
- The section on addressing leaders in *Emily Post's The Etiquette Advantage in Business: Personal Skills for Professional Success*, 2nd ed. (San Francisco: HarperCollins, 1999).

Games

One of the most unusual and enjoyable ways to learn about other religions is through playing board games or card games that test your skills while teaching key facts. The first of these is difficult to locate, but the second is readily available.

> Divine Madness: The World Religions Game. EMV Enterprises. PO Box 572, Farmington, CT 06304-0572. (860) 674-1172. Elizabeth J. M. Vecchio, 1995.
>
> Enlighten—Take a Spiritual Journey Around the World: A Game for Seekers ages 12 years and up. Enlighten Games Inc. 4A Cazneau Ave. Sausalito, CA 94965. (415) 331-3599. www.enlightengamesinc.com. Christa Reynolds, 2004.

Movies

The Hartley Film Foundation (see chapter 7 for contact information) has a wonderful collection of films, both specifically about particular traditions and also exploring interfaith themes. From their collection and through other sources, we recommend some of the following movies:

> *America's New Religious Landscape.* Alban Institute, PO Box 211, Annapolis Junction, MD 20701.
>
> *Beyond Theology: American Pluralism.* 2007. KTWU/Channel 11, Washburn University, Topeka, KS 66621.

Control Room, 2004. Lions Gate Entertainment, 2700 Colorado Ave., Santa Monica, CA 90404.

Dastaar: Defending Sikh Identity, 2005. Also Like Life Productions, www.alsolikelife.com.

Divan, 2003. Zeitgeist Films Ltd., 247 Centre St., New York, NY 10013

Divided We Fall: Americans in the Aftermath, 2006. New Moon Productions, www.dwf-film.com.

Faith & Belief: Five Major World Religions, 1992. Knowledge Unlimited Inc., PO Box 52, Madison, WI 53701.

God and Allah Need to Talk, 2007. 4219 Vinton Ave., Culver City, CA 90232.

Hiding and Seeking, 2004. Run Features, The Film Center Building, 630 9th Ave., Ste. 1213, New York, NY 10036.

Jews and Christians: A Journey of Faith. Auteur Productions, 10010 Newhall Rd., Potomac, Maryland 20854 (a study guide is also available).

Long Night's Journey into Day: South Africa's Search for Truth and Reconciliation, 2000. Iris Films, 2600 Tenth St., Ste. 413, Berkeley, CA 94710.

Me & the Mosque, 2005. National Film Board of Canada, Sales and Customer Service (D-10), PO Box 6100, Station Centre-ville, Montreal, QC, H3C 3H5 Canada.

Muhammad: Legacy of a Prophet, 2002. Kikim Media, 887 Oak Grove Ave., Ste. 201, Menlo Park, CA 94025.

Muslims (Frontline), 2003. Wellspring Media.

North of 49. Filmakers Library, 124 E. 40th St., New York, NY 10016.

Not in Our Town, 1995. California Working Group, 5867 Ocean View Dr., Oakland, CA 94618.

Three Faiths, One God: Judaism, Christianity, Islam. Auteur Productions, 10010 Newhall Rd., Potomac, Maryland 20854 (a study guide is also available).

Ties That Bind, 2006. Artistic Circles, 115 Linden Ave., Wilmette, IL 60091.

Trembling Before G-d, 2001. New Yorker Films.

Trust Me: Shalom, Salaam, Peace, 2003. Hartley Film Foundation, 49 Richmondville Ave., Ste. 204, Westport, CT 06880.

Posters

An interfaith "Golden Rule" poster is available from Scarboro Missions via Pflaum Publishing Group, 2621 Dryden Rd., Dayton, OH 45439. Tel: 1 (800) 543-4383, www.scarboromissions.ca/Store/index.php?cat=11.

An interfaith "Green Rule" poster is available from Faith & the Common Good, 47 Queen's Park Cres. E, Toronto, Ontario M5S 2C3, Canada. Tel: (416) 978-5306, www.faith-commongood.net/rule.

A whole collection of posters featuring multifaith festivals and information about particular religions is available from The Festival Shop at www.festivalshop.co.uk.

A "World Religion Map and Timeline," individual posters on the world's five major religions, and other resources are available from Knowledge Unlimited Inc., PO Box 52, Madison, WI 53701-0052. Tel: 1 (800) 356-2303, www.theKUstore.com.

Radio Shows and Podcasts

Several shows on the public airwaves and/or via podcast regularly address interfaith concerns:

Krista Tippet's *Speaking of Faith* on American Public Media
http://speakingoffaith.publicradio.org.

Welton Gaddy's *State of Belief* on AirAmerica Radio
www.airamerica.com/stateofbelief.

Maureen Fiedler's *Interfaith Voices* on independent stations throughout North America
www.interfaithradio.org.

Rowan Fairgrove's *Interfaith Today,* available as a podcast
www.interfaithtoday.org.

Religions for Peace-USA carries a series of podcasts that are interviews with renowned international religious leaders
www.rfpusa.org/podcast.

Bob Abernathy's PBS *Religion and Ethics Newsweekly*
www.pbs.org/wnet/religionandethics/rss/podcast.xml

Hartford Seminary features new podcasts regularly on its main site, www.hartsem.edu.

Appendix A

A Taxonomy of Interfaith

by Rev. Bud Heckman

Religions for Peace-USA undertook a survey of interfaith activities in the United States, building on the work done for the Pluralism Project at Harvard University by Lori Calmbacher and, much earlier, Christopher Coble. It confirmed what I'd already learned from my own experience—that virtually all interfaith activities and organizations tend toward one or the other of these poles on a continuum:

Dialogue	↔	Action
Right-brained/Arts/Heart-centered	↔	Left-brained/Reason/Head-centered
Formal	↔	Informal
Representative	↔	Grassroots
Organizational	↔	Personal
Staffed	↔	Unstaffed
Advocacy/Public Witness	↔	Conversation/Private Exploration
Particularistic/Differentiated	↔	Syncretistic/Blended

There are exceptions, of course. For example, some of the strongest and oldest interfaith organizations have developed a strong balance of both dialogue and action in their work, which I think is a key to their success. Some groups avoid advocacy altogether, often on account of an erroneous fear of violating the separation of church and state.

But almost all interfaith organizations fit into one of the eighteen different categories below. The categories in and of themselves do not mean anything. They are simply markers that help us understand the relationship between the different parts of the body that is the interfaith movement. Like class, gender, race, and other social categorizations, they help orient the reader, especially those struggling to define the shape of their interfaith work. The categories are guideposts to help find like-styled organizations or to aid in refining self-definition as the movement matures.

Chaplaincies. These include military chaplains, hospital chaplains, prison chaplains, and those at academic institutions.

Examples: Brown University's Office of the Chaplains and Religious Life; Newark's Interfaith Airport Chapel

As a measure of our country's growing diversity, in the year 2000, at the prompting of military representatives, Hartford Seminary started the country's first and only accredited program in Islamic chaplaincy. Its graduates serve both Muslims and non-Muslims alike in prisons, hospitals, and the military.

Ad-Hoc Groups. These organizations are formed by members of religious traditions for a specific purpose or in response to or for a one-time event, for example, 9/11 or the Iraq War. Many of them evolve into something more permanent.

Examples: Interfaith Association of Central Ohio (IACO); 9/11 Unity Walk or Interfaith Peace Walk

While the majority of interfaith organizations today were born in the mid-1990s or in reaction to 9/11, the IACO, interestingly enough, came together when then-president Reagan and then-president Gorbachev of the Soviet Union held a summit in Columbus in the mid-1980s, because someone wanted prayers offered from at least five faiths.

Congregationally Based Organizations. These groups are comprised of representatives from local congregations who meet to discuss issues of common concern, to build relationships, and to improve religious understanding among community members. It is one of the two most common forms of local interfaith organization.

Examples: Marin Interfaith Council; Inter-Faith Ministries of Wichita

For more than a century, the Inter-Faith Ministries of Wichita has been working with the support of dozens of local congregations. It is one of the best local interfaith organizations in the country to study if you are looking to start your own.

Resource Agencies. These organizations act as a source of religious information and education; many host dialogue events and other programs to educate the general public, promote religious discussion, and correct religious misconceptions.

Examples: Interfaith Center of New York; Tanenbaum Center for Interreligious Understanding

A handful of interfaith organizations are resource generators, publishing rich discussion guides and replicable do-it-yourself programs. Want a curriculum for introducing interfaith issues to elementary schoolchildren or a manual for handling religious diversity in the workplace? See the Tanenbaum Center for Interreligious Understanding. Want an interfaith calendar to keep track of events your local group is planning? See the Multifaith Action Society. Want to build a local interreligious council? See Religions for Peace-USA.

Interfaith Offices or Agencies (within one faith tradition). These agencies are run as a table or desk of a particular faith tradition to engage that tradition in interfaith work and issues.

Examples: General Commission on Christian Unity and Interreligious Concerns of The United Methodist Church; the U.S. Conference of Catholic Bishops, Secretariat of Ecumenical and Interreligious Affairs

These are some of the best places for you to get resources for and advice about local interfaith work, and increasingly these offices are appearing in other-than-Jewish-and-Christian faith traditions. To name a few, Covenant of the Goddess, Jains, Zoroastrians, Scientologists, and the Bahá'í all have an interfaith representative assigned to work with the public in the United States.

Dialogue Groups. These groups meet for discussion and mutual edification. They make up the bulk of interfaith organizations in the country. They are informal, unstaffed, and can be a bit sporadic about their meeting schedule.

Examples: Partners in Dialogue in Columbia, South Carolina; Jewish-Palestinian Living Room Dialogue Group of San Mateo County, California

There are also formal versions of these dialogues, like the ones sponsored by the Catholic Church described in chapter 1.

Interfaith Ministries/Seminaries. These groups have ministers who perform interfaith—or, as I have called them, multipath—services, addressing the needs of people with multiple belongings in one diverse grouping.

Examples: The Interfaith Seminary (of New York); The New Seminary

Small "house church" meeting groups and education centers are showing up in out-of-the-way places. At a big forum on immigration and religion in Maine, I remember being sidetracked by a peppering of questions about a new group that had formed in the area and its efforts to set up a satellite seminary in rented space at the local Christian theological school.

For-Profit Groups. These are money-making enterprises whose business is to provide resources for interfaith organizations.

Examples: Interfaith Marketplace; Interfaith Consulting Group; CoNexus Press (a former publishing and distribution engine for interfaith work)

Interfaith work is such a new area that there are few for-profit entities specifically focused on resourcing it. A handful of publishers, distributors, and consultants have sprouted up.

Media Groups. These are bodies whose objectives are to disseminate information about current religious/interfaith-related news and who effectively educate the public on U.S. religious diversity and issues.

Examples: Religion Communicators Council; Faith & Values Media

One sign of the broadening that is occurring in American religion is the expansion of membership of the National Interfaith Cable Coalition to include new faith traditions and interfaith groups. Both Religions for Peace-USA and the Islamic Society of North America have joined since 2004.

National and International Organizations. These bodies differ widely in their makeup and purposes but function as connection points in the web of interfaith activity.

Examples: Religions for Peace and Religions for Peace-USA; the Interfaith Alliance; International Association for Religious Freedom; Parliament of the World's Religions; United Religions Initiative

All of the contributors to this book have some affiliation with at least one of these organizations.

Chapters of National and International Organizations. These are local, state, or regional chapters that grow out of or belong to a larger interfaith entity on the national or international scene.

Examples: Tulsa Interfaith Alliance; Hawaii Conference of Religions for Peace; South Florida Interfaith Worker Justice

These groups are either dedicated solely to the mission of the parent organization or affiliated but also involved with a larger range of issues.

Umbrella Organizations. These are associations of interfaith organizations, formed by gathering separate, possibly unrelated interfaith organizations and/or representatives to develop and sustain dialogue about the interfaith movement and to engage in interfaith work.

Examples: North American Interfaith Network; Southern California Interfaith Network

These are great places to find the lay of the land. The North American Interfaith Network holds a popular annual meeting that attracts people from many different types of efforts. It is a colleague sharing forum, where one can learn new ideas.

Religious Leaders/Clergy Groups. These groups gather representatives of faith traditions to develop lines of communication for information exchange, mutual understanding, and common action.

Examples: InterFaith Conference of Metropolitan Washington (IFCMW); Lexington Interfaith Clergy Association

Chapter contributor Clark Lobenstine's IFCMW is one of the most exemplary groups in the country of this type. When religious leaders and clergy come together as official representatives of their faith traditions, we call these encounters "interreligious" rather than "interfaith." The term *interreligious* is rarely reflected in the name of the organization, however, owing to the broader acceptance and understanding of the term interfaith.

Retreat/Conference Centers. These places host interfaith gatherings, such as conferences and retreats, or provide services for the scope of religious traditions.

Examples: Mary & Joseph Retreat Center; Trinity Conference Center

To make ends meet and re-enliven their original missions, many religious centers that grew out of a particular tradition (usually Christian) are now catering to more diverse audiences.

Social Issue(s) and Action Groups. These organizations invite members of various traditions to address a single issue of common concern—for example homelessness, drug abuse, or the environment.

Examples: AIDS Interfaith Network of Sacramento; Interfaith Council for Homeless Families of Morris County; Maine Interfaith Power and Light

Many of these groups have been historically related to the national network called the Interfaith Community Ministries Network (ICMN), started by Christian ecumenical leaders. The ICMN is no longer in its heyday. The three largest and most vibrant networks of such organizations today are the Interfaith Alliance, Interfaith Worker Justice, and Interfaith Hospitality Network (now Family Promise).

Women's Groups. Obviously, this category includes all those groups that are comprised of female members only.

Examples: The Faith Club; Women Transcending Boundaries; Women of Faith

Having had the privilege of being one of only two male observers at the historic national interfaith conference "Women in Religion in the 21st Century" at the Interchurch Center in New York City in 2006, I have seen how women can uniquely approach interfaith dialogue when it is left entirely to their own gender.

Student/Youth Groups. These groups are run for, and usually by, youth or students at universities and academic institutions.

Examples: Campus Interfaith at Wilkes University; Interfaith Dialogue Student Association at Texas A&M University; North American Interreligious Youth Network; Interfaith Youth Core

At Princeton Theological Seminary in the winter of 2005, the first-ever summit of college interfaith groups was held under the banner "Coming Together." Organizers expected fifteen to twenty colleges to participate. They had three times that many. The group is expanding still and now meets on a yearly basis. Contact information for local college interfaith groups can be found through Interfaith Youth Core or Religions for Peace-USA.

Other Types. There are many new things in interfaith work coming onto the horizon or found off the beaten path.

For example, are you a quilter? Did you know that you can learn about other faiths through quilting? That is right, quilting. A Massachusetts-based group has started the Faith Quilts project, which brings people of different faiths together to integrate their faith sharing with the common activity of quilting. A how-to guide, video, and other resources are available.

While this book was in production a new group called Common Tables was formed by some friends in Colorado. Its focus? Bringing small groups together in homes for interfaith dialogue around a shared meal. It is a brilliant idea. While it must be done sensitively, meals provide a perfect environment for rubbing elbows and sharing traditions and beliefs.

Before you reinvent the wheel in your community, get on the Internet or on the phone and start hunting for models and asking questions. One of the best places to start is with the interfaith affairs office of your own religious community. Virtually every religious community has a person, office, or committee that handles interfaith relations. They are there to help you.

Appendix B

A Closer Look at Swidler's "Dialogue Decalogue"

By Rev. Dr. Francis Tiso

Just about everyone who becomes involved in interfaith dialogue comes across the guidelines for dialogue designed by Temple University's Leonard Swidler. His 1983 "Dialogue Decalogue" is a touchstone work from which many others have framed their approaches to interfaith dialogue. (See note 3 of chapter 1 for the original reference).

In a post-9/11 world, are these guidelines still relevant? Father Francis Tiso takes a closer look at this important contribution to the ground on which spoken dialogue has taken place.

First Commandment: The primary purpose of dialogue is to learn, that is, to change and grow in the perception and understanding of reality, and then to act accordingly.

Second Commandment: Interreligious, interideological dialogue must be a two-sided project—within each religious or ideological community and between religious or ideological communities.

Third Commandment: Each participant must come to the dialogue with complete honesty and sincerity. Conversely, each participant must assume a similar complete honesty and sincerity in the other partners.

Fourth Commandment: In interreligious, interideological dialogue we must not compare our ideals with our partner's practice, but our ideals with our partner's ideals, our practice with our partner's practice.

Fifth Commandment: Each participant must define himself. Conversely, the one interpreted must recognize herself in the interpretation.

Sixth Commandment: Each participant must come to the dialogue with no hard and fast assumptions as to where the points of disagreement are.

Seventh Commandment: Dialogue can take place only between equals.

Eighth Commandment: Dialogue can take place only on the basis of mutual trust.

Ninth Commandment: Persons entering into interreligious, interideological dialogue must be at least minimally self-critical of both themselves and their own religious or ideological traditions.

Tenth Commandment: Each participant eventually must attempt to experience the partner's religion or ideology "from within."

Swidler's "Decalogue" has inspired many interreligious activists over the years. But in the decades since these words were first published, have we learned anything more about the best ways to reach across faith lines? I think we have, and those of us who are committed to the long haul need to recognize that some aspects of the "Decalogue" need to be revised.

First Commandment

I think we have learned that the primary purpose of dialogue may not be simply to "learn, change, grow, and act" but something on the one hand more subtle and on the other more concrete. It would be difficult to say which is "primary" because in practice interreligious spoken dialogue has adopted many models corresponding to a broad spectrum of goals. Certainly, a search for common values and goals, and growth in the direction of interpersonal communion has been one very important purpose of dialogue. This is quite subtle and depends to a great extent on the spiritual authenticity of the persons in dialogue. But also—and this last point provides a real service to communities of faith—a primary purpose of dialogue would have to include the production of useful recommendations, reports, and common statements; there has to be a product to ensure a line of credible communication between those who do interreligious dialogue and those who are members of a particular religious community.

Second Commandment

The quality of communication not only between the dialogue partners but also between the dialogue partners and their own respective communities is thus crucial. Otherwise, spoken dialogue is not an interpersonal interface between two living communities of faith. Swidler saw this second commandment as a way of ensuring "that the whole community [will] eventually learn and change, moving towards an ever more perceptive insight into reality." As a background to this comment we easily detect the American innovator in the philosophy of science Thomas Kuhn's "paradigm shift" applied to the sociology of knowledge. There is an assumption here that religions on their own do not currently possess a sufficiently perceptive insight into reality, but that interreligious dialogue will in some way improve things. If the participants in spoken dialogue hold to that notion, then they will learn and change through dialogue. But if the participants are persuaded that their religion is sufficient unto itself, complete, and unalterable as to both means and ends, they may wish to restrict the goal of dialogue to social cooperation and mutual instruction so as to diminish intercommunity tensions. I have observed that Swidler's Second Commandment, itself taken as a paradigm, is applicable only in settings in which everyone comes from the same cultural matrix: progressive, postindustrial, university-educated persons sharing a common language. A very good example of this would be the Zen/Ch'an-Catholic Dialogue that meets in late January every year in Northern California. This group is particularly characterized by a desire to move together "towards an ever more perceptive insight into reality." Many other dialogue groups would not perceive themselves in this way, even though they may be sincerely committed to ongoing programs of dialogue.

Third Commandment

In any human relationship, complete honesty and sincerity are morally necessary for cooperation and mutual respect. However, human beings approach such a high level of morality only asymptotically. There is a Tibetan proverb to the effect that "since all human beings have both good and bad traits, the wise person knows how to work with the good and avoid the effects of the bad." In a paper for the MidWest Dialogue of Catholics and Muslims, Professor Anas Malik of John Carroll University showed how ambiguous elements in human interaction can, when properly acknowledged, actually contribute to a positive outcome. The real problem with what Swidler calls a "false front" lies in a certain kind of spiritual dishonesty in which a person who does not in fact practice the religion he or she is "representing" in a dialogue conversation actually corrupts the conversation with his or her own ambiguities. This phenomenon is worse than that of a person who upholds the ideal of a religion without having the ability to understand or practice it satisfactorily. At least the latter type of person will say things that other members of his or her faith community will recognize as coherent with their own beliefs. The sense that an interreligious dialogue is something coming from the heart of a community, and not merely a conversation among individuals who are cut off methodologically and ideologically from living traditions of religious life, is less injured by the clumsy but sincere believer than by the sophisticated revisionist.

Fourth Commandment

The habit of comparing bad practice on one side with high ideals on the other, or of comparing a "golden age" with a "dark age" is a characteristic of the worst kind of debating strategy: denigration, which always has a deadening effect on spoken dialogue. For this reason, accurate historical and doctrinal information must be made available to participants in dialogue. Putting this principle into practice, I have been working with a team of colleagues on a balanced and accurate chronology of Muslim–Christian interactions over the past two years. A few years ago, I worked with a Buddhist colleague to draw up glossaries of Buddhist and Catholic Christian terminology based on authoritative sources. Since historical behavior often differs widely from the ideals of religious traditions, it is important to know the facts and to respect the explanations given for the evident discrepancies by each side. This is the first step toward the "healing of memories" that humanity so greatly desires from the work of dialogue.

Fifth Commandment

Self-definition sounds like a good idea, but in practice it is dauntingly complex. First of all, there is the obvious problem of microsectarianism. There are individuals who have "declared" themselves to be bishops, high lamas, imams, enlightened masters, and so forth. On that basis, they may claim to represent authentically a particular tradition without in fact having a working relationship with any historic community of faith. Representatives of the Catholic Church are at times required to use the term the *Roman Catholic Church* in certain dialogues, especially in ecumenical milieu, since many Protestants consider themselves authentic instances of Catholic faith. However, the term *Roman Catholic* excludes a significant portion of Eastern or "Greek" Catholics who have every right to be considered an inherent part of historic Catholicism and, unlike Protestants, are in full communion with all Catholics of the various historic rites. So it is not so easy to define oneself in the dialogue milieu. A great amount of time can be spent on such exercises in clarification, sometimes distracting the participants from the topic set in the agenda.

However, Swidler is right that when, for example, a Catholic dialogue partner interprets or attempts to restate what a Muslim participant has just said, the Muslim has the right to affirm or deny the accuracy of the restatement, and vice versa. Fellow participants at the table may wish to refine what has been stated by both participants, to confirm or moderate the claims made, and to clarify what may not have been understood. Often, misunderstandings are the result of the context from which the speaker has set up his or her interpretation. A person rooted in a tradition with deep historical roots has to make substantial efforts to recognize when he or she is interpreting another religion in terms that have more to do with his or her own tradition than with the tradition being interpreted. Failure to make that effort can lead either to syncretism, in which basic differences are ignored or smoothed over by sly leveling tactics, or to exclusivism, in which even the most basic human commonalities are dismissed as irrelevant in light of the one true revelation from which the speaker is constructing his or her model of reality.

Sixth Commandment

The problem of "hard and fast assumptions as to where the points of disagreement are" would not exist if people came to the dialogue table properly prepared by prior study and conversation. Unfortunately, there is such an immediate need for interreligious dialogue that sometimes individuals come into the circle of conversation unprepared. Along with being unfamiliar with the issues being discussed, there are also deeply rooted problems of attitude. We still encounter religious leaders who are convinced that dialogue is an occasion for debate in which the winner will persuade the other participants to convert. The writings of Ismail Raji al-Faruqi, particularly his much reprinted book (edited by Ataullah Siddiqui), *Islam and Other Faiths* (Islamic Foundation), clearly outlines a set of rules that, were they to be implemented in Swidler's world, would completely undermine the current hard-won progress of dialogue with Muslims. In particular, chapter 9, "Rights of Non-Muslims Under Islam: Social and Cultural Aspects," presents an Islamic case for a kind of tolerance that on the surface seems quite rational, but that would in practice lead to the most gross violations of human rights imaginable, short of outright slavery. Al-Faruqi's spirited defense of Islamic rationality remains a major influence on contemporary Muslim thinking and has strong resonances with another widely read thinker, Tariq Ramadan, who is also convinced that Christianity is too dogmatic to be the basis for a modern civilization and that Islam should ally itself with Christianity's secularist critics. It should not come as a surprise to participants in dialogue with Muslims that this is the intellectual gymnasium in which many progressive or moderate Muslims have had their basic training. My counsel would be to take people as they are and be prepared with the chronologies, glossaries, and general bibliographies that will be necessary to bring all participants at the table toward a more dynamic approach to dialogue. Such a dynamic approach will lead to a softening of the hard edges based on those "hard and fast assumptions" about the other, without excluding voices that express the deeply felt concerns of the respective faith communities.

Seventh Commandment

Is there ever a dialogue between equals? Just as in legal terminology equality before the law is a valuable fiction that protects the basic rights of the individual, so too in the dialogue setting equality is a psychological fiction that enables participants to open up to the other participants in a conversation. As a basic attitude, it ensures that the listeners are working as hard as the speakers—that they are attentive to what is being said, that they have read the draft presentations before coming to the meeting, that they have done some additional research on their own, and above all that they believe that they can learn something of genuine value from those who are speaking. I once presented a paper to a dialogue of scholars in which it was clear that few of the participants had read the orientation text, which had been sent out several weeks before the meeting. One after another, participants asked questions that were clearly covered in the materials they had received, to the frustration of those who had done their homework. The lesson from this is that in spite of much work on dialogue preparation, theory and method, and concrete experience, we still need to be prepared to work with the obstacles to dialogue. In a way, there are no laws, no guidelines, no assumptions except practical ones of attitudinal and moral strategy. At best, you should strive to do unto others as you would have others do to you.

Eighth Commandment

The issue of mutual trust is again a matter more of attitude than of law. Over the years of Jewish–Catholic dialogue, guided with such care and insight by Dr. Eugene Fisher of the United States Conference of Catholic Bishops (USCCB), we have learned to deal with crises with great candor. Crises are inevitable. Whether asked or not, the question that occasionally appears at the edge of the forest is, "Do we trust you enough to believe that we can work through this crisis by speaking with one another honestly?" The alternative is to break off the relationship, which is always a serious risk because so much energy is required to reconstruct a broken dialogue. In theory we would prefer the psychological comfort of a serene and reasoned exchange of views, but in practice it is better to have an emotional dialogue than no dialogue at all. Mutual trust develops from those moments in dialogue when we are willing to be candid about the feelings that world events stir up in our communities. Candor and integrity in expressing our concerns discloses the degree of spiritual freedom in the hearts of those committed to dialogue.

Ninth Commandment

Is it possible to stand within a religious tradition with integrity and conviction but also to have a healthy attitude of self-criticism? In the dialogue setting, this is not easy to accomplish. In the first place, going back to the Fourth Commandment, we have to be sure that our self-criticism is directed toward the appropriate category of theory, practice, or history. Among members of a religious tradition, conversation about the disappointing ways the tradition is being lived in a particular setting are not uncommon. Moving from such in-house conversations to the dialogue table requires a great deal of mutual trust. To develop that degree of trust presupposes years of effort; the spirit of healthy self-criticism needs to be fostered over time. Unfortunately there are some people who engage in interreligious dialogue because they are committed to a critical and even destructive program within their own tradition. These are not very good representatives of the traditions, but they are part of the landscape and cannot be ignored. It should be obvious that someone representing a religious tradition should be deeply grounded in that tradition and be familiar with numerous aspects of the tradition, including areas of strength and weakness. However, even as a representative, it might not be appropriate to use a dialogue conversation as a sounding board for one's disagreements with a particular policy or belief in one's own religion. One of the problems of "activist" dialogue, in which speakers openly declare themselves to be "representing only myself," is precisely that such dialogues have little to say to the institutions that are struggling with issues of demographics, immigration, identity, legal challenges, and evolving structures of governance. If the dialogue does not speak with a voice of at least some authority within our communities, it is clear that over time, the relevance of interreligious dialogue for policy making and activism within the traditions will diminish. So perhaps dialogue participants need to ask who or what the "self" that is being criticized is when we engage in self-criticism.

Tenth Commandment

How do we, as dialogue participants, "attempt to experience the partner's religion ... 'from within'"? This is perhaps Swidler's most problematic commandment. He claims, following the lead of Raimondo Panikkar, that "a Christian will never fully understand Hinduism if he is not, in one way or another, converted to Hinduism." As we know from conversations with Buddhists and Hindus, Panikkar's remarks, which seem very open-minded to Christians, are seen as insidious to others, even without the reciprocal claim being articulated (i.e., that a

Hindu should become in some way a Christian to understand Christianity). I can recall a large-scale international dialogue in 1995 at which Panikkar's book, *The Unknown Christ of Hinduism*, was decried as a missionary tract designed to seduce Hindus and Buddhists into finding Christ and thereupon embracing the Christian faith. In fact, the book was meant to orient Christians toward a Christocentric encounter with Hinduism, but it is interesting that this good intention has been misread by both sides of the conversation. In reality, a Hindu will simply find a Hindu category for Jesus Christ and keep his or her Hinduism intact. Similarly, Christians devise "inclusivist" Christian theologies of world religions, keeping intact the universalistic claims of the gospel message while showing religious respect for the truths found in other traditions. Where Swidler and Panikkar have broken fertile ground, in my opinion, would be in a viable search for the authentically human in all religious experience. That search requires not only theological depth and clarity but also a strong and persistent engagement with the practice of the inner life in our respective traditions. Then, to articulate such experience in spoken dialogue, participants need to find or perhaps to hammer out a common philosophical language. This is a task that will require generations. Pope John Paul II, in the encyclical on philosophy's relationship to faith, *Fides et Ratio*, suggested that this would be a valuable project (section 72) that should engage philosophers, contemplatives, and activists working together in the dialogue setting. This project was begun in eleventh-century Spain among Jews, Muslims, and Christians, and led to the flowering of Western Scholastic theology in the thirteenth century. It seems that the thread of that conversation, frayed but not entirely broken, needs to be rewoven in our times.

Appendix C

A Formal Model
The West Coast Dialogue of Catholics and Muslims

by Rev. Dr. Francis Tiso

Appendix C offers a more detailed look at one formal bilateral interfaith dialogue described in shorter form by Father Francis Tiso in chapter 1. Of course, not everyone will be interested in creating such a structured dialogue. However, some of the planning processes and exercises of engagement described herein are adaptable to other forms of dialogue. It is a snapshot, if you will, of the world of religions as institutions relating to one another.

The West Coast Dialogue of Catholics and Muslims that was held on May 21–23, 2007, provides an excellent model of what goes into planning, organizing, convening, and running a spoken dialogue event.

Ground Rules

The following list of rules for setting up formal dialogue was the underlying agreement that brought these groups together:

1. A single "round" of Muslim–Catholic dialogue will be set up to take up a topic of mutual interest, concluding with the publication of a common document.

2. In this way, we can contribute solid recommendations to our leadership that will bear fruit as our communities grow in their faith commitment.

3. The round will be limited to four years, a quadrennium.

4. There will be at least eight and at most ten official members from each side. Each official member of the dialogue will make a commitment to being present for the four-year round at all sessions; each annual session will last approximately two days.

5. Each official member will present a paper at least once in the quadrennium, and will contribute to the drafting of common documents, recommendations, and press releases in support of the work of staff.

6. Each official member will be approved by the respective co-chairs on the basis of the ability of the member-candidate to work actively and effectively with an interreligious dialogue group.

7. The sponsoring organizations will work out an agreement on shared funding for housing, meals, and travel.

8. Observers are permitted to attend the meetings of the dialogue, but must be approved by the respective co-chairs. Observers do not give presentations, but may participate in discussion.

9. If necessary, a member who must be absent from a dialogue may appoint a substitute with the approval of the respective co-chair. Substitutes are to be briefed by the co-chair (or other members) before coming to the dialogue meeting.

10. Each member will understand that active communication with staff and with other members of the dialogue is crucial for the success of the quadrennium.

11. Whenever possible, members will have a working partner from the other faith in order to promote dialogue on the local level between annual meetings.

12. The dialogue meeting takes place once a year. It is a regional dialogue of experts who exchange ideas and experiences in order to bring suggestions, observations, information, and recommendations to their local communities. The goal of the dialogue is to produce sound documents such as press releases, talking points, reports, and resources that represent the beliefs, values, and best practices of our respective communities. In this way, we hope to advance and deepen the commonalities that unite us as people of faith.

13. Local initiatives will be reported at the start of every annual meeting, thus providing an opportunity to encourage, evaluate, and reflect on the experiences of our communities.

14. An annual regional dialogue is not the best instrument for carrying out activist programs, which are more effectively implemented on the local level. However, the regional dialogue benefits greatly from shared reflection on new initiatives, trends in our communities, special challenges, and local needs.

15. Advantages to both sides:

  • We gain personal knowledge of key leadership.
  • Our respective teachings are accurately conveyed to leadership.
  • We produce recommendations and reports to strengthen our communities in the face of challenges.
  • Everyone gets a working knowledge of the way each community functions: structures, authority, law, communication, and agencies.
  • We gain access to the international connections that are important to the way we live our faith.
  • It gives us an opportunity to articulate concerns, issues, values, and difficulties that have arisen in our communities.

Schedule

The following schedule with accompanying recommendations offers a model for such dialogue. It was sent out as a memorandum to all participants in the West Coast Dialogue in March 2007:

MONDAY, MAY 21

2:00 p.m. Check in
3:00 Welcome remarks by co-chairs.
Reports on local initiatives and shared concerns at this time.
4:30 Muslim prayer time
5:00 Catholic Eucharist and Vespers
6:00 Dinner
7:00 Presentation: "Joseph"
8:00 p.m. Muslim prayer time
8:20–9:15 Discussion

TUESDAY, MAY 22

7:45 a.m. Catholic morning prayer
8:30 Breakfast
9:30 Presentation: "Yusuf"
Discussion

10:30 Break
10:45–11:30 Discussion on these narratives and related.
11:30 Catholic midday prayer
12:00 p.m. Lunch
1:00 Muslim prayer time.
1:30 Presentation: "Christian Virtue Ethics in Narrative Context"
Discussion

2:30 Break
2:45 Presentation: "Muslim Virtue Ethics in Narrative Context"
Discussion

4:00 Break
4:30 Muslim prayer time
4:30 Catholic Eucharist and Vespers
6:00 Catered dinner offered by the local mosque community
7:30–8:30 Open Discussion: Conclusions on our work on narrative and
   virtue ethics.

WEDNESDAY MAY 23

7:45 a.m. Catholic morning prayer Eucharist
8:30 Breakfast
9:15 Future Plans
10:30 Departures for those who need to
12:00 p.m. Lunch and last departures

Guidelines

As a further example of process, the following directions were provided along with the schedule in order to involve more participants
actively in the dialogue:

Focus points: The virtues, values, and issues that we find in these
narratives include, but are not restricted to: courage, family soli-

darity, social engagement, reconciliation after betrayal, self-discipline, immigration, how communities address problems, and how communities appropriate faith and apply faith to life.

A new role in the dialogue: The moderators are asked to regulate question-and-answer periods and discussion, with particular attention to timing and to orderly inclusion of all who wish to speak.

Volunteers have been assigned to organize prayer services, set up the catered meal, assist with premeeting communications, and prepare welcome packets.

Name signs are used to facilitate communication; the cards are large enough to be read from across the room.

All presenters should send out an abstract, outline, or full text about three to four weeks before the meeting.

Copies of the full presentation should be made available to all participants.

Fr. Tiso will take minutes during sessions and will draft a press release.

Questionnaire

The following questionnaire, designed to streamline the planning process, was handed out to each participant at the introductory session. It was to be completed and returned after lunch on Tuesday so that the future planning session could be prepared for Wednesday morning. In fact, this procedure greatly improves the planning session. Data from the questionnaire are written on a newsprint paper easel before the session to facilitate the conversation that must arrive at consensus. The method gives due recognition to all suggestions and allows them to be critiqued in a relatively short amount of time. As a written document, it becomes part of the record of this meeting. Those participants who could not stay for the final morning are still "counted in" the planning process by their responses on the questionnaire, which contains the following, as an example:

- Please update and correct your contact information and that of any members of the dialogue who may be absent.
- What would be your preferred location and dates for next year's dialogue?

- The topic for next year should conclude our quadrennium of study on narratives. In previous meetings, we have explored Methods of Scriptural Interpretation; Narratives Observed and Put into Practice; Virtue Ethics in Narrative Context. Perhaps our next topic could be to relate narrative to theology and/or spirituality? Or should we look at ways to apply our study of narrative to pastoral situations that we are encountering? Other ideas?
- Who should be our presenters and what themes should they take up?
- Who should be chosen to facilitate prayer and liturgy next time?
- Evaluations: What could we be doing better? What would you like to do for this dialogue that you have not yet been able to do?
- Nominations of new participants, to be approved by the co-chairs.
- How would you like to publish the results of our presentations over the past quadrennium?

What Kind of Environment Do the Dialogue Participants Inhabit?

An anthropologist observer might expect this to be a temporary encampment for hunters and gatherers in the bush. In reality, the participants have elected to continue nearly a decade of these annual meetings in the manner of a religious retreat. The setting this year is a Catholic retreat center on a pleasant ridge not far from the California coastline. The architecture is reminiscent of a monastery, with guest rooms set up along a central garden area, somewhat like a cloister. The whole environment is beautifully landscaped. Another group, Catholic candidates for the diaconate and their wives, are meeting in other facilities of the retreat center, giving the participants a glimpse of Catholic diversity in Southern California. The dialogue meetings take place in a large room with tables set up in a square that allows everyone to be face to face. Meals are taken in a large refectory adjacent to the meeting room.

How Did They Get There?

Most of the participants arrive by motor vehicle from nearby parts of Southern California; some must fly in from San Jose, Seattle, Yakima, and San Francisco.

How Were They Appointed or Evaluated for This Work?

This dialogue group was set up about a decade ago through collaborative planning by the Secretariat of Ecumenical and Interreligious Affairs (SEIA) of the United States Conference of Catholic Bishops and Muslim leaders in Southern California from the Islamic Society of Orange County and the Islamic Education Center of Orange County. The SEIA, working through the associate director for Interreligious Affairs, was carrying out a mandate from the Bishops' Committee on Ecumenical and Interreligious Affairs, which is the agency of the national Bishops' Conference authorized to promote dialogue. Thus, this is a formal dialogue, authorized officially by the Catholic Church in the United States and engaging experts and leadership at a high level. Participants in the dialogue are selected in consultation with the co-chairs of the meeting; participants are named by the co-chairs themselves, by the associate director of SEIA, or by other leaders in the respective communities. The co-chairs approve the naming of participants and occasional observers. On the Catholic side, the diocesan bishop or religious superior of each participant is asked to approve nominees by sending SEIA a letter confirming that the nominee is a Catholic in good standing who has already contributed significantly to interreligious relations.

What Preparatory Work Is Done and by Whom Before the Meeting?

The SEIA associate director and his staff do most of the logistical work, following through on suggestions given at the final session of each meeting. The final session also determines the dates of the next meeting, recommended locations, overall scheduling suggestions, recommendations for presenters and moderators of sessions, and topics. Presenters draft their papers beforehand and, ideally, send them to the associate director, who forwards them electronically or in any other required format to participants about a month before the meeting. He also collects valuable documentation that might support the dialogue and sends it to participants in the course of the year. From time to time, he advises the co-chairs on preparations for the dialogue and makes suggestions to the presenters on their topics. Some logistical matters and communications are facilitated by volunteers on the Muslim side.

What Are the Participants' Qualifications?

Participants usually have an advanced academic or theological degree from accredited institutions. One group of participants consists of the Ecumenical and Interreligious Officers of the participating Catholic Dioceses of the region; the Catholic officer is partnered with a leading imam who collaborates with the Catholic officer in the course of the year. The idea is to maintain working contact from one annual regional meeting to the next. At the start of every annual meeting, partners report on local activities to the regional group. Other participants are not partnered, but are involved in interreligious teaching or community activities. Some participants have taken training courses in interreligious and ecumenical dialogue, such as those sponsored by SEIA.

What Do They Do in Formal Sessions?

Formal sessions begin with prayer, followed by an oral presentation of twenty to thirty minutes on the selected topic. There are four major presentations in the course of two days of dialogue. A moderator guides discussion of the presentation, which can continue for approximately an hour, with time for a break of fifteen to twenty minutes. While the moderator ensures that discussion is orderly and that interruptions are kept to a time limit, the associate director takes notes on a laptop that will be preserved as the official minutes of the dialogue. These notes will also be mined for the press release and for suggestions for future meetings.

What Do They Do Informally Between Sessions?

During breaks, the participants share tea, coffee, and informal conversation in small groups in and around the meeting room. After the evening session, participants may take walks, again in small groups of two or three, to discuss the day's events and to reflect on what worked and what was less helpful. Conversations also address personal concerns and problems that have emerged in our communities in recent months. There are frequent discussions of Islamophobia in the American mass media, with its consequences in terms of concrete acts of disrespect and violence against persons and institutions.

Are There Hierarchies in Place Before the Meeting?

Yes, the co-chairs are all recognized leaders in their respective communities. Official participants or "members" of the dialogue are imams, scholars, ecumenical officers, or other trained personnel. Observers may be community activists, lay leaders, teachers, or young or newly ordained clergy.

What Are the Divisions of Labor within the Structure of a Meeting?

We have indicated the roles of co-chairs, moderators, the SEIA associate director, members, and observers. Co-chairs are distinguished from the moderators of sessions; the moderators keep the discussion orderly by assuring that all who wish to speak are called on in order and by limiting the time each person may speak. Here is a description of the overall responsibilities of co-chairs in service to the dialogue:

a. The co-chairs make a keynote presentation at the introductions session by way of orientation to the theme of the meeting, bringing in current issues and concerns in our communities.
b. They intervene from time to time in their own voices, responding to inquiries that require their expertise.
c. They intervene to remind the dialogue group of the particular needs of our communities, thus representing the official voice of the faith communities convened at the dialogue table.

Then, between meetings, the co-chairs have additional duties:

a. They approve the appointment of new members to the dialogue.
b. They approve the presence of new observers.
c. They report to appropriate oversight groups (e.g., Shura Council, umbrella organizations, Bishops' Council on Ecumenical and Interreligious Affairs) on the contents of the dialogue; talking points are prepared to accompany the press release.

d. They make inquiries and forward important information to the general convener or staff person.

e. They approve and promote knowledge of the dialogue in mass media where appropriate.

f. They assist in resolving difficulties and misunderstandings that may emerge in the faith communities, in mass media, or among dialogue members.

What Rituals Are Enacted?

There is usually a short prayer at the start of sessions and at meals. Islamic prayer times and Catholic Eucharist and Liturgy of the Hours are incorporated into the schedule. Participants may observe the prayer rituals of each side. Persons who arrive late are welcomed by the associate director. Packets with the schedule, the text of presentations, a pad and pencil, and name signs are prepared and given out as part of the welcoming process.

What Happens at Meal Time?

Food is halal and served buffet style. Apart from a short blessing, formality is kept to a minimum. Catholics and Muslims mingle at table and continue their informal conversations, in some cases building on years of friendship and collaboration. One catered halal meal is offered by the Muslim side.

Roles of Men? Roles of Women?

The male participants are in the majority. Approximately four out of ten on the Muslim side and one out of nine on the Catholic side are women. However, the women are engaged as presenters and are very active in the discussion process.

How Is the Work of a Meeting Concluded?

The final session, which is dedicated to future planning, makes extensive use of the questionnaire (which also serves as a way to affirm attendance and to record corrections in contact information). The SEIA associate director plans the final session on the basis of the information given in the questionnaire, which is collected at lunch on the second day. He also works through informal consultation with participants over meals. At the session, participants are presented with viable alternatives in terms of dates, topics, and presenters taken from the questionnaires. Usually the planning session is not well attended; many participants return home before this session. This has the effect of allowing those who stay to function informally as a steering committee. A focused discussion of ways to improve dialogue also takes place at this final meeting.

What Goes on in the Days and Weeks Immediately Following a Meeting?

A press release is drafted and shared with all participants to be sure that it accurately reflects the contents of the dialogue. When everyone approves it, the press release goes up on the website of the participating groups. Recently, we have been summing up the dialogue meetings with talking points that our respective leadership can use on the local level to encourage dialogue activities. The minutes are also circulated in electronic format so that all participants can concur on the dynamic aspects of spoken dialogue and make corrections in the historic record of the meeting. A fresh participant list is drawn up based on revised information and planning for the next meeting goes on, especially reserving space and confirming dates. Members exchange information supportive of the work of the dialogue via e-mail or through collaborative efforts at other meetings and conventions. Some participants write collaborative articles for periodicals and journals. The press release then sums up the main themes of the meeting.

Talking Points

Talking points enable the leadership of our communities to be able to speak with unity of voice when they discuss the work of the dialogue group in other settings.* They are sent out in a special, restricted electronic mailing. The five talking points from this session follow:

---

* They are an essential bridge between the dialogue interface and the "intra" communitarian environment. They enable the leadership of the communities—those who did and those who did not attend the dialogue—to say something in their environment, for example, at an interfaith event, to the press, or in preaching.

1. By discussing the story of Joseph in the Bible and in the Qur'an, the dialogue group was able to explore the boundaries between Muslim and Catholic views of prophetic figures. Catholics emphasized the fallibility of prophets and their exemplary repentance; only Christ is perfect.

2. Shi'a and Sunni Muslims articulated different theologies of sanctity, but equally affirmed the impeccability and infallibility of prophets.

3. Both sides recognized that the Joseph narratives teach perennial values and virtues such as forgiveness, patience, resistance to temptation, skillful use of intelligence to benefit others, and faithfulness to God and family.

4. The discussion of dream episodes in the Joseph narratives opened up the topic of spiritual discernment. Both Muslims and Catholics agree that authentic interior experiences and dreams will conform to revealed scripture and moral norms.

5. The Joseph story has inspired a wealth of literature in European and South Asian cultures, such as in the historical novels of Thomas Mann and in the classic romantic Urdu epic, *Joseph and Zulekha*.

Notes

Introduction

Portions of the introduction are revised from an unpublished presentation entitled "The Contemporary U.S. as a Multi-Religious Society and Culture: The Landscape" made to the Conference of Major Superiors of Men (a Catholic men's leadership organization) on August 4, 2005, in Scottsdale, Arizona.

1. For an example of work in the schools, see the work done under the administration of former U.S. Secretary of Education Richard W. Riley (www.ed.gov/inits/religionandschools/v-guide.html) and that of Charles Haynes at the First Amendment Center of the Freedom Forum (www.freedomforum.org/templates/document.asp?documentID=12815). For an example of the progress in the workplace, consult the Tanenbaum Center's guidelines (www.tanenbaum.org/workplace.html).

2. Interestingly, there are almost never more than two faiths in question, perhaps as a practical result of the complexity of getting to know, understand, and own even one.

3. David Roozen, director of the Hartford Institute for Religion Research, notes that this is an aggressive and linear translation of the trend data. But even the well-respected National Opinion Research Council's General Social Survey trend in religion preference shows a notable drop in Christian market share beginning in 1990 that if projected forward would have Christianity dropping below 50 percent within the next five to six decades. It is an alarming shift either way.

4. Specific organizations are referenced in part III, "Interfaith Organizations and the Web."

5. After 9/11, a group of theater folks interviewed New Yorkers to discover what they were experiencing. The result was a play called *In Their Own Words*. Intrigued by its unexpected religious subtexts, they interviewed more than a hundred New Yorkers about their religious conceptions of themselves and others and distilled 2,300 pages of transcript into a one-hour play, *Same Difference*. The play captured those real prejudices that people are only willing to articulate in anonymous interviews; at the same time, it helped to spark profound dialogues and fostered real understanding.

1 Dialogue through Conversation—Spoken Dialogue

1. J. Hoeberichts, *Francis and Islam* (Quincy, IL: Franciscan Press, 1997).
2. Refer to www.thedialogueproject.org.
3. Leonard Swidler, *Theoria → Praxis: How Jews, Christians, and Muslims Can Together Move from Theory to Practice* (Leuven, Belgium: Peeters, 1998).
4. See the excellent discussion in Abraham Vélez De Cea, "A New Direction for Comparative Studies of Buddhists and Christians: Evidence from Nagarjuna and John of the Cross," *Buddhist Christian Studies*, Vol. 26, 2006: 139–55.

2 Dialogue through Arts—"Opening the World's Door"

1. John Dewey, *Art as Experience* (New York: Perigee Books, 1934).
2. Daniel Yankelovich, *The Magic of Dialogue: Transforming Conflict into Cooperation* (New York: Simon & Schuster: 2001).
3. Maria Hornung, *Encountering Other Faiths* (Mahwah, NJ: Paulist Press, 2007).
4. Dr. Norman J. Cohen, *Moses and the Journey to Leadership: Timeless Lessons of Effective Management from the Bible and Today's Leaders* (Woodstock, VT: Jewish Lights Publishing, 2006).

3 Dialogue through Observation and Participation—Interfaith Prayer Services

1. The beautiful prayers offered at the Day of Prayer for World Peace at Assisi, Italy can be found at www.hds.harvard.edu/spiritual/peace.html.
2. You can also find the "Guidelines for Interfaith Prayer Services" at the InterFaith Conference's website: www.ifcmw.org/default.asp?page=Interfaith_Prayer_ Guidelines.
3. My address at an interfaith conference in Kyoto, Japan, on why I am compelled as a Christian to be in relationship with those of other faiths describes this in more detail. It can be read at www.ifcmw.org.
4. Over the years we have added the names of new member faith communities in the third paragraph, but made no other changes. When the Washington Area Buddhist Network joined in October 2006, we added the words "or our particular experience of sacred truth*" to the second paragraph, at the suggestion of members of this nontheistic tradition. Through this responsive they also recommended placing "*" after each time the word "God" or "Creator" appears rather than repeating "or our particular experience of sacred truth."

   Permission to reproduce or modify this reading is granted if the context is maintained, you give credit to the Interfaith Conference of Metropolitan Washington, and you send a copy of the program or service in which it is used to: Executive Director, InterFaith Conference, 1426 Ninth St., NW, Washington, DC 20001-3330.

5. Yes, an offering is taken even when the service is in the synagogue. It is not held on the Sabbath when money is not used. The temple does rely on our ushers both to bring the offering plates and to collect the gifts since the church's ushers know how to do it.

6. In this case, I do use a multireligious service as opposed to an interfaith one because there are a number of Christian–Jewish or Christian–Jewish–Muslim services for his birthday. Some of these interfaith services are very well planned, such as the one a large synagogue hosts, using its regular Friday night Shabbat service before the Martin Luther King federal holiday and engaging several African American churches. Others are really Christian services with one or two people of another faith participating.

7. Please refer to www.childrensdefense.org/site/PageServer?pagename=What_CDF_Does_Childrens_Sabbaths_Resources.

8. The text and list of signers of the Alexandria Declaration are available at the Anglican Communion's Network for Inter Faith Concerns website: http://nifcon.anglicancommunion.org/work/declarations/alexandria.cfm.

4 Action through Service—From Shared Values to Common Action

1. Martha Nussbaum, *The Clash Within: Democracy, Religious Violence, and India's Future* (Cambridge, MA: The Belknap Press of Harvard University Press, 2007).

2. Martin Luther King Jr., "The Nobel Prize 1964 Acceptance Speech," December 10, 1964, available at the Nobel Foundation website http://nobelprize.org/nobel_prizes/peace/laureates/1964/king-acceptance.html.

3. Ashutosh Varshney, *Ethnic Conflict and Civic Life* (New Haven, CT: Yale University Press, 2003).

4. Wilfred Cantwell Smith, *The Faith of Other Men* (San Francisco: Harper, 1963).

5. From "The World House" in Martin Luther King Jr., *Where Do We Go from Here: Chaos or Community?* (Boston: Beacon Press, 1967).

6. Stanley Hauerwas, *A Community of Character: Toward a Constructive Christian Social Ethic* (South Bend, IN: University of Notre Dame Press, 1981).

7. Eboo Patel and Mariah Neuroth, "The Interfaith Youth Core: Building Chicago as a Model Interfaith Youth City," in *Building the Interfaith Youth Movement: Beyond Dialogue to Action*, eds. Eboo Patel and Patrice Brodeur (Lanham, MD: Rowman & Littlefield Publishers, 2006), 172.

About the Contributors

Rev. Dr. C. Welton Gaddy is the president of the Interfaith Alliance and the Interfaith Alliance Foundation. Rev. Gaddy has held numerous positions of leadership both within and outside of the Baptist movement and is a member of the Council of 100 Leaders, which seeks to bridge the gap between Islam and the West. The author of more than twenty books and the host of a nationally syndicated radio show, Rev. Gaddy focuses on promoting religion as a positive force in national life.

Rabbi Carol Harris-Shapiro is the author of the controversial book *Messianic Judaism: A Rabbi's Journey through Religious Change in America*, which examines the validity of Messianic Judaism as a form of Judaism. Rabbi Harris-Shapiro has taught courses at several major universities and currently serves as an assistant professor of contemporary Jewish studies at Gratz College in Melrose Park, Pennsylvainia.

Rev. Bud Heckman is an ordained United Methodist clergyman from Ohio, currently serving as the chief development officer at Hartford Seminary in Connecticut, a unique theological school that focuses on interreligious dialogue and enjoys a diverse student body of Christians, Muslims, and Jews. He is the former executive director of Religions for Peace-USA, where he started as a consultant working with local U.S. communities on interfaith issues. He delights in the relationships established with fellow contributors during these times.

April Kunze is the vice president of programs for the Interfaith Youth Core. A young woman with extensive background in grassroots community building and youth leadership, April joined the IFYC in 2000 as a volunteer and later became its first staff member. Her articles about interfaith work among young adults have been published in a multitude of publications, and she is the founder of the Crib Collective, which seeks to create social entrepreneurship among the youth of Chicago.

Rev. Dr. Clark Lobenstine is the executive director of the InterFaith Conference of Metropolitan Washington and also a parish associate at Silver Spring Presbyterian Church in Maryland. With thirty years of experience working with religious leaders of diverse faiths and traditions, Rev. Lobenstine lends his experience to many groups throughout the Washington, D.C., community, and is a member of the Mayor's Interfaith Council. After 9/11, Rev. Lobenstine organized more than a hundred lectures, many given by Muslims, in hopes of expanding the public's understanding of Islam.

Dr. Eboo Patel is the founder and director of the Interfaith Youth Core and is one of the world's most sought-after speakers on the subject of the interfaith movement and the interfaith youth movement in particular. He serves as a board member for several major interfaith associations and holds membership in such exclusive organizations as the Council on Foreign Relations and the EastWest Institute. Dr. Patel is currently working on a book on the role of religious youth in the modern era.

Rori Picker Neiss is program coordinator for the Jewish Orthodox Feminist Alliance and former lead staff of Religions for Peace-USA. A graduate of the Macaulay Honors College at Hunter College in New York City, Rori researched interfaith dialogue among Orthodox Jews and wrote her thesis concentrating on Rabbi Joseph B. Soloveitchik's seminal treatise "Confrontation" on the barriers to Jewish participation in interfaith dialogue.

Noah Silverman is the content coordinator for the Outreach Education & Training Program of the Interfaith Youth Core. Among his many accomplishments, Noah managed the 2006 National Days of Interfaith Youth Service, organized the fourth National Conference on

Interfaith Youth Work, and co-taught a course on interfaith peace-building in DePaul University's Peace Studies Department in Chicago.

Abby Stamelman Hocky, MSW, is the executive director of the Interfaith Center of Greater Philadelphia. She has worked toward fostering interfaith dialogue, particularly between Muslims, Jews, and Christians, in the Philadelphia area and beyond. Abby is currently working on a project with synagogues in New York that will ultimately seek to reimagine the current model of Jewish youth education.

Rev. Susan Teegen-Case is the founder and director of the Arts & Spirituality Center, an organization comprised of both artists and spiritual leaders that focuses on the interplay of artistic and spiritual avenues as a path to healing. Her experiences as an interfaith chaplain helped shape her theories about the power of creative expression to fuel nonviolence and community revitalization.

Rev. Dr. Francis Tiso is an interfaith relations specialist at the United States Conference of Catholic Bishops, originating from the Diocese of Isernia-Venafro in Italy and having served in the archdiocese of San Francisco. He holds various degrees from some of the world's finest academic institutions, and has traveled and lectured extensively for two decades, doing much of his work in Italy. Speaking upwards of ten languages, Father Tiso's academic and spiritual interests are largely in the reconciliation of Buddhist spirituality with Christian theology.

About Religions for Peace

Interfaith activity, like faith itself, is about relationships. The editors and contributors to this guidebook all found solace and safety in relationships that bridge faith lines, often through the auspices of Religions for Peace.

Religions for Peace came into being originally as the World Conference on Religion and Peace through a series of meetings of senior religious leaders and other civil society actors in the early 1960s. These efforts culminated into an organizing conference in Kyoto, Japan, in 1970. Only a scant handful of other interfaith organizations existed at this time.

Over time Religions for Peace, as it came to be known, established offices in New York City, directly across the plaza from the United Nations, and began building a representative model of leadership for doing interfaith work. For the next several decades it worked to establish action-oriented and program-driven interreligious councils of religious leaders in countries all over the globe.

Today, Religions for Peace is arguably the largest interfaith entity and is organized on several levels: the International Secretariat in New York; regional conferences in Africa, Asia, Europe, and now Latin America and the Caribbean; and more than sixty affiliates at the national level, as well as a number of local units. Moreover, Religions for Peace enjoys consultative status with the Economic and Social Council (ECOSOC) of the United Nations, with UNESCO, and with UNICEF.

Religions for Peace recognizes that religious communities are our largest social institutions. It lives in the hope that there are still yet untapped resources, infrastructures, and cultural understandings and motivations for achieving peace, especially when religious communities come together.

Religions for Peace-USA

As the International Secretariat of the World Conference of Religions for Peace came to be located in the United States, a growing number of U.S. religious communities became interested in distinctive models of interreligious relations presented by Religions for Peace. A U.S. Conference of Religions for Peace rose up from within the WCRP's auspices and grace. What is now called Religions for Peace-USA was formed, eventually expanding to include a broad and diverse table of representatives from more than sixty U.S. religious communities. Religions for Peace-USA focuses on building community, addressing diversity, and examining the role of the United States in the world.

Index

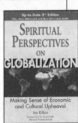
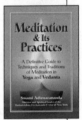

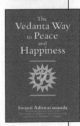

Children's Spiritual Biography

Ten Amazing People
And How They Changed the World
by Maura D. Shaw; Foreword by Dr. Robert Coles
Full-color illus. by Stephen Marchesi

For ages
7 & up

Black Elk • Dorothy Day • Malcolm X • Mahatma Gandhi • Martin Luther King, Jr. • Mother Teresa • Janusz Korczak • Desmond Tutu • Thich Nhat Hanh • Albert Schweitzer

This vivid, inspirational and authoritative book will open new possibilities for children by telling the stories of how ten of the past century's greatest leaders changed the world in important ways.

8½ x 11, 48 pp, HC, Full-color illus., 978-1-893361-47-8 **$17.95**
For ages 7 & up

Spiritual Biographies for Young People—For ages 7 and up

 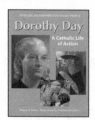 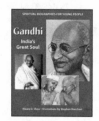 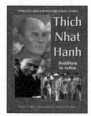

Black Elk: Native American Man of Spirit
by Maura D. Shaw; Full-color illus. by Stephen Marchesi
Through historically accurate illustrations and photos, inspiring age-appropriate activities and Black Elk's own words, this colorful biography introduces children to a remarkable person who ensured that the traditions and beliefs of his people would not be forgotten.
6¾ x 8¾, 32 pp, HC, Full-color and b/w illus., 978-1-59473-043-6 **$12.99**

Dorothy Day: A Catholic Life of Action
by Maura D. Shaw; Full-color illus. by Stephen Marchesi
Introduces children to one of the most inspiring women of the twentieth century, a down-to-earth spiritual leader who saw the presence of God in every person she met. Includes practical activities, a timeline and a list of important words to know.
6¾ x 8¾, 32 pp, HC, Full-color illus., 978-1-59473-011-5 **$12.99**

Gandhi: India's Great Soul
by Maura D. Shaw; Full-color illus. by Stephen Marchesi
There are a number of biographies of Gandhi written for young readers, but this is the only one that balances a simple text with illustrations, photographs, and activities that encourage children and adults to talk about how to make changes happen without violence. Introduces children to important concepts of freedom, equality and justice among people of all backgrounds and religions.
6¾ x 8¾, 32 pp, HC, Full-color illus., 978-1-893361-91-1 **$12.95**

Thich Nhat Hanh: Buddhism in Action
by Maura D. Shaw; Full-color illus. by Stephen Marchesi
Warm illustrations, photos, age-appropriate activities and Thich Nhat Hanh's own poems introduce a great man to children in a way they can understand and enjoy. Includes a list of important Buddhist words to know.
6¾ x 8¾, 32 pp, HC, Full-color illus., 978-1-893361-87-4 **$12.95**

Children's Spirituality—Board Books

Adam and Eve's New Day (A Board Book)
by Sandy Eisenberg Sasso; Full-color illus. by Joani Keller Rothenberg
A lesson in hope for every child who has worried about what comes next. Abridged from *Adam and Eve's First Sunset*.
5 x 5, 24 pp, Full-color illus., Board Book, 978-1-59473-205-8 **$7.99** *For ages 0–4*

How Did the Animals Help God? (A Board Book)
by Nancy Sohn Swartz; Full-color illus. by Melanie Hall
Abridged from *In Our Image*, God asks all of nature to offer gifts to humankind—with a promise that they will care for creation in return.
5 x 5, 24 pp, Board Book, Full-color illus., 978-1-59473-044-3 **$7.99** *For ages 0–4*

Where Is God? (A Board Book) *by Lawrence and Karen Kushner; Full-color illus. by Dawn W. Majewski* A gentle way for young children to explore how God is with us every day, in every way. Abridged from *Because Nothing Looks Like God*.
5 x 5, 24 pp, Board Book, Full-color illus., 978-1-893361-17-1 **$7.99** *For ages 0–4*

What Does God Look Like? (A Board Book)
by Lawrence and Karen Kushner; Full-color illus. by Dawn W. Majewski
A simple way for young children to explore the ways that we "see" God. Abridged from *Because Nothing Looks Like God*.
5 x 5, 24 pp, Board Book, Full-color illus., 978-1-893361-23-2 **$7.99** *For ages 0–4*

How Does God Make Things Happen? (A Board Book)
by Lawrence and Karen Kushner; Full-color illus. by Dawn W. Majewski
A charming invitation for young children to explore how God makes things happen in our world. Abridged from *Because Nothing Looks Like God*.
5 x 5, 24 pp, Board Book, Full-color illus., 978-1-893361-24-9 **$7.99** *For ages 0–4*

What Is God's Name? (A Board Book)
by Sandy Eisenberg Sasso; Full-color illus. by Phoebe Stone
Everyone and everything in the world has a name. What is God's name? Abridged from the award-winning *In God's Name*.
5 x 5, 24 pp, Board Book, Full-color illus., 978-1-893361-10-2 **$7.99** *For ages 0–4*

What You Will See Inside ...

This important new series of books, each with many full-color photos, is designed to show children ages 6 and up the Who, What, When, Where, Why and How of traditional houses of worship, liturgical celebrations, and rituals of different world faiths, empowering them to respect and understand their own religious traditions—and those of their friends and neighbors.

What You Will See Inside a Catholic Church
by Reverend Michael Keane; Foreword by Robert J. Keeley, EdD
Full-color photos by Aaron Pepis
8½ x 10½, 32 pp, Full-color photos, HC, 978-1-893361-54-6 **$17.95**

Also available in Spanish: **Lo que se puede ver dentro de una iglesia católica**
8½ x 10½, 32 pp, Full-color photos, HC, 978-1-893361-66-9 **$16.95**

What You Will See Inside a Hindu Temple
by Dr. Mahendra Jani and Dr. Vandana Jani; Full-color photos by Neirah Bhargava and Vijay Dave
8½ x 10½, 32 pp, Full-color photos, HC, 978-1-59473-116-7 **$17.99**

What You Will See Inside a Mosque
by Aisha Karen Khan; Full-color photos by Aaron Pepis
8½ x 10½, 32 pp, Full-color photos, HC, 978-1-893361-60-7 **$16.95**

What You Will See Inside a Synagogue
by Rabbi Lawrence A. Hoffman and Dr. Ron Wolfson; Full-color photos by Bill Aron
8½ x 10½, 32 pp, Full-color photos, HC, 978-1-59473-012-2 **$17.99**

Children's Spirituality

Remembering My Grandparent: A Kid's Own Grief Workbook in the Christian Tradition *by Nechama Liss-Levinson, PhD, and Rev. Molly Phinney Baskette, MDiv* 8 x 10, 48 pp, 2-color text, HC, 978-1-59473-212-6 **$16.99** *For ages 7–13*

Does God Ever Sleep? *by Joan Sauro, CSJ; Full-color photos*
A charming nighttime reminder that God is always present in our lives.
10 x 8½, 32 pp, Quality PB, Full-color photos, 978-1-59473-110-5 **$8.99** *For ages 3–6*

Does God Forgive Me? *by August Gold; Full-color photos by Diane Hardy Waller*
Gently shows how God forgives all that we do if we are truly sorry.
10 x 8½, 32 pp, Quality PB, Full-color photos, 978-1-59473-142-6 **$8.99** *For ages 3–6*

God Said Amen *by Sandy Eisenberg Sasso; Full-color illus. by Avi Katz*
A warm and inspiring tale of two kingdoms that shows us that we need only reach out to each other to find the answers to our prayers.
9 x 12, 32 pp, HC, Full-color illus., 978-1-58023-080-3 **$16.95**
For ages 4 & up (a Jewish Lights book)

How Does God Listen? *by Kay Lindahl; Full-color photos by Cynthia Maloney*
How do we know when God is listening to us? Children will find the answers to these questions as they engage their senses while the story unfolds, learning how God listens in the wind, waves, clouds, hot chocolate, perfume, our tears and our laughter.
10 x 8½, 32 pp, Quality PB, Full-color photos, 978-1-59473-084-9 **$8.99** *For ages 3–6*

In God's Hands *by Lawrence Kushner and Gary Schmidt; Full-color illus. by Matthew J. Baeck*
9 x 12, 32 pp, Full-color illus., HC, 978-1-58023-224-1 **$16.99** *For ages 5 & up (a Jewish Lights book)*

In God's Name *by Sandy Eisenberg Sasso; Full-color illus. by Phoebe Stone*
Like an ancient myth in its poetic text and vibrant illustrations, this award-winning modern fable about the search for God's name celebrates the diversity and, at the same time, the unity of all the people of the world.
9 x 12, 32 pp, HC, Full-color illus., 978-1-879045-26-2 **$16.99**
For ages 4 & up (a Jewish Lights book)

Also available in Spanish: El nombre de Dios
9 x 12, 32 pp, HC, Full-color illus., 978-1-893361-63-8 **$16.95**

In Our Image: God's First Creatures
by Nancy Sohn Swartz; Full-color illus. by Melanie Hall
A playful new twist on the Genesis story—from the perspective of the animals. Celebrates the interconnectedness of nature and the harmony of all living things.
9 x 12, 32 pp, HC, Full-color illus., 978-1-879045-99-6 **$16.95**
For ages 4 & up (a Jewish Lights book)

Noah's Wife: The Story of Naamah
by Sandy Eisenberg Sasso; Full-color illus. by Bethanne Andersen
This new story, based on an ancient text, opens readers' religious imaginations to new ideas about the well-known story of the Flood. When God tells Noah to bring the animals of the world onto the ark, God also calls on Naamah, Noah's wife, to save each plant on Earth.
9 x 12, 32 pp, HC, Full-color illus., 978-1-58023-134-3 **$16.95** *For ages 4 & up (a Jewish Lights book)*

Also available: Naamah: Noah's Wife (A Board Book)
by Sandy Eisenberg Sasso; Full-color illus. by Bethanne Andersen
5 x 5, 24 pp, Board Book, Full-color illus., 978-1-893361-56-0 **$7.99** *For ages 0–4*

Where Does God Live? *by August Gold and Matthew J. Perlman*
Using simple, everyday examples that children can relate to, this colorful book helps young readers develop a personal understanding of God.
10 x 8½, 32 pp, Quality PB, Full-color photo illus., 978-1-893361-39-3 **$8.99** *For ages 3–6*

Spiritual Biography / Reference

Spiritual Leaders Who Changed the World
The Essential Handbook to the Past Century of Religion
Edited by Ira Rifkin and the Editors at SkyLight Paths; Foreword by Dr. Robert Coles
An invaluable reference to the most important spiritual leaders of the past 100 years.
6 x 9, 304 pp, 15+ b/w photos, Quality PB, 978-1-59473-241-6 **$18.99**

Spiritual Biography—SkyLight Lives

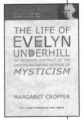

SkyLight Lives reintroduces the lives and works of key spiritual figures of our time—people who by their teaching or example have challenged our assumptions about spirituality and have caused us to look at it in new ways.

The Life of Evelyn Underhill
An Intimate Portrait of the Groundbreaking Author of Mysticism
by Margaret Cropper; Foreword by Dana Greene
Evelyn Underhill was a passionate writer and teacher who wrote elegantly on mysticism, worship, and devotional life.
6 x 9, 288 pp, 5 b/w photos, Quality PB, 978-1-893361-70-6 **$18.95**

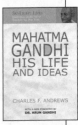

Mahatma Gandhi: His Life and Ideas
by Charles F. Andrews; Foreword by Dr. Arun Gandhi
Examines from a contemporary Christian activist's point of view the religious ideas and political dynamics that influenced the birth of the peaceful resistance movement.
6 x 9, 336 pp, 5 b/w photos, Quality PB, 978-1-893361-89-8 **$18.95**

Simone Weil: A Modern Pilgrimage
by Robert Coles
The extraordinary life of the spiritual philosopher who's been called both saint and madwoman.
6 x 9, 208 pp, Quality PB, 978-1-893361-34-8 **$16.95**

Zen Effects: The Life of Alan Watts
by Monica Furlong
Through his widely popular books and lectures, Alan Watts (1915–1973) did more to introduce Eastern philosophy and religion to Western minds than any figure before or since.
6 x 9, 264 pp, Quality PB, 978-1-893361-32-4 **$16.95**

More Spiritual Biography

Bede Griffiths: An Introduction to His Interspiritual Thought
by Wayne Teasdale
The first study of his contemplative experience and thought, exploring the intersection of Hinduism and Christianity.
6 x 9, 288 pp, Quality PB, 978-1-893361-77-5 **$18.95**

The Soul of the Story: Meetings with Remarkable People
by Rabbi David Zeller
Inspiring and entertaining, this compelling collection of spiritual adventures assures us that no spiritual lesson truly learned is ever lost.
6 x 9, 288 pp, HC, 978-1-58023-272-2 **$21.99** *(a Jewish Lights book)*

Spiritual Practice

Soul Fire: Accessing Your Creativity *by Rev. Thomas Ryan, CSP*
Shows you how to cultivate your creative spirit as a way to encourage personal growth.
6 x 9, 160 pp, Quality PB, 978-1-59473-243-0 **$16.99**

Running—The Sacred Art: Preparing to Practice
by Dr. Warren A. Kay; Foreword by Kristin Armstrong
Examines how your daily run can enrich your spiritual life.
5½ x 8½, 160 pp, Quality PB, 978-1-59473-227-0 **$16.99**

Hospitality—The Sacred Art: Discovering the Hidden Spiritual Power
of Invitation and Welcome *by Rev. Nanette Sawyer; Foreword by Rev. Dirk Ficca*
Explores how this ancient spiritual practice can transform your relationships.
5½ x 8½, 192 pp, Quality PB, 978-1-59473-228-7 **$16.99**

Thanking & Blessing—The Sacred Art: Spiritual Vitality through
Gratefulness *by Jay Marshall, PhD; Foreword by Philip Gulley*
Offers practical tips for uncovering the blessed wonder in our lives—even in trying circumstances. 5½ x 8½, 176 pp, Quality PB, 978-1-59473-231-7 **$16.99**

Everyday Herbs in Spiritual Life: A Guide to Many Practices
by Michael J. Caduto; Foreword by Rosemary Gladstar Explores the power of herbs.
7 x 9, 208 pp, 21 b/w illustrations, Quality PB, 978-1-59473-174-7 **$16.99**

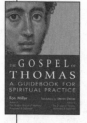

Divining the Body: Reclaim the Holiness of Your Physical Self *by Jan Phillips*
8 x 8, 256 pp, Quality PB, 978-1-59473-080-1 **$16.99**

Finding Time for the Timeless: Spirituality in the Workweek
by John McQuiston II Simple stories show you how refocus your daily life.
5½ x 6¾, 208 pp, HC, 978-1-59473-035-1 **$17.99**

The Gospel of Thomas: A Guidebook for Spiritual Practice
by Ron Miller; Translations by Stevan Davies
6 x 9, 160 pp, Quality PB, 978-1-59473-047-4 **$14.99**

Earth, Water, Fire, and Air: Essential Ways of Connecting to Spirit
by Cait Johnson 6 x 9, 224 pp, HC, 978-1-893361-65-2 **$19.95**

Labyrinths from the Outside In: Walking to Spiritual Insight—A Beginner's Guide
by Donna Schaper and Carole Ann Camp
6 x 9, 208 pp, b/w illus. and photos, Quality PB, 978-1-893361-18-8 **$16.95**

Practicing the Sacred Art of Listening: A Guide to Enrich Your Relationships
and Kindle Your Spiritual Life—The Listening Center Workshop
by Kay Lindahl 8 x 8, 176 pp, Quality PB, 978-1-893361-85-0 **$16.95**

Releasing the Creative Spirit: Unleash the Creativity in Your Life
by Dan Wakefield 7 x 10, 256 pp, Quality PB, 978-1-893361-36-2 **$16.95**

The Sacred Art of Bowing: Preparing to Practice
by Andi Young 5½ x 8½, 128 pp, b/w illus., Quality PB, 978-1-893361-82-9 **$14.95**

The Sacred Art of Chant: Preparing to Practice
by Ana Hernández 5½ x 8½, 192 pp, Quality PB, 978-1-59473-036-8 **$15.99**

The Sacred Art of Fasting: Preparing to Practice
by Thomas Ryan, CSP 5½ x 8½, 192 pp, Quality PB, 978-1-59473-078-8 **$15.99**

The Sacred Art of Forgiveness: Forgiving Ourselves and Others through God's Grace
by Marcia Ford 8 x 8, 176 pp, Quality PB, 978-1-59473-175-4 **$16.99**

The Sacred Art of Listening: Forty Reflections for Cultivating a Spiritual Practice
by Kay Lindahl; Illustrations by Amy Schnapper
8 x 8, 160 pp, b/w illus., Quality PB, 978-1-893361-44-7 **$16.99**

The Sacred Art of Lovingkindness: Preparing to Practice
by Rabbi Rami Shapiro; Foreword by Marcia Ford 5½ x 8½, 176 pp, Quality PB, 978-1-59473-151-8 **$16.99**

Sacred Speech: A Practical Guide for Keeping Spirit in Your Speech
by Rev. Donna Schaper 6 x 9, 176 pp, Quality PB, 978-1-59473-068-9 **$15.99**
HC, 978-1-893361-74-4 **$21.95**

Prayer / Meditation

Sacred Attention: A Spiritual Practice for Finding God in the Moment
by Margaret D. McGee
Framed on the Christian liturgical year, this inspiring guide explores ways to develop a practice of attention as a means of talking—and listening—to God.
6 x 9, 144 pp, HC, 978-1-59473-232-4 **$19.99**

Women Pray: Voices through the Ages, from Many Faiths, Cultures and Traditions
Edited and with Introductions by Monica Furlong
5 x 7¼, 256 pp, Quality PB, 978-1-59473-071-9 **$15.99**

Women of Color Pray: Voices of Strength, Faith, Healing, Hope and Courage *Edited and with Introductions by Christal M. Jackson*
Through these prayers, poetry, lyrics, meditations and affirmations, you will share in the strong and undeniable connection women of color share with God.
5 x 7¼, 208 pp, Quality PB, 978-1-59473-077-1 **$15.99**

Secrets of Prayer: A Multifaith Guide to Creating Personal Prayer in Your Life *by Nancy Corcoran, CSJ*
This compelling, multifaith guidebook offers you companionship and encouragement on the journey to a healthy prayer life. 6 x 9, 160 pp, Quality PB, 978-1-59473-215-7 **$16.99**

Prayers to an Evolutionary God
by William Cleary; Afterword by Diarmuid O'Murchu
Inspired by the spiritual and scientific teachings of Diarmuid O'Murchu and Teilhard de Chardin, reveals that religion and science can be combined to create an expanding view of the universe—an evolutionary faith.
6 x 9, 208 pp, HC, 978-1-59473-006-1 **$21.99**

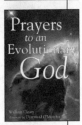

The Art of Public Prayer: Not for Clergy Only *by Lawrence A. Hoffman*
6 x 9, 288 pp, Quality PB, 978-1-893361-06-5 **$18.99**

A Heart of Stillness: A Complete Guide to Learning the Art of Meditation
by David A. Cooper 5½ x 8½, 272 pp, Quality PB, 978-1-893361-03-4 **$16.95**

Meditation without Gurus: A Guide to the Heart of Practice
by Clark Strand 5½ x 8½, 192 pp, Quality PB, 978-1-893361-93-5 **$16.95**

Praying with Our Hands: 21 Practices of Embodied Prayer from the World's Spiritual Traditions *by Jon M. Sweeney; Photographs by Jennifer J. Wilson; Foreword by Mother Tessa Bielecki; Afterword by Taitetsu Unno, PhD*
8 x 8, 96 pp, 22 duotone photos, Quality PB, 978-1-893361-16-4 **$16.95**

Silence, Simplicity & Solitude: A Complete Guide to Spiritual Retreat at Home
by David A. Cooper 5½ x 8½, 336 pp, Quality PB, 978-1-893361-04-1 **$16.95**

Three Gates to Meditation Practice: A Personal Journey into Sufism, Buddhism, and Judaism *by David A. Cooper* 5½ x 8½, 240 pp, Quality PB, 978-1-893361-22-5 **$16.95**

Prayer / M. Basil Pennington, OCSO

Finding Grace at the Center, 3rd Ed.: The Beginning of Centering Prayer *with Thomas Keating, OCSO, and Thomas E. Clarke, SJ; Foreword by Rev. Cynthia Bourgeault, PhD*
A practical guide to a simple and beautiful form of meditative prayer.
5 x 7¼, 128 pp, Quality PB, 978-1-59473-182-2 **$12.99**

The Monks of Mount Athos: A Western Monk's Extraordinary Spiritual Journey on Eastern Holy Ground *Foreword by Archimandrite Dionysios*
Explores the landscape, the monastic communities, and the food of Athos.
6 x 9, 256 pp, 10+ b/w drawings, Quality PB, 978-1-893361-78-2 **$18.95**

Psalms: A Spiritual Commentary *Illustrations by Phillip Ratner*
Reflections on some of the most beloved passages from the Bible's most widely read book. 6 x 9, 176 pp, 24 full-page b/w illus., Quality PB, 978-1-59473-234-8 **$16.99**
HC, 978-1-59473-141-9 **$19.99**

The Song of Songs: A Spiritual Commentary *Illustrations by Phillip Ratner*
Explore the Bible's most challenging mystical text.
6 x 9, 160 pp, 14 b/w illus., Quality PB, 978-1-59473-235-3 **$16.99**; HC, 978-1-59473-004-7 **$19.99**

Spirituality & Crafts

The Knitting Way
A Guide to Spiritual Self-Discovery
by Linda Skolnik and Janice MacDaniels
Examines how you can explore and strengthen your spiritual life through knitting.
7 x 9, 240 pp, Quality PB, b/w photographs, 978-1-59473-079-5 **$16.99**

The Scrapbooking Journey
A Hands-On Guide to Spiritual Discovery
by Cory Richardson-Lauve; Foreword by Stacy Julian
Reveals how this craft can become a practice used to deepen and shape your life.
7 x 9, 176 pp, Quality PB, 8-page full-color insert, plus b/w photographs
978-1-59473-216-4 **$18.99**

The Painting Path
Embodying Spiritual Discovery through Yoga, Brush and Color
by Linda Novick; Foreword by Richard Segalman
Explores the divine connection you can experience through creativity.
7 x 9, 208 pp, 8-page full-color insert, plus b/w photographs
Quality PB, 978-1-59473-226-3 **$18.99**

The Quilting Path
A Guide to Spiritual Discovery through Fabric, Thread and Kabbalah
by Louise Silk
Explores how to cultivate personal growth through quilt making.
7 x 9, 192 pp, Quality PB, b/w photographs and illustrations, 978-1-59473-206-5 **$16.99**

Contemplative Crochet
A Hands-On Guide for Interlocking Faith and Craft
by Cindy Crandall-Frazier; Foreword by Linda Skolnik
Illuminates the spiritual lessons you can learn through crocheting.
7 x 9, 192 pp (est), b/w photographs, Quality PB, 978-1-59473-238-6 **$16.99**

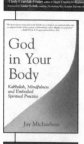

Kabbalah / Enneagram
(from Jewish Lights Publishing)

God in Your Body: Kabbalah, Mindfulness and Embodied Spiritual Practice
by Jay Michaelson 6 x 9, Quality PB Original, 978-1-58023-304-0 **$18.99**

Cast in God's Image: Discover Your Personality Type Using the Enneagram and Kabbalah
by Rabbi Howard A. Addison 7 x 9, 176 pp, Quality PB, 978-1-58023-124-4 **$16.95**

Ehyeh: A Kabbalah for Tomorrow *by Dr. Arthur Green*
6 x 9, 224 pp, Quality PB, 978-1-58023-213-5 **$16.99**

The Enneagram and Kabbalah, 2nd Edition: Reading Your Soul
by Rabbi Howard A. Addison 6 x 9, 192 pp, Quality PB, 978-1-58023-229-6 **$16.99**

The Gift of Kabbalah: Discovering the Secrets of Heaven, Renewing Your Life on Earth
by Tamar Frankiel, PhD 6 x 9, 256 pp, Quality PB, 978-1-58023-141-1 **$16.95**
HC, 978-1-58023-108-4 **$21.95**

Kabbalah: A Brief Introduction for Christians
by Tamar Frankiel, PhD 5½ x 8½, 176 pp, Quality PB, 978-1-58023-303-3 **$16.99**

Zohar: Annotated & Explained *Translation and Annotation by Dr. Daniel C. Matt*
Foreword by Andrew Harvey 5½ x 8½, 176 pp, Quality PB, 978-1-893361-51-5 **$15.99**
(a SkyLight Paths book)

Spirituality

Next to Godliness: Finding the Sacred in Housekeeping
Edited and with Introductions by Alice Peck
Offers new perspectives on how we can reach out for the Divine.
6 x 9, 224 pp, Quality PB, 978-1-59473-214-0 **$19.99**

Bread, Body, Spirit: Finding the Sacred in Food
Edited and with Introductions by Alice Peck
Explores how food feeds our faith. 6 x 9, 224 pp, Quality PB, 978-1-59473-242-3 **$19.99**

Renewal in the Wilderness: A Spiritual Guide to Connecting with God in the Natural World *by John Lionberger*
Reveals the power of experiencing God's presence in many variations of the natural world. 6 x 9, 176 pp, b/w photos, Quality PB, 978-1-59473-219-5 **$16.99**

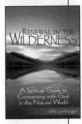

Honoring Motherhood: Prayers, Ceremonies and Blessings
Edited and with Introductions by Lynn L. Caruso
Journey through the seasons of motherhood. 5 x 7¼, 272 pp, HC, 978-1-59473-239-3 **$19.99**

Soul Fire: Accessing Your Creativity *by Rev. Thomas Ryan, CSP*
Learn to cultivate your creative spirit. 6 x 9, 160 pp, Quality PB, 978-1-59473-243-0 **$16.99**

Technology & Spirituality: How the Information Revolution Affects Our Spiritual Lives *by Stephen K. Spyker* 6 x 9, 176 pp, HC, 978-1-59473-218-8 **$19.99**

Money and the Way of Wisdom: Insights from the Book of Proverbs
by Timothy J. Sandoval, PhD 6 x 9, 192 pp (est), Quality PB, 978-1-59473-245-4 **$16.99**

Awakening the Spirit, Inspiring the Soul
30 Stories of Interspiritual Discovery in the Community of Faiths
Edited by Brother Wayne Teasdale and Martha Howard, MD; Foreword by Joan Borysenko, PhD
6 x 9, 224 pp, HC, 978-1-59473-039-9 **$21.99**

Creating a Spiritual Retirement: A Guide to the Unseen Possibilities in Our Lives
by Molly Srode 6 x 9, 208 pp, b/w photos, Quality PB, 978-1-59473-050-4 **$14.99**
HC, 978-1-893361-75-1 **$19.95**

Finding Hope: Cultivating God's Gift of a Hopeful Spirit
by Marcia Ford 8 x 8, 200 pp, Quality PB, 978-1-59473-211-9 **$16.99**

The Geography of Faith: Underground Conversations on Religious, Political and Social Change *by Daniel Berrigan and Robert Coles* 6 x 9, 224 pp, Quality PB, 978-1-893361-40-9 **$16.95**

Jewish Spirituality: A Brief Introduction for Christians *by Lawrence Kushner*
5½ x 8½, 112 pp, Quality PB, 978-1-58023-150-3 **$12.95** *(a Jewish Lights book)*

Journeys of Simplicity: Traveling Light with Thomas Merton, Bashō, Edward Abbey, Annie Dillard & Others *by Philip Harnden* 5 x 7¼, 144 pp, Quality PB, 978-1-59473-181-5 **$12.99** 128 pp, HC, 978-1-893361-76-8 **$16.95**

Keeping Spiritual Balance As We Grow Older: More than 65 Creative Ways to Use Purpose, Prayer, and the Power of Spirit to Build a Meaningful Retirement *by Molly and Bernie Srode* 8 x 8, 224 pp, Quality PB, 978-1-59473-042-9 **$16.99**

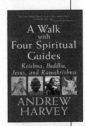

Spirituality 101: The Indispensable Guide to Keeping—or Finding—Your Spiritual Life on Campus *by Harriet L. Schwartz, with contributions from college students at nearly thirty campuses across the United States* 6 x 9, 272 pp, Quality PB, 978-1-59473-000-9 **$16.99**

Spiritually Incorrect: Finding God in All the Wrong Places *by Dan Wakefield; Illus. by Marian DelVecchio* 5½ x 8½, 192 pp, b/w illus., Quality PB, 978-1-59473-137-2 **$15.99**

Spiritual Manifestos: Visions for Renewed Religious Life in America from Young Spiritual Leaders of Many Faiths *Edited by Niles Elliot Goldstein; Preface by Martin E. Marty* 6 x 9, 256 pp, HC, 978-1-893361-09-6 **$21.95**

A Walk with Four Spiritual Guides: Krishna, Buddha, Jesus, and Ramakrishna
by Andrew Harvey 5½ x 8½, 192 pp, 10 b/w photos & illus., Quality PB, 978-1-59473-138-9 **$15.99**

What Matters: Spiritual Nourishment for Head and Heart
by Frederick Franck 5 x 7¼, 128 pp, 50+ b/w illus., HC, 978-1-59473-013-9 **$16.99**

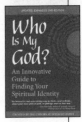

Who Is My God?, 2nd Edition: An Innovative Guide to Finding Your Spiritual Identity
Created by the Editors at SkyLight Paths 6 x 9, 160 pp, Quality PB, 978-1-59473-014-6 **$15.99**

Spirituality of the Seasons

Autumn: A Spiritual Biography of the Season
Edited by Gary Schmidt and Susan M. Felch; Illustrations by Mary Azarian
Rejoice in autumn as a time of preparation and reflection. Includes Wendell Berry, David James Duncan, Robert Frost, A. Bartlett Giamatti, E. B. White, P. D. James, Julian of Norwich, Garret Keizer, Tracy Kidder, Anne Lamott, May Sarton.
6 x 9, 320 pp, 5 b/w illus., Quality PB, 978-1-59473-118-1 **$18.99**

Spring: A Spiritual Biography of the Season
Edited by Gary Schmidt and Susan M. Felch; Illustrations by Mary Azarian
Explore the gentle unfurling of spring and reflect on how nature celebrates rebirth and renewal. Includes Jane Kenyon, Lucy Larcom, Harry Thurston, Nathaniel Hawthorne, Noel Perrin, Annie Dillard, Martha Ballard, Barbara Kingsolver, Dorothy Wordsworth, Donald Hall, David Brill, Lionel Basney, Isak Dinesen, Paul Laurence Dunbar. 6 x 9, 352 pp, 6 b/w illus., Quality PB, 978-1-59473-246-1 **$18.99**

Summer: A Spiritual Biography of the Season
Edited by Gary Schmidt and Susan M. Felch; Illustrations by Barry Moser
"A sumptuous banquet.... These selections lift up an exquisite wholeness found within an everyday sophistication."— ★ *Publishers Weekly* starred review
Includes Anne Lamott, Luci Shaw, Ray Bradbury, Richard Selzer, Thomas Lynch, Walt Whitman, Carl Sandburg, Sherman Alexie, Madeleine L'Engle, Jamaica Kincaid.
6 x 9, 304 pp, 5 b/w illus., Quality PB, 978-1-59473-183-9 **$18.99**
HC, 978-1-59473-083-2 **$21.99**

Winter: A Spiritual Biography of the Season
Edited by Gary Schmidt and Susan M. Felch; Illustrations by Barry Moser
"This outstanding anthology features top-flight nature and spirituality writers on the fierce, inexorable season of winter.... Remarkably lively and warm, despite the icy subject." — ★ *Publishers Weekly* starred review
Includes Will Campbell, Rachel Carson, Annie Dillard, Donald Hall, Ron Hansen, Jane Kenyon, Jamaica Kincaid, Barry Lopez, Kathleen Norris, John Updike, E. B. White.
6 x 9, 288 pp, 6 b/w illus., Deluxe PB w/flaps, 978-1-893361-92-8 **$18.95**
HC, 978-1-893361-53-9 **$21.95**

Spirituality / Animal Companions

Blessing the Animals: Prayers and Ceremonies to Celebrate God's Creatures, Wild and Tame *Edited by Lynn L. Caruso* 5 x 7¼, 256 pp, HC, 978-1-59473-145-7 **$19.99**

Remembering My Pet: A Kid's Own Spiritual Workbook for When a Pet Dies
by Nechama Liss-Levinson, PhD, and Rev. Molly Phinney Baskette, MDiv; Foreword by Lynn L. Caruso
8 x 10, 48 pp, 2-color text, HC, 978-1-59473-221-3 **$16.99**

What Animals Can Teach Us about Spirituality: Inspiring Lessons from Wild and Tame Creatures by Diana L. Guerrero 6 x 9, 176 pp, Quality PB, 978-1-893361-84-3 **$16.95**

Spirituality—A Week Inside

Come and Sit: A Week Inside Meditation Centers
by Marcia Z. Nelson; Foreword by Wayne Teasdale
6 x 9, 224 pp, b/w photos, Quality PB, 978-1-893361-35-5 **$16.95**

Lighting the Lamp of Wisdom: A Week Inside a Yoga Ashram
by John Ittner; Foreword by Dr. David Frawley
6 x 9, 192 pp, 10+ b/w photos, Quality PB, 978-1-893361-52-2 **$15.95**

Making a Heart for God: A Week Inside a Catholic Monastery
by Dianne Aprile; Foreword by Brother Patrick Hart, ocso
6 x 9, 224 pp, b/w photos, Quality PB, 978-1-893361-49-2 **$16.95**

Waking Up: A Week Inside a Zen Monastery
by Jack Maguire; Foreword by John Daido Loori, Roshi
6 x 9, 224 pp, b/w photos, Quality PB, 978-1-893361-55-3 **$16.95**; HC, 978-1-893361-13-3 **$21.95**

Sacred Texts—SkyLight Illuminations Series

Offers today's spiritual seeker an accessible entry into the great classic texts of the world's spiritual traditions. Each classic is presented in an accessible translation, with facing pages of guided commentary from experts, giving you the keys you need to understand the history, context and meaning of the text. This series enables you, whatever your background, to experience and understand classic spiritual texts directly, and to make them a part of your life.

CHRISTIANITY

The End of Days: Essential Selections from Apocalyptic Texts—
Annotated & Explained *Annotation by Robert G. Clouse*
Helps you understand the complex Christian visions of the end of the world.
5½ x 8½, 224 pp, Quality PB, 978-1-59473-170-9 **$16.99**

The Hidden Gospel of Matthew: Annotated & Explained
Translation & Annotation by Ron Miller
Takes you deep into the text cherished around the world to discover the words and events that have the strongest connection to the historical Jesus.
5½ x 8½, 272 pp, Quality PB, 978-1-59473-038-2 **$16.99**

The Lost Sayings of Jesus: Teachings from Ancient Christian, Jewish, Gnostic and Islamic Sources—Annotated & Explained
Translation & Annotation by Andrew Phillip Smith; Foreword by Stephan A. Hoeller
This collection of more than three hundred sayings depicts Jesus as a Wisdom teacher who speaks to people of all faiths as a mystic and spiritual master.
5½ x 8½, 240 pp, Quality PB, 978-1-59473-172-3 **$16.99**

Philokalia: The Eastern Christian Spiritual Texts—Selections Annotated & Explained *Annotation by Allyne Smith; Translation by G. E. H. Palmer, Phillip Sherrard and Bishop Kallistos Ware*
The first approachable introduction to the wisdom of the Philokalia, which is the classic text of Eastern Christian spirituality.
5½ x 8½, 240 pp, Quality PB, 978-1-59473-103-7 **$16.99**

The Sacred Writings of Paul: Selections Annotated & Explained
Translation & Annotation by Ron Miller
Explores the apostle Paul's core message of spiritual equality, freedom and joy.
5½ x 8½, 224 pp, Quality PB, 978-1-59473-213-3 **$16.99**

Sex Texts from the Bible: Selections Annotated & Explained
Translation & Annotation by Teresa J. Hornsby; Foreword by Amy-Jill Levine
Offers surprising insight into our modern sexual lives.
5½ x 8½, 208 pp, Quality PB, 978-1-59473-217-1 **$16.99**

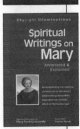

Spiritual Writings on Mary: Annotated & Explained
Annotation by Mary Ford-Grabowsky; Foreword by Andrew Harvey
Examines the role of Mary, the mother of Jesus, as a source of inspiration in history and in life today. 5½ x 8½, 288 pp, Quality PB, 978-1-59473-001-6 **$16.99**

The Way of a Pilgrim: The Jesus Prayer Journey—Annotated & Explained
Translation & Annotation by Gleb Pokrovsky; Foreword by Andrew Harvey
This classic of Russian spirituality is the delightful account of one man who sets out to learn the prayer of the heart, also known as the "Jesus prayer."
5½ x 8½, 160 pp, Illus., Quality PB, 978-1-893361-31-7 **$14.95**

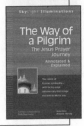

Sacred Texts—cont.

MORMONISM

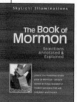

The Book of Mormon: Selections Annotated & Explained
Annotation by Jana Riess; Foreword by Phyllis Tickle
Explores the sacred epic that is cherished by more than twelve million members of the LDS church as the keystone of their faith.
5½ x 8½ , 272 pp, Quality PB, 978-1-59473-076-4 **$16.99**

NATIVE AMERICAN

Native American Stories of the Sacred: Annotated & Explained
Retold & Annotated by Evan T. Pritchard
Intended for more than entertainment, these teaching tales contain elegantly simple illustrations of time-honored truths.
5½ x 8½, 272 pp, Quality PB, 978-1-59473-112-9 **$16.99**

GNOSTICISM

Gnostic Writings on the Soul: Annotated & Explained
Translation & Annotation by Andrew Phillip Smith; Foreword by Stephan A. Hoeller
Reveals the inspiring ways your soul can remember and return to its unique, divine purpose.
5½ x 8½, 144 pp, Quality PB, 978-1-59473-220-1 **$16.99**

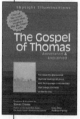

The Gospel of Philip: Annotated & Explained
Translation & Annotation by Andrew Phillip Smith; Foreword by Stevan Davies
Reveals otherwise unrecorded sayings of Jesus and fragments of Gnostic mythology.
5½ x 8½, 160 pp, Quality PB, 978-1-59473-111-2 **$16.99**

The Gospel of Thomas: Annotated & Explained
Translation & Annotation by Stevan Davies Sheds new light on the origins of Christianity and portrays Jesus as a wisdom-loving sage.
5½ x 8½, 192 pp, Quality PB, 978-1-893361-45-4 **$16.99**

The Secret Book of John: The Gnostic Gospel—Annotated & Explained
Translation & Annotation by Stevan Davies The most significant and influential text of the ancient Gnostic religion.
5½ x 8½, 208 pp, Quality PB, 978-1-59473-082-5 **$16.99**

JUDAISM

The Divine Feminine in Biblical Wisdom Literature
Selections Annotated & Explained
Translation & Annotation by Rabbi Rami Shapiro; Foreword by Rev. Cynthia Bourgeault, PhD
Uses the Hebrew books of Psalms, Proverbs, Song of Songs, Ecclesiastes and Job, Wisdom literature and the Wisdom of Solomon to clarify who Wisdom is.
5½ x 8½, 240 pp, Quality PB, 978-1-59473-109-9 **$16.99**

Ethics of the Sages: *Pirke Avot*—Annotated & Explained
Translation & Annotation by Rabbi Rami Shapiro Clarifies the ethical teachings of the early Rabbis. 5½ x 8½, 192 pp, Quality PB, 978-1-59473-207-2 **$16.99**

Hasidic Tales: Annotated & Explained
Translation & Annotation by Rabbi Rami Shapiro
Introduces the legendary tales of the impassioned Hasidic rabbis, presenting them as stories rather than as parables. 5½ x 8½, 240 pp, Quality PB, 978-1-893361-86-7 **$16.95**

The Hebrew Prophets: Selections Annotated & Explained
Translation & Annotation by Rabbi Rami Shapiro; Foreword by Zalman M. Schachter-Shalomi
Focuses on the central themes covered by all the Hebrew prophets.
5½ x 8½, 224 pp, Quality PB, 978-1-59473-037-5 **$16.99**

Zohar: Annotated & Explained *Translation & Annotation by Daniel C. Matt*
The best-selling author of *The Essential Kabbalah* brings together in one place the most important teachings of the Zohar, the canonical text of Jewish mystical tradition.
5½ x 8½, 176 pp, Quality PB, 978-1-893361-51-5 **$15.99**

Sacred Texts—cont.

ISLAM

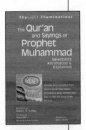

The Qur'an and Sayings of Prophet Muhammad
Selections Annotated & Explained
Annotation by Sohaib N. Sultan; Translation by Yusuf Ali; Revised by Sohaib N. Sultan
Foreword by Jane I. Smith
Explores how the timeless wisdom of the Qur'an can enrich your own spiritual journey.
5½ x 8½, 256 pp, Quality PB, 978-1-59473-222-5 **$16.99**

Rumi and Islam: Selections from His Stories, Poems, and Discourses— Annotated & Explained
Translation & Annotation by Ibrahim Gamard
Focuses on Rumi's place within the Sufi tradition of Islam, providing insight into the mystical side of the religion.
5½ x 8½, 240 pp, Quality PB, 978-1-59473-002-3 **$15.99**

EASTERN RELIGIONS

The Art of War—Spirituality for Conflict
Annotated & Explained
by Sun Tzu; Annotation by Thomas Huynh; Translation by Thomas Huynh and the Editors at Sonshi.com; Foreword by Marc Benioff; Preface by Thomas Cleary
Highlights principles that encourage a perceptive and spiritual approach to conflict.
5½ x 8½, 256 pp, Quality PB, 978-1-59473-244-7 **$16.99**

Bhagavad Gita: Annotated & Explained
Translation by Shri Purohit Swami; Annotation by Kendra Crossen Burroughs
Explains references and philosophical terms, shares the interpretations of famous spiritual leaders and scholars, and more.
5½ x 8½, 192 pp, Quality PB, 978-1-893361-28-7 **$16.95**

Dhammapada: Annotated & Explained
Translation by Max Müller and revised by Jack Maguire; Annotation by Jack Maguire
Contains all of Buddhism's key teachings.
5½ x 8½, 160 pp, b/w photos, Quality PB, 978-1-893361-42-3 **$14.95**

Selections from the Gospel of Sri Ramakrishna
Annotated & Explained
Translation by Swami Nikhilananda; Annotation by Kendra Crossen Burroughs
Introduces the fascinating world of the Indian mystic and the universal appeal of his message.
5½ x 8½, 240 pp, b/w photos, Quality PB, 978-1-893361-46-1 **$16.95**

Tao Te Ching: Annotated & Explained
Translation & Annotation by Derek Lin; Foreword by Lama Surya Das
Introduces an Eastern classic in an accessible, poetic and completely original way.
5½ x 8½, 192 pp, Quality PB, 978-1-59473-204-1 **$16.99**

STOICISM

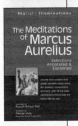

The Meditations of Marcus Aurelius
Selections Annotated & Explained
Annotation by Russell McNeil, PhD; Translation by George Long; Revised by Russell McNeil, PhD
Offers insightful and engaging commentary into the historical background of Stoicism.
5½ x 8½, 288 pp, Quality PB, 978-1-59473-236-2 **$16.99**

Judaism / Christianity / Interfaith

Talking about God: Exploring the Meaning of Religious Life with Kierkegaard, Buber, Tillich and Heschel *by Daniel F. Polish, PhD*
Examines the meaning of the human religious experience with the greatest theologians of modern times. 6 x 9, 176 pp, HC, 978-1-59473-230-0 **$21.99**

Interactive Faith: The Essential Interreligious Community-Building Handbook
Edited by Rev. Bud Heckman with Rori Picker Neiss
A guide to the key methods and resources of the interfaith movement.
6 x 9, 400 pp (est), HC, 978-1-59473-237-9 **$40.00**

The Jewish Approach to Repairing the World (*Tikkun Olam*)
A Brief Introduction for Christians *by Rabbi Elliot N. Dorff, PhD*
A window into the Jewish idea of responsibility to care for the world.
5½ x 8½, 192 pp (est), Quality PB, 978-1-58023-349-1 **$16.99** (a Jewish Lights book)

Modern Jews Engage the New Testament: Enhancing Jewish Well-Being in a Christian Environment *by Rabbi Michael J. Cook, PhD*
A look at the dynamics of the New Testament.
6 x 9, 416 pp, HC, 978-1-58023-313-2 **$29.99** (a Jewish Lights book)

Disaster Spiritual Care: Practical Clergy Responses to Community, Regional and National Tragedy
Edited by Rabbi Stephen B. Roberts, BCJC, & Rev. Willard W.C. Ashley, Sr., DMin, DH
The definitive reference for pastoral caregivers of all faiths involved in disaster response.
6 x 9, 384 pp, Hardcover, 978-1-59473-240-9 **$40.00**

The Changing Christian World: A Brief Introduction for Jews
by Rabbi Leonard A. Schoolman
5½ x 8½, 176 pp, Quality PB, 978-1-58023-344-6 **$16.99** (a Jewish Lights book)

The Jewish Connection to Israel, the Promised Land: A Brief Introduction for Christians *by Rabbi Eugene Korn, PhD*
5½ x 8½, 192 pp, Quality PB, 978-1-58023-318-7 **$14.99** (a Jewish Lights book)

Christians and Jews in Dialogue: Learning in the Presence of the Other
by Mary C. Boys and Sara S. Lee; Foreword by Dorothy C. Bass
Inspires renewed commitment to dialogue between religious traditions.
6 x 9, 240 pp, HC, 978-1-59473-144-0 **$21.99**

Healing the Jewish-Christian Rift: Growing Beyond Our Wounded History
by Ron Miller and Laura Bernstein; Foreword by Dr. Beatrice Bruteau
6 x 9, 288 pp, Quality PB, 978-1-59473-139-6 **$18.99**

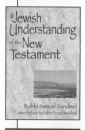

Introducing My Faith and My Community
The Jewish Outreach Institute Guide for the Christian in a Jewish Interfaith Relationship
by Rabbi Kerry M. Olitzky 6 x 9, 176 pp, Quality PB, 978-1-58023-192-3 **$16.99** *(a Jewish Lights book)*

The Jewish Approach to God: A Brief Introduction for Christians
by Rabbi Neil Gillman 5½ x 8½, 192 pp, Quality PB, 978-1-58023-190-9 **$16.95** *(a Jewish Lights book)*

Jewish Holidays: A Brief Introduction for Christians
by Rabbi Kerry M. Olitzky and Rabbi Daniel Judson
5½ x 8½, 176 pp, Quality PB, 978-1-58023-302-6 **$16.99** *(a Jewish Lights book)*

Jewish Ritual: A Brief Introduction for Christians
by Rabbi Kerry M. Olitzky and Rabbi Daniel Judson
5½ x 8½, 144 pp, Quality PB, 978-1-58023-210-4 **$14.99** *(a Jewish Lights book)*

Jewish Spirituality: A Brief Introduction for Christians *by Rabbi Lawrence Kushner*
5½ x 8½, 112 pp, Quality PB, 978-1-58023-150-3 **$12.95** *(a Jewish Lights book)*

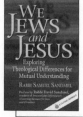

A Jewish Understanding of the New Testament
by Rabbi Samuel Sandmel; new Preface by Rabbi David Sandmel
5½ x 8½, 368 pp, Quality PB, 978-1-59473-048-1 **$19.99**

We Jews and Jesus: Exploring Theological Differences for Mutual Understanding
by Rabbi Samuel Sandmel; new Preface by Rabbi David Sandmel A Classic Reprint
6 x 9, 192 pp, Quality PB, 978-1-59473-208-9 **$16.99**

Show Me Your Way: The Complete Guide to Exploring Interfaith Spiritual Direction
by Howard A. Addison 5½ x 8½, 240 pp, Quality PB, 978-1-893361-41-6 **$16.95**